AF662121

Emerging Dimensions of Business

About the book

The present business environment is vastly different from what it was a decade ago. In the wake of liberalisation and globalisation, the domestic industry and business has to gear itself for the new challenges of global competitiveness and quality. Sustainable growth, social justice and ethical issues are the other challenges that need to be met.

India is witnessing a paradigm shift in the business environment. The forces of globalisation, information technology, privatisation and knowledge explosion have transformed the business scenario. The challenge of change is multi-faceted and the rate of change is very fast. Only those industries and organisations are going to survive and grow in future which will be able to proactively respond and adjust to the new circumstances. The fast changing business environment has significant implications for the human, financial, operational, commercial and managerial dimensions of trade, commerce and industry.

The topics covered in this book relate to the whole range of emerging issues in the functional areas of business, namely finance, marketing, human resources and information technology. The present volume, it is hoped, will be of great use and benefit to the researchers, practitioners, policy makers, business executives and students.

About the editors

Dr. Mohi-ud-Din Sangmi is a Reader in the Department of Commerce, University of Kashmir, Srinagar. He obtained his Ph.D. degree from the same University in 1998. He has sixteen years of teaching experience in the area of management accounting, management control systems, and security analysis. He was the editor of the journal *Business Review* (1999-2002). Dr. Sangmi is associated with several professional bodies including ICWAI and IFCAI.

Dr. Nazir A. Nazir is **a** Reader in the Department of Commerce, University of Kashmir, Srinagar. He secured his Ph.D. degree from the Faculty of Management Studies, University of Delhi. He has contributed articles in reputed journals including *Indian Journal of Industrial Relations*. He has conducted various sessions in his field of specialisation – human resource development, and labour management relations.

Emerging Dimensions of Business

Edited by
Dr. Mohi-ud-Din Sangmi
Dr. Nazir A. Nazir

New Century Publications
Delhi India

NEW CENTURY PUBLICATIONS
34, Gujranwala Town, Part-2,
Delhi - 110 009 INDIA
Tel.: 27247805, 27138192
Fax: +91-11-27464774
E-mail: indiatax@del2.vsnl.net.in

Copyright © 2004 by Department of Commerce, University of Kashmir

All rights reserved. No part of this book may be reproduced, stored in a retrieval system, or transmitted in any form or by any means, mechanical, photocopying, recording, or otherwise without the prior written permission of the publisher.

First Published 2004

ISBN: 81-7708-061-x

Published by New Century Publications and printed at Singhal Print Media Pvt. Ltd, Delhi -110 007

PRINTED IN INDIA

The University of Kashmir

ce-Chancellor

Foreword

At the dawn of new millennium, the forces shaping the world have reached a critical level where their implications will be realized with amazing speed. These forces are exposing us to various economic, social, technological, ethical, political and cultural changes, as a result of which the business environment is changing at a faster pace, reflecting a multitude of trends at the national and the global levels. The aggregate of these trends may create a new milieu for the trade, commerce, business and industry and pose new challenges for them.

The globalisation policy adopted by the country made it possible to integrate the Indian economy with the world economy. This has opened wide gates for the multi national companies to start production here and market their products at the doors of the Indian consumers. The Indian industry which was swimming hitherto in the protected waters, has to face now competition in the new environment where the survival of the fittest has become the order of the day. This has posed a new challenge for the Indian business houses.

The fast developments in the information technology have revolutionized the commerce and business practices through out the world. The information technology has transformed the world into a global village wherein information can be instantly acquired, transformed, retrieved, transferred and stored for decision making and for carrying out the business operations anywhere in the world. The processing of information at one place for multiple locations or at several places for one location, is becoming common. This will change the very nature of corporate offices and give rise to a new corporate culture. Besides, the commercial practices will get totally transformed with the help of information technology, from a market place to anywhere buying and selling Since the internet era giving birth to E-commerce is changing the rules of the game of business and commerce, the business organisations are left with no alternative but to develop and train their manpower to face these challenges.

Global trade environment is becoming complex with the interplay of multi-lateralism, regionalism and bilateral initiatives which come through the WTO. The results of the Uruguay Round of Negotiations have resulted into the Trade in goods, including TRIMS (Trade Related Investment Measures), Agreement on TRIPS (Trade Related Intellectual Properties), trade in services, trade policy review mechanism, dispute settlement mechanism, Industrial tariff, e-commerce, Government procurement, etc.

The changes made in the financial sector front are totally visible nowadays. The permission of foreign banks and private sector banks to operate in the Indian financial market has posed new challenges and provided new opportunities. The new scenario of banking has forced the public sector banks to consolidate their position, redefine their objectives, re-formulate their strategies and re-invent themselves in the new market place. In this way, new products are being designed by the banks, new activities - which hitherto were out of the domain of commercial banks, like Merchant banking, factoring, leasing etc. - are being undertaken and new markets explored. Even the developmental financial institutions like the IDBI, ICICI, IFCI etc. are re-engineering themselves to the new financial scenario. In such a situation, the sources of finance and other business opportunities have compounded.

The present book, "Emerging Dimensions of Business" edited by Dr. Mohi-ud-Din Sangmi and Dr. Nazir A. Nazir, senior faculty members in the Department of Commerce of our University, is a solid contribution in this direction. The editors, I am pleased to learn, have done a commendable job by editing and compiling the papers presented in the

National level seminar conducted by the Department of Commerce of our University on a similar theme.

I hope the book would contribute in understanding the latest developments in business environment and will be useful to the faculty, students, researchers and businessmen alike.

(Prof. Jalees A. K. Tareen)

Acknowledgements

We are greatly indebted to Prof. Jalees Ahmad Khân Tareen, the Vice-Chancellor of the University of Kashmir, Srinagar for acceding to our request to write the forword to this book.

Prof. S. Fayyaz Ahmad, Head, Department of Commerce is thanked for the perennial inspiration, encouragement and logistics for completing this work.

The paper writers whose names are given in the list of contributors are greatly acknowledged for their contributions without which this book would have been impossible.

We are felicated to put on record the names of the faculty members of our Department viz. Dr. Khurshid Ahmad Bhat, Dr. Riyaz Ahmed, Dr. Mushtaq Ahmed, Dr. Bashir Ahmad, Mr. Mohammad Shafi and Er. Qaiser Rashid who made lot of contribution in making the book to see the light of the day.

We are highly grateful to our family members for their constant support, cooperation and moral help to take this work to completion.

Thanks are due to M/s Computer Vision, Srinagar for computer-typesetting the manuscript. M/s New Century Publications, New Delhi are thanked to publish the book so neatly and on time

While acknowledging a number of people who made one or the other contribution, the authors admit that if there are any mistakes/errors in the book, the responsibility of that lies on the authors only.

Dr. Mohiud-Din Sangmi
Reader/Associate Professor

Dr. Nazir A. Nazir
Reader/Associate Professor

Preface

We are at present witnessing a paradigm shift in the business environment. The forces of globalization, information technology, privatization and knowledge explosion have transformed the business scenario. The challenge of change is multi-faceted and the rate of change is very fast. Only those industries and organizations are going to survive and grow in future which will be able to proactively respond and adjust to the new circumstances. The fast changing business environment has significant implications for the human, financial, operational, commercial and managerial dimensions of trade, commerce and industry.

To assess the implications of the new environment, the Department of Commerce, University of Kashmir organized a National level two day seminar on the theme *Commerce Education in the New Millennium*. The topics covered the whole range of emerging issues relating to different functional areas of business like finance, marketing, human resources and information technology.

I am highly thankful to Dr. Mohi-ud-Din Sangmi and Dr. Nazir Ahmad, for completing their assignment in spite of a number of other pressing academic engagements. I also thank the paper writers for making their valuable contributions. We express our gratitude to the Vice-chancellor of our University Professor Jalees A.K. Tareen for inspiring and motivating us to complete this task.

The present volume, it is hoped, will be of great use and benefit to the researchers, practitioners, policy makers, business executives and students. I also expect that the educational policy makers will, in particular, take note of the suggestions and policy implications outlined in this book and will accord to business education its due place in the educational set-up, so that the problems of unemployment and industrial backwardness can be mitigated.

Srinagar
October, 2003

Professor S. Fayyaz Ahmad
Head, PG Department of Commerce
University of Kashmir
Srinagar

Contributors

Badar Alam Iqbal
Professor
Department of Commerce, Aligarh Muslim University, Aligarh

Mehraj-ud-Din
Director
Academic Staff College, University of Kashmir, Srinagar

Sayyed Fayyaz Ahmad
Professor and Head
Department of Commerce, University of Kashmir, Srinagar

G.M. Bhat
Professor
Department of Economics, University of Kashmir, Srinagar

G.Q. Mir
Professor
Department of Law, University of Kashmir, Srinagar

M.R. Sofi
Principal
Government Degree College, Handwara, Kashmir

Mohi-ud-Din Sangmi
Reader
Department of Commerce, University of Kashmir, Srinagar

Nazir A. Nazir
Reader
Department of Commerce, University of Kashmir, Srinagar

Zeenat Ara
Lecturer (Selection Grade)
Department of Commerce, Government Degree College for Women, Nawakadal, Srinagar

M.A. Bhat
Lecturer

Department of Commerce, University of Kashmir, Srinagar

Bashir Ahmad
Lecturer
Department of Commerce, University of Kashmir, Srinagar

Nisar Ahmad Yatoo
Lecturer
Government Degree College, Sopore, Kashmir

G.M. Baqal
Lecturer (Selection Grade)
Government Women's College, Nawakadal, Srinagar

Riyaz A. Rainaye
Lecturer
Department of Commerce, University of Kashmir, Srinagar

F.A. Mir
Head, Department of Commerce
Government Degree College for Boys, Anantnag, Kashmir

Syed Javed Iqbal Kamili
Head, Department of Commerce
Gandhi Memorial College, Srinagar

Zahoor Ahmad Chatt
Lecturer (Selection Grade)
Department of Commerce and Management
Government Degree College, Bemina, Srinagar

Farooq A. Shah
Senior Lecturer
Department of Commerce and Management
Government Degree College, Bemina, Srinagar

Mohammad Ayub Dar
Lecturer
Department of Law, University of Kashmir, Srinagar

N.A. Gilkar
Senior Lecturer

Department of Commerce and Management
Government Degree College, Bemina, Srinagar

Mohammad Shafi
Lecturer
Department of Commerce, University of Kashmir, Srinagar

Parvez A. Shah
Lecturer
Department of Commerce, Gandhi Memorial College, Srinagar

Kalim Wahidi
Chartered Accountant, Wahidi Associates, Srinagar

L.K. Jha
Chartered Accountant, Jammu & Kashmir Bank Ltd, Srinagar

Surjeet Singh Risam
Development Officer, New India Assurance Co. Ltd., Srinagar

Khavar Mehraj Handoo
Manager (IT)
Jammu & Kashmir Bank Ltd.

Arif A. Shah
Department of Commerce, University of Kashmir, Srinagar

G.R. Akhoon
Radio Kashmir, Srinagar

Contents

01

INTRODUCTION

Before 1991, Indian economy was not as it is today. Most of the important commodities like oil, fertilizer, cement, steel, sugar etc. were under controlled price regime (suggestive). Capacities were always falling behind the growth of demand. The licensing system was very rigid, the import policy very stringent, tariff barriers very high and the capacity creation very difficult. But once capacity was created, the profits were almost assured as the inefficiencies could be passed on to the customer. The whole system was based on cost plus structure and supplier- market dominated India for at least 54 years even after independence. The fragmented capacity creation ensured unviable economies of scale. The light commercial vehicle manufacturers were given licence for 12,500 vehicles each and 4 such units came up with foreign collaboration. It was definitely not an economy of scale. Similarly, cement plants were initially allowed to produce 2 lac tonnes per year and then 4 lac tonnes and finally 10 lac tonnes per year. This was again a case of dis-economy of scale. Same is true of steel. Despite having highest iron ore deposits of very high quality, India could not achieve competitive advantage in this industry because of lower economies of scale. In similar fashion, textile, sugar, oil, consumer goods, in short, the whole area of industry was treated. With the result, the cost of production always remained high and it was possible to pass it on to the consumer. This made Indian industry complacent and lazy. The product and technological development was pushed into the background. The Indian economy was brought to high cost-low-quality economy. The products were scarce in the market. It would take 5-6 years for getting a scooter delivered after booking. Car used to take at least 2 years. The customer hadn't had any say but the industry continued to make money.

The other related aspect which governed the business environment was related to MRTP and FERA. The industrial houses were not allowed to expand beyond 100 crores and hence with the belief that this would create monopoly. The provisions of the Foreign Exchange Regulation Act were discretely used to harass the people without any impact on the major capital flight. It coupled with an inefficient and uneconomic industrial operations which gave rise to non-competitive export, leading to a Balance of Payment crisis. The corporate tax rates were very high which discouraged an inflow of foreign capital. Thus the rupee depreciated and depreciated and depreciated. Ultimately, the Indian economy reached to a brink of bankruptcy in 1991 with only 1.1 billion dollars worth of foreign currency assets, just enough for 2 weeks trade for the country.

Then a new era started, which is generally considered to be a great historic period of the Indian economy. It was the time when from all corners of the country only one slogan came: "Re-engineer the economy, rejuvenate the country, the paradise lost should be regained." In this way, at the macro-level Structural Adjustment Programme (SAP) dovetailed and all the sectors of the economy got a new direction and a fresh lease of life. The new economic conjectures came to surface: Liberalization - liberating the industry from the License Raj and de-reservations of certain industries from the government list; Privatization - dis-investment of government owned business houses; and Globalisation - opening up the economy to foreign business houses to establish their bases and trade operations in this country. Incidentally, the period was supplemented with the information technology. All these forces taken together have had a profound impact upon the managerial, commercial and industrial practices.

No doubt the reforms were initiated in the agriculture, industrial, financial and government sectors which gave birth to a new scenario of business and commerce. These changes made fresh demands for new skills. Thus the commerce and business educational institutions have no alternative but to respond to these new needs and supply the manpower as per the new requirements after re-designing their courses and re-tooling their institutions. Towards this end, the Department of Commerce, University of Kashmir organised a two-day national seminar in which a large number of academicians,practioners and professionals participated and presented their papers, the present book is the collection of the selected papers presented in the seminar and for the sake of convenience have been divided into the following five sections :-

- Information technology & E- commerce
- Human Resource Management
- Corporate Governance
- Marketing & International Trade
- Finance and Accounting
- Business and Commerce Education

All the above facets are described in the book as follows:

Information Technology and E-Commerce

In this digital age, there is no aspect of life which has not been affected by the electronic revolution and information technology which have stepped into our homes, offices, businesses, and almost in all spheres of public life. Not only this, the advancement in IT has changed the definition of commerce and business. With just a click of the mouse, we can enter into commercial and business transactions anywhere and at any time. The turnover of business transactions based on electronic commerce now is in billions of dollars. The papers included in this section throw light on the impact of IT on business and bring forth *inter alia*, the legal implications related to E-Commerce.

In his paper, Fayez Ahmad Mir, while discussing the concept of E-Commerce emphasizes that the traditional mode of commerce should be retained by at least small business houses as they can not afford the risk of any payment security through cybernetics. He, however, asserts that the fully developed companies must shift to E-Commerce to boost their businesses.

Mehraj-ud-Din Mir, highlights certain cyber issues within the purview of IT Act 2000. He identifies certain weaker aspects of the Act and asserts that the Act is deficient in certain aspects in relation to Indian contract Act, 1872. He concludes that owing to the inadequacy of the existing legislation for the present day e-commerce, the cyber violations are bound to occur.

Mr. Khavar Mehraj Handoo has attempted to discuss the various classes of payment systems necessary for internet commerce. All the practicalities and technicalities related to the operational part of internet payment system have been aptly described.

Human Resource Management

Human being is the most important component of all commercial organizations. With the new changes in business, a lot of new jobs got created. Lots of existing jobs got eliminated, giving birth to unlearning and re-learning of different skills. With the result, the traditional role of organizations has moved from managing personnel to developing human resources. The structural adjustment programme (SAP) started in line with new economic policy, put added challenges to human resources departments of the organizations in the country. These aspects have been thoroughly dealt with in this section.

G. M. Bhat lays stress on the need for recognizing human and social element in the contemporary global industrial scenario. The author critically evaluates the efforts made at the macro level for the social sector and human development and concludes that under the second generation economic reforms, much more remains to be done for the progress of this vital aspect.

Nazir A. Nazir pleads for a change in the labour laws and mind set of organizational leaders which is required for minimizing the labour unrest leading to strikes and lockouts.

Riyaz A. Rainayee advocates for a paradigm shift in the organizational thinking which, he argues is a must for effective utilization of human resources by pooling together talents, skills and teamwork spirit to be competitive in the new century.

Syed Pervaiz Ahmed Shâh highlights various issues that are emerging on the HRD scenario in recent years. The HR professionals, in order to be globally acceptable, need to capitalize their efforts on the development of required skills, competencies and attitudes in order to have sustainable competitive advantage, the author concludes.

Farooq A. Shâh's paper dealing with role stress concludes that effective management of role stress warrants immediate attention of human resources and behavioral experts in the backdrop of human and economic loss to the organization.

Nisar A. Yattoo stresses the need for effective handling of trade and labour unions towards improvements in organizational performance. Taking a case of banking industry, the author suggests that to achieve a competitive advantage, the HR should be developed in such a manner that the better customer services are provided and profitability is improved.

Corporate Governance

With the growth of corporate organizations characterized by the separation between ownership and control, their internal organizational problems, as also their external relations to the society, have acquired new dimensions, not envisaged in the early era of the corporation. A company is now considered a social institution, interacting with the society in many ways and affecting all stakeholders -- shareholders, employees, creditors, customers, the government and the general public. It has to come up to the expectations of all these stakeholders which needs a new mantra of corporate governance to be adopted, having in its fold environmental consciousness, business ethics, fair play, transparency and social responsibility.

Mohd Ayub Dar tries to unearth the myths of corporate criminal liability under the Indian Environmental Laws. With the great disaster of Bhopal gas tragedy (Union Carbide Corporation), the Indian companies became conscious of eco-system and environmental requirements to be complied with in the work setting. Over the years, what have been the lapses of the corporations towards this aspect and how the environmental law has dealt with them is the crux of this paper.

Arif A. Shâh delineates the new role of directors in the modern corporations. The author argues that with the drastic amendments in the Indian companies Act, 1956, the role of directors has increased manifold. In fact, the directors are now expected to testify every right or wrong in the company which they govern or are connected with. The SEBI laws and Indian Accounting Standards are also charging the corporate directors with added responsibilities. The paper expects that with rules in operation, the ever increasing corporate scams would get dwindled in the years to come.

Marketing and International Trade

The process of globalization has widened the customer base and the operations of the companies. The Indian companies, as a sequel to this process of internationalization could not remain dormant. Moreover, because of depression in the value of rupee and its partial convertibility, removal of quantity restrictions, easing of tariffs and other trade barriers, the composition of international trade in the country has changed over the years. This has put a lot of pressure on Indian economy which is forced to understand the new challenges of the global markets, to push exports and safeguard, as far as possible, against imports. This section deals with this aspect.

M. R. Sofi criticizes the industrially developed countries like the USA, UK, Germany, Italy and France for creating impediments (tariff and non-tariff barriers) against third world countries in their efforts to enter global market. He also urges upon both India and Pakistan to apply the methods adopted by Japan for having a considerable share in the world market.

Zahoor Ahmad Chatt shows clearly with evidence that Indians could venture into technology export trade particularly in the areas of arts and crafts. He states that technology exports are becoming increasingly important in the matrix of globalization of business. The thrust areas of technology exports for India could be setting up of turnkey projects and infrastructure exports. However, he sounds a caution that the technology should not be exported unless it is tried and proved successful within the indigenous country. He makes many suggestions for improving the status of technology exports by India.

Mushtaq Ahmad Bhat discusses the service quality practices of commercial banks in India. The author has come up with some pragmatic suggestions to improve the service quality in the banking institutions operating in the country, in view of the changing economic scenario.

Accounting and Finance

Over the years, the field of Accounting and Finance has undergone a revolutionary transformation. Accounting standards have become the order of the day in almost all organizations of the world. Even the common Accounting language is emphasized to avoid confusion and ensure transparency in the accounting and reporting practices. The transnationalisation of businesses have brought severe challenges for tax imposing and tax collecting machineries. Moreover, the innovations in the financial products and the changes in financial sector have posed new challenges to the business communities. All these issues have been addressed in this section.

In their joint paper, Mohi-ud-Din Sangmi & S.Javid Kamili highlight certain gaps in the Indian Accounting Standards as compared to the International ones. They assert that there is a need to bridge gap that exists between Indian GAAP and that of the world to ensure better harmonization of accounting practices required in present times.

L. K. Jha has differentiated the Indian GAAP with the US GAAP. The author has shown that the conversion of financial statements from Indian to US GAAP needs a Herculean exercise.

Kalim Wahidi pleads for an emphasis for observance of professional ethics in all professions including accounting. The author suggests five principles in this direction viz. integrity, objectivity, independence, confidentiality and professional competence.

Badar Alam Iqbal shows the innovative tax practices adopted by various countries in the new global economic scenario. The author, after comparing the Indian tax system and the world, suggests a framework for taxing global business.

G. Q. Mir underlines various pros and cons of direct and indirect taxes. The author concludes that due to tax evasion, the revenue collection from these taxes has not been upto the mark which needs to be looked into for financing the developmental needs of the country.

Bashir Ahmad gives an analysis of commodity taxation as prevalent in India. He suggests a frame-work for developing VAT system in the field of commodity taxation.

Mohammad Shafi evaluates the merits and demerits of FDI. The author is of the opinion that FDI is more a bane than a boon under Indian conditions. The author emphasizes that in order to be fruitful, FDI should be channelised in areas like engineering projects, infrastructure projects etc.

Nazir Ahmed Gilkar suggests some strategies for launching mutual fund products in the state of Jammu & Kashmir. The author is of the opinion that ethical funds could be a better option for the state investors who are still ignorant about the investment in mutual fund channels.

Surjeet Singh Risam describes the emerging dimensions of risk coverage under the changing conditions where MNCs have already flooded the insurance sector. He suggests certain measures for the Indian public sector insurance companies for facing the new onslaught of competition unleashed by private players.

Business/Commerce Education

In the light of the changes in economic environment, the very definition of business/commerce has changed in the new millennium. The new millennium has in its kitty new threats and opportunities for the business houses. The business houses have to safeguard themselves against these threats and have to tap these opportunities which in the long run pose severe challenges for the institutions imparting business/commerce education. In this backdrop, the various issues of business/commerce education in the changed social and economic milieu have been discussed in its totality in this section.

Sayyid Fayyaz Ahmad outlines that a historical transition at the global level is witnessed in all spheres of human activity. The focus of globalization, privatization and information technology in particular, has started revolutionizing the trade, commerce and industry. The time demands that the students of business and commerce should be exposed to the global environmental issues like WTO, FDI, ISO quality standards, International Accounting Standards (IAS), etc. All these issues need to be incorporated in the business/commerce curriculum. He finally concludes that the institutions imparting business and commerce education must adopt a futuristic and proactive approach towards promoting educational standard, in the discipline of business and commerce.

G. R. Akhoon highlights the development status of commerce education in India, USA and Britain. He attempts to make a study of various problems faced by commerce education in the country.

Zeenat Ara states that the scheme of vocational education adopted by the UGC is a nice doze for developing entrepreneurship skills among the students. However, owing to some difficulties at the operational level, the scheme has not been successful to obtain the desired results.

G. M. Bakal while citing the success of the scheme of vocational education in Japan and Germany concludes that in the state of Jammu & Kashmir, the students of this stream have not achieved any distinction because of the examination oriented teaching-learning methodology, lack of on-the-job-training, conventional teaching methods, lack of demand for vocational student pass-outs etc.

ooo

Section I: Information Technology & E-commerce

02

CYBERNATICS DEVOID OF PAYMENT SECURITY - AN UNDERSTANDING

Fayaz Ahmad Mir

Abstract

This paper attempts to study the mechanism of online commerce. A peep into various aspects of cybernatics help to identify that payment security protocols are sufficient in building confidence among the consumers who feel more scared, as their financial information are exposed globally on network before large number of internet users. Various protocols have been launched which have shown considerable improvement. It has led to confidence building measures and encouragement to consumers, to transact business electronically. Various other issues like custom charges, taxation payments, insufficient regulations for piracy, fraud, and protection of intellectual property rights, has not been taken care of. The paper concludes that new protocols Secured Socket Layout (SSL) and Secure Transaction technology STT and Secure Electronic Transaction (SET) have shown upward trend in online business. The grown up companies should adopt the online commerce with an aim to expand their business on the net.

Introduction

Cybernetics has undergone a sea change, which already gained momentum at the fag end of the last millennium. It did not concentrate on information, communication, education and entertainment (ICEE) but tempted business and industry as well. It demolished the strong and conventional business and commerce concepts, customs, models, tools, aids, etc. The basic objectives of commerce, however, were not changed which refer to combination of various economic activities so as to make goods and services reach to the ultimate consumers who are at two distinct ends without any difficulty. Infotech has not only made it fast, efficient and economical but also user friendly.

In 1996 websites became status symbol and companies, therefore, setup web services. The web commerce popularly known as 'E-commerce' grew considerably in the year 1999 as mainstream necessity, which has remained an academic curiosity from 1996 to 1998. Yankee Group Research (USA) predicated in 1996 to cover business worth $137 billion by the year March, 2001 which proved a reality. It is expected to touch business volume of $1000 billion by the year 2005. Peter Drucker also predicted "by 2020 the residential universities with fair campuses would have disappeared and may become only educational tourist potential. Learning will take place through E-learning super market".

On line business popularly known as (E-commerce) refers to total application of the computer and the process of conducting commercial transactions through internet. Electronic commerce consists of two phases. First phase comprises conducting commerce with the help of electronic medium such as TV, Fax. The second phase is the internet. The TV and Fax mode were in operation for decades, but the internet is recent development which combines commerce, data management and security capabilities. Thus E-commerce, in wider sense, is an integration of communications, data management and security capabilities, which permit organizations to exchange information about sale of goods and services. E-commerce, therefore, has three important distinct features known as CSD.

- **Communication:** This helps the organizations to transfer information from buyer to seller. It replaced sharing the same spoken language in traditional commercial transactions to digital language that is by use of transactions.
- **Security:** This mechanism authenticates the source of information and guarantees the integrity and privacy of information. This is of paramount importance as it has eliminated the physical presence of buyer and seller at one place to complete commercial transactions.
- **Data Management:** It refers to format of information which helps to establish common digital language to successfully complete electronic transactions.

The E-Business is broadly divided into two models: (1) B2B (Business to Business) (2) B2C (Business to Customer) as detailed in Box I. As regards on line payments, customers feel more scared while transacting electronically as their financial information is exposed to the large number of internet users. The main payment modes (i) The cash model (ii) The check model, and (iii) The credit model. The credit model is more popular but most sensitive one, which needs confidence building tools to encourage the consumers and credit card holders to continue their business beyond any apprehensions. Therefor, the objectives of the Present Paper are:

i) to study the online payment mechanism

ii) to understand the genuineness of the apprehensions of the information leakage.

iii) to assess the sufficiency of various tools to guard the interests of the consumers.

iv) to assess scope for improving the current tools and framing new tools to strengthen further payment security.

Mechanism of E-Commerce

The basic objective of E-commerce (web based enterprise) is to achieve the set business goals and expectations

Box – I: Modes of E-business

(B 2 B) Business to Business

Under this model of E-commerce, Business is conducted between two separate businesses i.e. two different business entities. In this model company allows its purchases department to buy office supplies online. Company can setup open purchase order with office supplier and allow its employees responsible for purchases to access the suppliers internet site for making such purchases. This model of e-commerce is characterized by high volume and low price margin. In Windows we open Browsers and enter www.merisel.com in URL section where by Merisel website views. It is setup for retailers, value added resellers and other business users to order computer components over the Internet.

(B 2 C) Business to Consumer

Under this model, Commerce is conducted between business and consumer. A home user carries commercial transaction on home PC with a retailer. Thus it is a commercial transaction between buyer and seller on internet. For example a consumer has to buy a book, he accesses to bookseller by opening internet site and makes on spot purchases. This model is characterized by low volume and high price margin.

which are not fully achieved by traditional mode of commerce. It boosts business already functioning under traditional commerce mode web provides all facets required to turn normal business into e-com enabled enterprise. It provides opportunities to traditional mode of business to move ahead successfully. In virtual enterprise web connects islands of information from within corporate internets and across the internet. It facilitates sharing of information without physical contacts and location. This opportunity has tempted and promoted new form of social endeavour and virtual business. It is formed without membership formalities and geographical locations popularly known as Value Added Network (VAN) and Virtual Private Network (VPN).

The success of E-commerce depends on web storefront. The web storefront can be successfully launched if it possesses the following characteristics given in Fig. A:

Fig. A Storefront Characteristics

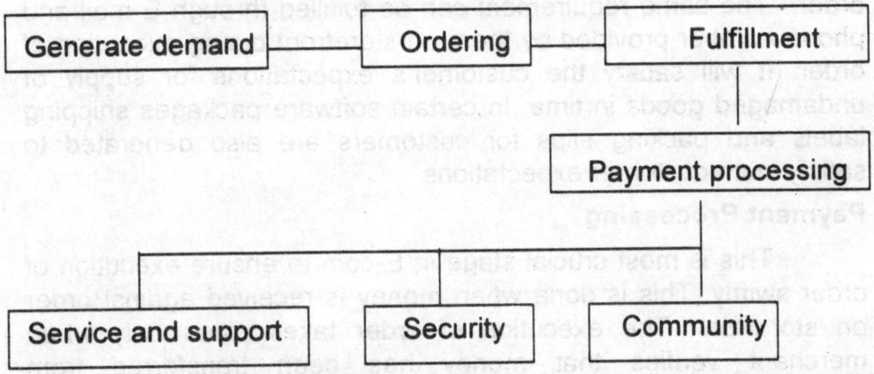

Generate Demand

It is possible when online advertisement will attract large number of consumers towards web storefront. Success in generating demand will depend on the following two conditions:

- traffic must be attracted towards storefront
- lookers must be converted into customers

Success of banner ads is measured by click through rates 3% of it is treated as very high in web advertising industry.

Ordering

Success of banner ads leads to customers persuasion to order storefront should be simple to use and in accordance with latest designs and human psychology. Storefront can achieve desired target if it follows the following guidelines:

- Consistent in look and background, foreground colours, front size and logos.
- Eliminate redundant information
- Make shopping easy by carts and cookies.
- Payment mechanism must accept many substitutes like the Credit Card mode, the check mode, Debit/ ATM Card or COD
- Bailout mechanism i.e. provide phone use to consumer to clarify his doubts or questions without turning back.

Fulfillment

The customers are always worried about the progress of order. The same requirement can be fulfilled through E-mail and phone number provided by them on storefront during execution of order. It will satisfy the customer's expectations for supply of undamaged goods in time. In certain software packages shipping labels and packing slips for customers are also generated to satisfy such customer expectations.

Payment Processing

This is most crucial stage in E-com to ensure execution of order swiftly. This is done when money is received against order on storefront. The execution of order takes place only when merchant verifies that money has been transferred from customer's through any payment mode like the cash mode, the check mode, the credit card mode or Debit/ATM or merchant Bank. Main popular payment modes are:

The Cash Mode

Difficult and unpopular payment mode known as web E-cash, wherein electronic money or tokens are used by buyers and sellers guaranteed by some third party an usually established Bank. In this model cash is transferred immediately from buyers through digital wallet. No back end process is required. The leading vendor of this model is Digicash communicated as (http://www.digicash.com).

The Check Mode

In this payment mode customer's provide digital version "the check" to web storefront. The digital check is encrypted by using appropriate techniques available in security system. Web storefront verifies the check" through its financial institutions to ensure availability of funds and consults customer's financial, institution too. In this mode funds are not transferred immediately, but ordering software automatically deducts the requisite amount from wallet. The leading vendor in this mode of payment is check free communicated as (www.checkfree.com).

The Credit Mode

It is most convenient and very popular mode of web payment known as Credit Card. Once a consumer enter the credit

Card number on web order form, the internet is used to deliver that information to an authorization server. When authorization succeeds and signal for enough funds availability in customers account is received, a capture transfers the funds from consumers Bank account to merchants Bank account. The credit card facility is in use for long but E-com linked it on the internet is the recent development.

Service and Support

Consumer satisfaction is the essence of future business which is possible when service and support is satisfactorily provided by software package in pre sales, inquires, order tracking and post sales support. The web page need to be designed in such a manner that a merchant can have easy contact via online form, E-mail address and phone number. This facility is available in many software packages namely:

- Automatic Call back
- Click to deal
- Co browsing

Community

Customer is the focal point in all business. Business needs to be more loyal to the customer, to win and encourage him to repeat business. Sales and support services should provide "stickiness" which can be achieved by offering special discounts Sales promotion measures and new items to be added to business. It is why Amazon.com generates 58 percent of its sales from repeat customers.

Web-business is carried under two ways depending on financial strength and volume:

- An in-house technology model
- An instant storefront technology model

An In-house Technology Model

In this model business buy, develop and implement software package, a service platform, redundant internet connection, secure payment processing network connections and round the clock maintenance. It is a personal E-commerce setup possible in large business houses by engaging professional and supporting staff with much more one time cost approximately $ 3 lack. It makes business independent and provides full control and coordination in software and hardware infrastructure. This model facilitates easy and convenient integration in existing and end enterprise system. High cost does not permit most of small business to have their own in-house technology.

Instant Storefront Technology Model

This model is used by those business who cannot afford to have "An in house technology model" to carry out E-commerce. In this model business use vendors or providers of software packages which are available at low cost and require little technical know how. Business has to focus on sale of goods and services only. The instant storefront packages are mainly two:

- Online storefront
- Offline storefront
- Online storefront

In online store front, the entire E-com package is on the service providers infrastructure. Business entities access through internet browsers. The favourable feature in this mode is that business can be managed from anywhere, having internet connection facility available. Business is free from upgradation, supervision and other allied services to storefront. However, the overall control does not rest with business but with service providers or vendors. The maintenance can be time consuming as it depends on speed of internet connection.

Offline Storefront

This mode requires installation of software on the business computing infrastructure. The business builds and maintains the business itself. Business is connected to internet and transmits the website when business wants to publish the changes made in business. In this method business maintains its own speed and control. However, it may be noted that software can not be easily upgraded and re-installed. It is not suitable for small business as they do not have enough time and energy to upgrade or work on such technology.

Security

It is the most sensitive function of E-com. Consumer is more scared about the security as he is transacting money electronically and his financial information is downloaded on internet which is used by large number of internet users. Customer is apprehensive about fraud or misuse of this digital information. This security requires the attention towards following points:

- Data confidentiality
- Authentication and identification
- Access control
- Data integrity
- Non repudiation

Besides security from the view point of consumers, there are various other issues confronting online business as discussed hereunder:-

Intellectual property rights: Intellectual properties are not protected as it is easy to duplicate information and create illegal copies of even copyright protected materials. Confidentiality is not guarded.

Taxation: Commercial transactions are subject to taxation payment almost globally. In on line trade questions like, who pays, who receives, who collects, what is the agency, what is rate of tax-all. These conundrums are still un-addressed so far.

Customs: It violates existing custom rules as no laws are made or amended which are meant to protect domestic industry as a national commitment. Here no such restrictions are imposed by any country.

Regulations: No effective regulations are available till date to prevent privacy or strictly impose certain restrictions to ensure efficient desired security.

Fraud: Mischief or fraud takes place in ordinary course of business. As such, there is no strict rule to punish crimes and frauds. Under 'United States Electronic Funds Transfer Act', a maximum fine of $50 is available for credit card fraud made by credit card holder. For other frauds there is no legislation at all.

Security: In E-com, the pattern of authentication, non-repudiation, accountability and physical delivery are dealt quite differently. No consistent base line is available till date.

Trust: In normal commercial transactions the terms and conditions are fixed face to face by buyers and sellers and suppliers are assured regularity. No such terms and conditions are available on line. It is easy to setup and easy to turn down.

Ubiquitous availability: The E-com results service disruption most of times which is full of risk and causes loss to traders. Business opportunities can be missed till further communications and accessibility will be restored.

Sufficiency of Tools

Cryptography is a useful tool in protecting wide variety of attacks on communication between two ends i.e. merchant and customer. The electronic payment system functions on the basis of cryptography application techniques like S/MIME, SSL, SET. The message of human card reader is called plain text and process of making message unreadable to human is called encryption and decryption in vice versa. Cipher is a mathematical function in cryptography and all modern encryption algorithms use a key. These tools which grant security to payment transactions are explained as under.

Security Socket Layer (SSL)

This protocol is developed by Netscape Communications and submitted to IETF as a standard security protocol. It provides privacy over the network. It provides client server applications in such a way that it prohibits data transmission from being disclosed or altered. It provides both encryption and authentication and operates on TCP transport. It is obvious when transport is secured, the whole data operated on that transport is secured too. When two hosts are communicating on SSL secured transport, all traffic between them is secured. SSL uses three port process:-

- Information is encrypted to prevent un-authorised disclosures.
- Information is authenticated to ensure that same is being sent and received by transacting parties

- SSL provides message integrity to prevent information from being altered during interchange between source and destination.

The typical exchange between SSL server and SSL client is shown in Fig. B.

Fig. B: Secure Socket Layer Protocol transactions between an SSL server and an SSL client

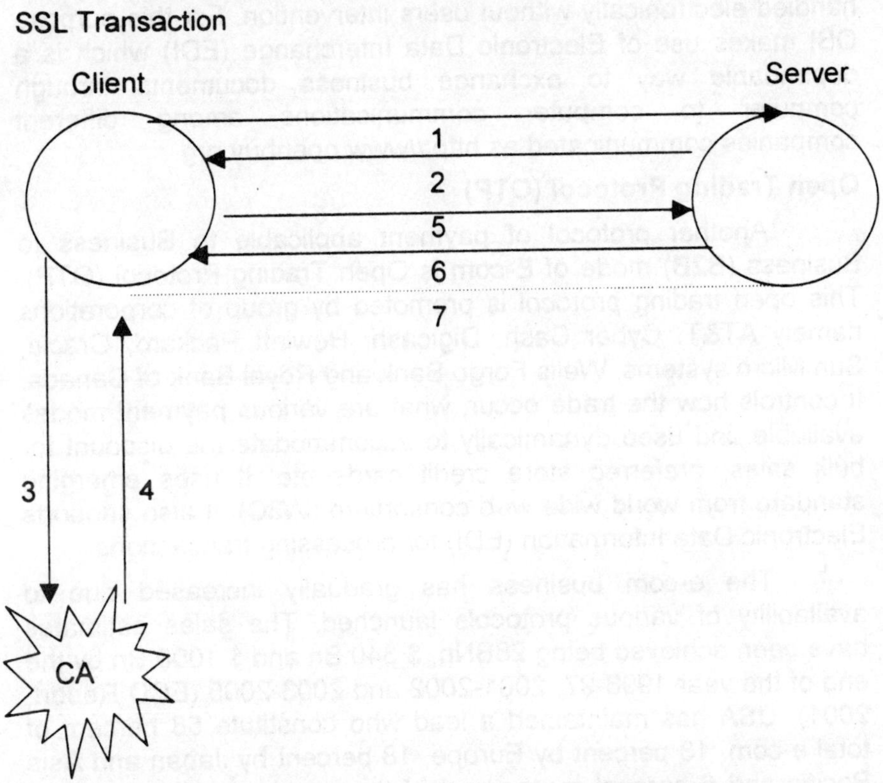

The Fig. B has clearly shown that in the SSL clients exchange session key for transaction and is given up after the transaction is complete. New session keys are opted and exchanged in another transactions by same client on same server. It is transparent to user, easy to operate once browsers are developed. This is feasible in B2C business mode.

Open Buying on Internet (OBI)

This payment security tool is applicable to B2B mode of business. It is sponsored by American Express especially designed to meet high volume transactions at low price in business. The 80 percent of companies business is covered by this protocol. It ensures that purchaser is identified appropriately and his spending capabilities are authorised before purchase process is complete. In this protocol invoicing and payments are handled electronically without users intervention. For this purpose OBI makes use of Electronic Data Interchange (EDI) which is a dependable way to exchange business documents through computer to computer communications among different companies communicated as http://www.openbuy.org.

Open Trading Protocol (OTP)

Another protocol of payment applicable to Business to Business (B2B) mode of E-com is Open Trading Protocol (OTP). This open trading protocol is promoted by group of corporations namely AT&T, Cyber Cash, Digicash, Hewlett Packard, Oracle, Sun Micro systems, Wells Forgo Bank and Royal Bank of Canada. It controls how the trade occur, what are various payment modes available and used dynamically to accommodate the discount for bulk sales, preferred store credit cards etc. It uses emerging standard from world wide web consortium (W3C). It also supports Electronic Data Information (EDI) for processing transactions.

The e-com business has gradually increased due to availability of various protocols launched. The sales estimates have been achieved being 26BNn, $ 340 Bn and $ 1000 Bn by the end of the year 1996-97. 2001-2002 and 2003-2005 (ECD Report, 2001). USA has maintained a lead who constitute 58 percent of total e-com. 18 percent by Europe, 18 percent by Japan and Asia Pacific and 6 percent by the rest of the world as shown in ECD Report, 2001. Studies have also revealed that the use of e-com in business is more popular in youngesters as compared to children and elders. The percentage of youngesters is highest with 49 percent in the age group of 18 to 20 years followed by 28 percent in the age group of 15 to 37 and lowest 3 percent in the age group of above 55 years the same (NASSCOM Report, 2001). Researches have identified that in India e-com users are more professionals in terms of percentage followed by students and lowest by housewives with 38, 43 and 4 percent respectively (NASSCOM Report, 2001).

New Trends

E-com has potential to increase speed, accuracy and efficiency of business as well as personal transactions. Establishment of web storefront can be as simple as allowing internet service provider (ISPs) to host electronic storefront to lease a speed low-concentration Internet access line (T1). The main gains of this mechanism are:-

- Provides Instant world wide availability
- Focuses more on consumer needs
- Permits direct interaction and simplified communications between buyer and seller
- Reduces errors, time and over head costs in information processing by eliminating redundant data entry requirements
- Provides new business opportunities as entrepreneurs design innovative ways to exploit the internet for commerce
- Helps to enter new markets including geographically remote areas.
- Helps wider access to assistance and advice from experts and peers.
- Helps to send and receive online orders for purchase and sale at minimum cost by automatic purchasing.

Since E-com does not provide physical contact, between buyers and sellers, offers great challenges for trustworthiness. Payment security, thus, demands, to address the following:

- Confidence of payment information
- Integration of payment information transmitted over public networks
- Verification regarding account holder using legitimate account.

- Verification regarding merchants acceptances to particular account
- Inter operation between software and network providers.

In view of the above issues in payment security, many protocols were developed from time to time. In 1995 the first protocol known as Secured Electronic Payment Protocol (SEPP) was jointly developed by "Netscape Communication, IBM, Alliance of Master Card. In the same year Visa and Microsoft consortium of a different network payment was launched called Secure Transaction Technology (STT). In January 1996 new protocol was launched to accommodate the SEPP and STT which had created confusion in market called Secure Electronic Transaction (SET). SET was further strengthened when strong global credit card market holder American Express endorsed it. SET became very popular in Europe first but finally got its place in United States too. It relies on existing credit card infrastructure for payments but does not take note of transfer of funds between individuals. It is specific purpose protocol where CMT model applies which refer to buyers, merchant and acquirer. SET assumes the existence of conventional credit card transactions (in which card holder forwards his details to the merchant who sends it to acquirer to obtain clearance for the payment which he gets from the institution who has issued the credit card) facility and only specifies the subset of dialogues between the customer and merchant, and merchant and entity called payment gateway.

In this protocol card holder watch SET transactions on their credit card statements. Acquirer will also see the transactions as an extension of his current relationship with merchant customers. The current version of SET is 1.0. It is also performing complex transactions. It cancels the Authorization of an amount , when merchant fails to make supply of goods. It is further clear from the model as shown in Fig. C and D, that once card holder and merchant are connected, it opens ways for payment on financial network. SET assumes that links are already existing with computer hardware and gateway.

Fig. C: Various phases of Credit Card payment addressed by Secure Electronic Transactions Standard.

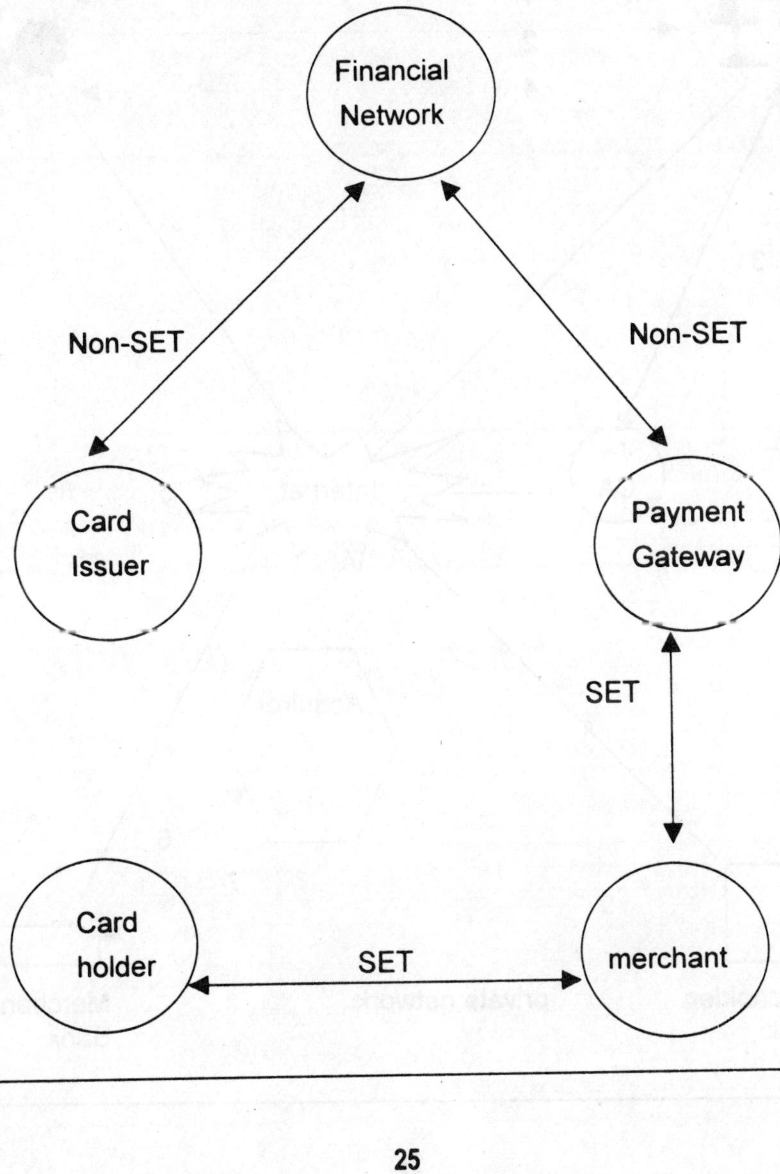

Fig. D: Identical transactions used by SET

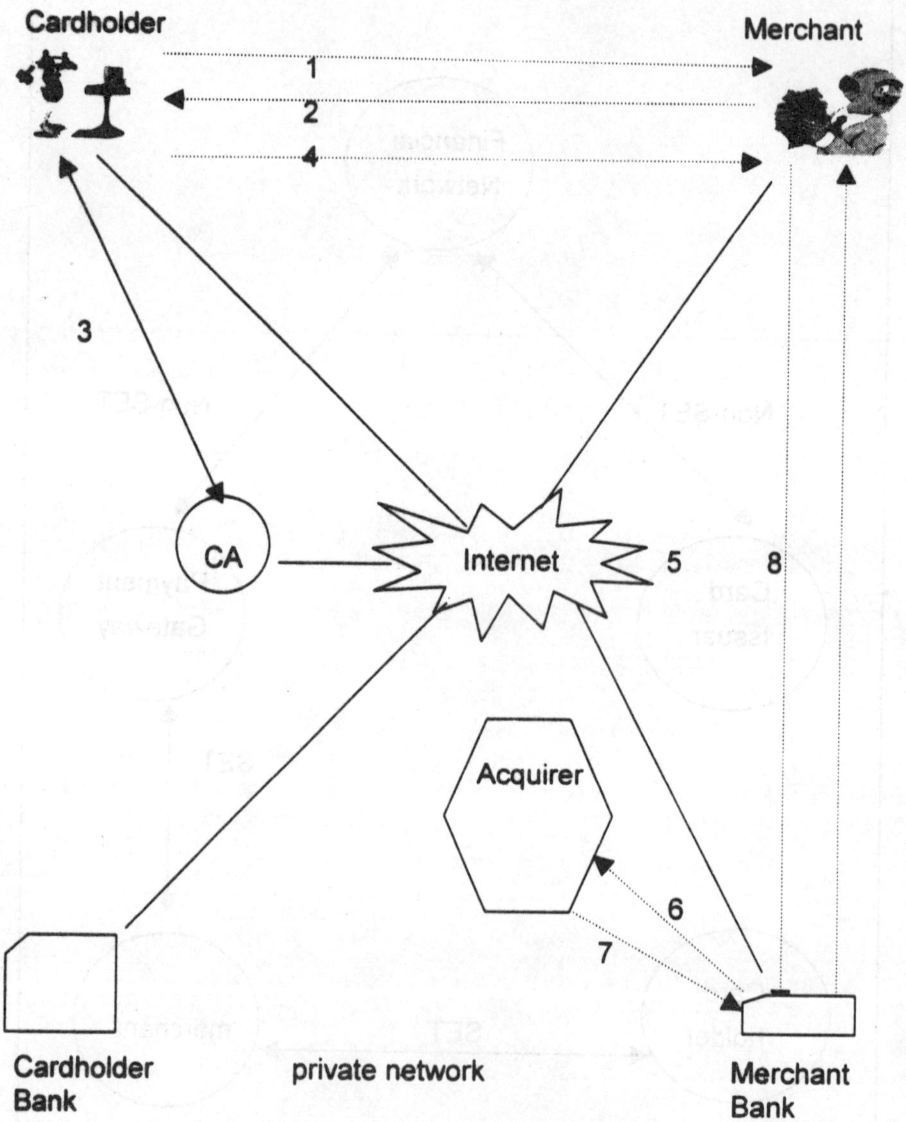

Conclusion

E-commerce has significant impediment on the grounds of establishment of efficient standards. Many standards have been fixed and implemented which seem to have been accepted, as E-commerce shows upward trend in the total business transacted. The existing standards include cryptography, S/MME, SSL, SEPP, STT, and SET etc. Some of these standards are matured and available, while others are in infancy. Standard is still a concern for users, but the paper suggests that many more standards or new protocols need to be devised. Various Associations, individuals, committees researchers and legislators in India and abroad are fully devoted and show concern about it. This is clear from the various reports, recommendations and suggestions made in this regard by various concerned agencies. The availability of Internet is wholly responsible for the growth of E-commerce. In 2000, 36 percent of world population have access to the internet in which India contributes only 0.37 percent. It is observed that attraction is at younger age. Professionals are toppers in the total usage of internet and housewives at the bottom. The new standards are seriously considered to be established and internet protocol version 6 (IPVE) is not sufficient to coup up with the future requirements by 2005. This was disclosed by European Task Force study in May 2001. Information technology Act 2000 has come into force in India from 17th October, 2000 which shows seriousness and regulation efforts towards e-com. E-com help to build competitive advantage by easy access to global market and supplies which ultimately leads to economic growth. At present out of total Internet users, 56 percent are holding credit card who transact 48 percent for books, 25 percent for cinema tickets and 23 percent for music. This clearly indicates very little response to general business i.e. Other than education and entertainment. The traditional way of commerce can be successfully converted into web enabled commerce organisations, provided all facets work well together, and business have well defined targets. It will be a grave lapse if established business in traditional mode is not converted into online mode as the same can help to expand existing business. The established customers should not be disappointed by closing down physical outlets, showrooms or shops where customers physically wish to be present after walking to such departmental outlets for shopping purposes. Web com can assist in selling infrastructure and advertisement and not for total business. The further improvement in the online business could be affected by putting in practice the following suggestions:

i) to push internet penetration
ii) to provide infrastructure status to managed services like ASP's and DSP's
iii) to encourage small scale industries to invest in information technology
iv) to formulate comprehensive rules and regulations regarding Direct and Indirect taxes to encompass electronic transactions.
v) to direct state governments to review sales tax rules
vi) to frame regulations for payment system to decide the pattern of payment of tax.
vii) to give legal sanctions to internet banking
viii) to augment banking technology infrastructure
ix) to lower down the cost of PC's and internet connections
x) to improve poor communication breakdowns.

References

Cris Infae Study, published in Hindustan Times dated 9th Sept, 2000, New Delhi.

Forster, Research Report, New York, Published in the Hindustan Times Business, dated 18th May, 2001 (New Delhi Edition).

Gandhi, Rohit (1998) Advertising on the Web, Still a Bumby Road, Siliconindia Magazine, Oct, 1998.

Interview of Central Minister of State for Commerce in India published in the Hindustan Times on 13th June, 2001 (New Delhi Edition).

Minoli, Daniel and Emma Minoli, Web Commerce Technology Handbook, New York

President, IPV6 Forum report in Ottawa on 16.5.2001, The Hindustan Times Business, (New Delhi Edition).

Report of CII Chief Published in The Hindustan Times Business dated 13 June, 2001 (New Delhi Edition).

Report of CII, published in Hindustan Times dated 10th June, 2001

Report of NASSCOM Chief published in Hindustan Times Business in New Delhi on 3rd August, 2001

Shikeley David, E-Commerce Strategy, Technology and Application

Wilson, Ralph F. Review, I/Cat Commerce on Line

--oOo--

03

COPYRIGHT LAWS AND INFORMATION TECHNOLOGY: AN ANALYTICAL REVIEW

Mehraj Uddin

Introduction

Information Technology in the present century has attained new heights and has penetrated very deep in almost every sector of the society. The information technology is growing faster and faster and the challenges of cybernetics, internet revolution, rapid spinning of the World Wide Web (WWW), mass reeling of hyper text transfer protocol(http) and hypertext marking language (html) have given birth to serious judicial issues of techno-legal dimensions, especially in the area of intellectual property rights (IPR) regime.[1]

The entire world has shrunk into a global village and the communication net-work has become very strong and effective. It is true that at the close end of 20th century, we witnessed major changes, primarily because of cyber technology, cyber commercial transactions, cyber piracy, cyber pornography and other related issues. Information technology and fast communication links have revolutionized the whole world with its tremendous impact on the global commercial transactions. The business class can't run their business effectively with out modern hi-tech aids. The consumers, sellers, manufactures and others are using computers to create, transmit and store information in the electronic form. The age old reliable method of pen, paper and ledger is being replaced by hard and software and in the advanced countries, it has been already replaced. In fact, the traditional pattern of paper documents are being discarded for the reasons that electronic method is cheaper in cost, easier to store and retrieve, faster to transmit and communicate.

No doubt, advantages of electronic medium are obvious, but business community, by and large have been reluctant to transact business in the electronic form, because of some apprehensions regarding validity of such transactions. The business transactions for their validity, enforcement and adjudication, in case of any breach by either of the two parties, need a proper paper documentation failing which such transactions have no value in the eyes of law. It is true that there was a time, when all the commercial transactions were carried out on the basis of oral communications and oral commitments, and there was hardly any chance of breach. The common phrase in the business community was that 'it is my word' and normally no one dared to retreat from one's word/stand. Honesty was regarded as the best policy and dishonestly was an exception.

However, with the dawn of modern era, selfishness, greed and materialistic tendencies changed the entire scenario and business transactions did often come under the clouds of breach followed by claims and counter claims and hence the need for written documentation, as the adjudicator or court can't arrive to the conclusions, unless 'facts' and 'arguments' asserted by the parties are supported by the documentary evidence. The law of evidence is based on paper documents for which writing and signature is an essential requirement for the enforcement. The parties, because of all these facts were very much apprehensive to facilitate and promote e-commerce. However, despite all the apprehensions, the business through electronic gadgets continues to boom with the growth in information technology.

The business through electronic medium at the National and International level is growing rapidly with a very vast and wide ambit to cover almost all major business transactions and as the e-commerce eliminates the paper documentation, hence the need for a change in legal procedure and legal frame work to deal with emerging trends in commerce became an urgent necessity to remove all the apprehensions and to facilitate e-commerce. The efforts have been made to change laws both at National and International level. It became need of the hour to bring all electronic transactions within the legal framework and to give a legal shape to such transactions, legal rights and obligations that flow thereof. Hence, legal movement to cover the issues posed by e-medium in general and e-commerce in particular gained momentum.

2. The Copyright Law

2.1 The Perspective

The development of various methods to deal with and to enforce the commercial transactions has a long drawn history. Copyright laws, Intellectual Property laws and IT laws have a number of common issues and all these laws have developed with the development of modern technology. It is a fact that in the ancient days, greed and materialism was hardly any body's concern and creative persons like artists, musicians and writers made, composed or wrote their works for fame and recognition rather than to make money out of it. The issue of copyright never arose, but it assumed significance with the invention of the printing press. [2]

Importance of copyright in fact, was recognised only with the invention of printing press, which enabled the reproduction of books in large quantity. Moreover, production and re-production of the creative work in large quantity was abused to the detriment of the authors or creative works. The first Copyright law, known as Statute of Anne, was enacted in 1710 in England and subsequently known as UK Copyright Act 1911. A number of countries through out the globe followed the suit and enacted laws to check copyright violations. India, in order, to safe guard the interests of the author or creator of some work, enacted the first legislation in 1914, which was mainly based on the UK Copyright Act 1911.

However, in a span of more than four decades (1914-1957) a lot of changes took place in the area of broadcasting, television, and cinematography, etc. and mode of printing. The Copyright Act 1914 did not visualize the changes in the communications, cinematography and other related sectors. The movement for the development of the copyright law and moreover, in order to cope-up with the post independence scenario, constitutional mandate of independent India and to fulfill international obligations in the field of copyright, a complete revision of copyright law was under-taken and finally Copyright Act 1957 was enacted. The said Act, no doubt has in a way re-arranged the basic principles of the existing laws but it has been tailored to cover all the developments in the area of copyright from 1914-1957. The aim and object of the copyright law is to balance two extreme and hostile situations i.e. the exclusive monopoly of the copyright on one hand and the necessity of the public access and free flow of information on the other hand.

The ostensible purpose of the copyright laws is not for denying or restricting information, but to make the information available for common and public good and also to encourage authors in their intellectual contribution and to secure value for their endeavours.[3] The Act has been amended on several occasions in 1983, 1984, 1992 and 1999.

2.2 The main features

The main features of the existing copyright law of 1957 with the update amendments are as under:-

i) Copyright Office:

The Act provided for establishment of the 'Copyright Office' under the control of the Registrar of Copyrights.[4]

ii) Registration:

The Copyright Act 1957 under Sec.44 provides for registration of the work in a prescribed format. However, the registration is not mandatory.

iii) Copyright Board:

The Act provides for establishment of the Copyright Board.[5] The Board shall be deemed to be a Civil Court for the purposes of the Code of Criminal Procedure 1973[6] and all proceedings before the Board shall be deemed to be judicial proceedings within the meaning of the Indian Penal Code 1860 [7]

4) Scope of the Copyright:

The scope of the definition of copyright has been enlarged, to include exclusive right to communicate works by radio diffusion. It also includes broadcast and re-broadcast. The original literary, dramatic, musical and artistic works, cinematograph films, sound recording etc. brought within the purview of the Copyright laws. [8]

Further, under various amendments, a number of new dimensions have been given to the concept of copyright. It is now provided that communication to the public means, making any work available for being seen or heard or otherwise enjoyed by the public directly or by any means of display or diffusion other than by issuing copies of such work regardless of whether any member of the public actually sees, hears or otherwise enjoys the work so made available.[9]

v) Computer Programme:

The computer programme has been also brought within the purview of the copyright law. The Act provides that computer includes any electronic or similar device having information processing capabilities. Computer Programme as per the Act means a set of instructions expressed in words, codes, schemes or in any other form, including a machine readable medium, capable of causing a computer to perform a particular task or to achieve a particular result. It further defines that duplicating equipment means any mechanical contrivance or device used or intended to be used for making copies of any work. Literary work as per provisions of the Act, includes computer programmes, tables and compilations.[10]

The amendment of 1999 has introduced some more expectations within the ambit of Sec.52, that are specifically applicable to computer programmes. Moreover, certain acts under the provisions of the Act, do not constitute infringement of the copyright.

vi) Copyright with the Author:

The first owner of copyright shall be the author. However, this is subject to the provisions of the Copyright Act[11]

vii) Term of Copyright:

The Act has fixed the term of the copy right as life of the author and 25 years after death. However, in case of a literary, dramatic or musical or artistic work, which is published anonymously or pseudonymously, the copyright shall subsist until sixty years from the beginning of the calendar year next following the year in which the work is first published. However, where identity of the author is disclosed before expiry of the said copyright then in that case, it shall subsist until sixty years from the beginning of the calendar year following the year in which the author dies.[12]

It is further provided that in case of posthumous work, the copyright shall subsist until sixty years from the beginning of the calendar year next following the year in which the work is first published.[13]

The Act also deals separately with term of copyright in case of photographs, cinematograph films, sound recording, works of public undertakings, Government works and works of international organisations.[14]

viii) Right of Assignment:

The Act gives right of assignment to the author. It is now provided that the owner of the copyright may assign to any person the copyright either wholly or partially and either generally or subject to limitations and either for the whole of the copyright or any part thereof. However, no assignment of the copyright in any work shall be valid unless it is in writing, signed by assignor or by his duly authorised agent.[15]

ix) Right to Relinquish:

The Act provides that subject to the provisions of the Act, the author has a right to relinquish all or any of the rights.[16]

x) License to Produce/Publish Translations:

The Act provides for issuance of license to produce or reproduce and publish translations. However, the issuance of license is subject to the provisions of the Act and can be terminated as per provisions of the Act [17]

xi) License for Public Performances:

The Act provides for issuance of special or general license for public performance of any work by means of radio receiving set or any mechanical tools. It deals with broadcast reproduction right and provides for performer's rights.[18]

xii) License to Library:

The Act provides that a license may be issued to any library to make or cause to be made one copy of any book in which copyright subsists.

xiii) Copyright Societies:

The Act provides for registration of the Copyright Societies. It also deals with administration of rights of owner, payment of remuneration and control by copyright society.[19]

xiv) International Copyright.

The Act provides power to extend copyright to foreign works. It deals with the power of the Central Government in respect of broadcasting organisa-tions and performers in certain other countries. The provisions have been also made in respect of works of certain foreign International organisations and foreign authors.[20] As per the amended law (w.e.f. 15.1.2000) the Central Government has the power to issue direction to the effect that all or any provision of the Act relating to work first published in any territory outside India to which the order relates in like manner, as if the authors were citizens of India. This equally applies to unpublished work. The content spinned under WWW, http and html can be brought within the scope of International copyright administration.

xv) Offences:

The Copyright Act provides that any person who knowingly infringes or abets the infringement of the copyright in a work or any other right conferred by this Act shall be liable as per provisions of the Act.[19] Further, any person who knowingly makes use on a computer of an infringing copy of a computer programme shall be liable.[21]

xvi) Powers of the Police

The Act has empowered the police officer, not below the rank of a sub-inspector, may if he is satisfied, seize with out warrant, all copies of the work, and all other related material used for the purpose. [22]

xvii) Remedies

The following remedies are available to the owner of the work, whose right under the Copyright Act has been violated.

a) Injunction

b) Damages

c) Accounts or

d) Any other right which may be conferred by law.

Scope of the remedies provided under Section 55 are narrowed down by the provisions of the Section itself. The Section provides that if the Defendant proves that as on the date of infringement, he was not aware and no reasonable ground to believe that copyright subsisted in the work, the plaintiff shall not be entitled to any work. Further, remedy in case of ground-less threat given by the owner to the Defendant also gives a negative effect to the remedy available under the section.

xviii) Appeals

The Act also provides detailed procedure for appeal to the party aggrieved by order of the Court or Registrar. The appeal against certain orders of the Magistrate can be made in the higher court and against the Registrar to

Copyright Board.[23] The appeal against Copyright Board can be made in the High Court.[24]

03 Cyber Legislations

The modern legislation regarding information technology dates back to 1977 when the World Intellectual Property Organisation (WIPO) drafted Model provisions for the protection of computer software by encompassing three major components of IT such as computer programmes, programme description and supporting materials.

The Model law 1977 defines 'Computer programmes' as a set of instructions capable, when incorporated in a machine-readable to have information-processing capabilities to indicate, perform or achieve a particular function, task or result. The 'programme description' means a complete procedural representation in verbal, schematic or other form, insufficient detail to determine a set of instructions, constituting a corresponding computer programme. The 'supporting material' entails any matter other than a computer programme or a programme description, created for aiding the understanding or application of a computer programme, for example a problem descriptions and user instructions.[25]

The National Commission on New Technology uses of copyrighted work, (CONTU) 1978. The Commission, subscribed that computer programmes are not analogous to literary works.[26] Even the most important international copyright convention i.e. Berne Convention does not protect the communication to public or publication right of the author in the digital context, under the convention. Copyright-protection covers all 'literary and artistic work' encompassing diverse forms of original creativity, such as fiction and non-fiction, scientific and technical texts, computer programmes, data base musical works audio-visual works, fine art, drawings painting and photograph.[27]

The convention provides that collection of literary or artistic work such as encyclopaedias and anthologies which be reason of the selection and arrangement of their contents constitute intellectual creations shall be protected as such, without prejudice to the copyright in each of the work forming part of such collection.[28]

The developed countries saw intellectual property as the fruit of the creative capacity and intellectual efforts of their individual citizens and companies, as a legitimate basis for these companies and individual to earn a trading advantage. Trade related aspects of Intellectual Property Rights (TRIPS) harmonised the National trade and intellectual property laws, including copyright law.[29]

Part-11 of the Agreement deals in depth with the various aspects of copyright and imposes an obligation on members of the World Trade Organisation (WTO) to comply with Art/1 to 21 of the Berne Convention 1971[30] Art. 10 of TRIPS deals with computer programmes and stipulates that computer programmes shall be treated as literary works under the Berne Convention. It is further provided that 'compilation of data' or other material, whether in machine readable or other form, which by reason of the selection or arrangement of their contents constitute intellectual creations shall be protected as such. The protection which shall not extend to the data or material itself, shall be without prejudice to any copyright subsisting the data or material itself.

The Agreement basically envisages for a copyright protection not only for the databases, but also for the manner in which the database has been arranged. The World Intellectual Property Organisation (WIPO) Internet Treaties namely (a) WIPO Copy right Treaty WCT; and (b) WIPO Performances and Phonograms Treaty (WPPT) both address to the issues pertaining to the challenges of online enforcement and licensing. The drafts of the WIPO copyright treaty were able to comprehend a situation whereby the question of relationship between the copyright laws and the internet was brought to the forefront. The Treaty contains a provision which provides that compilation of data or other material, in any form, which by reason of the selection or arrangement of their contents constitute intellectual creations, are protected as such. It takes into account the internet.[31]

04. The Juristic Issues

The cyber communications gained momentum in the developed countries and e-commerce replaced the paper based transactions. The developing countries were left with no option, but to jump in the race. The cyber transactions and violations thereof have posed new challenges to the legal system and has given birth to numerous issues pertaining to procedure, implementation and enforcement. The basic issues, however being as under:

a) Validity of the electronic contracts;
b) Enforcement of electronic contracts;
c) Copyright parameters;
d) Rights and duties of the parties;
e) Limitations of the liability;
f) Extra-territorial jurisdiction;
g) Right of liberty;
h) Right of privacy;
i) Powers of the police;
j) Right of information;
k) Excludes NIA;
l) Penalties and adjudication; and
m) Various other issues.

The Legal Movement

In order to address to the juristic issues, the legal movement both at National and International level was initiated and it gained momentum through out the world. The United Nations Commission on International Trade Law (UNCITRAL) in view of the growing trend of the commercial transactions through electronic medium drafted a model law that covers the issues pertaining to such commercial transactions. The Model law of UNCITRAL was adopted in the year 1996 and the General Assembly of the United Nations recommended that all the States should give favourable considerations to the said Model Law, when they enact or revise their laws.[32]

The UNCITRAL Model Law on electronic commerce provides for equal treatment of the user of the electronic communications and paper based communications. Further, in pursuance to a recent declaration by member countries, the World Trade Organisation (WTO) also provided inputs in this direction. The member countries, keeping in view the growing trend of the e-commerce recognised the need for bringing suitable amendments in their existing laws.

05. Indian Scenario:

The development of various methods to deal with and to enforce the commercial transactions has a long drawn history. Copyright laws, Intellectual Property laws and IT laws have a number of common issues and all these laws have developed with the development of modern technology. It is a fact that in the ancient days, greed and materialism was hardly any body's concern and creative persons like artists, musicians and writers made, composed or wrote their works for fame and recognition rather than to make money out of it. The issue of copyright never arose, but it assumed significance with the invention of the printing press.[2] The first Copyright law, known as Copyright Act 1914 finally Copyright Act 1957 was enacted. The said Act, no doubt has in a way re-arranged the basic principles of the existing laws but it has been tailored to cover all the developments. The Act has been amended on several occasions in 1983, 1984, 1992 and 1999. Further, most of the issues raised by the modern technological revolution do not fit within the scope of the commercial laws.

India in the light of growing trend of e-commerce, enacted Information Technology Act 2000 [33] The Act is based on functional equivalent approach and attempts to address to the apprehensions of the business community. The basic features of the IT Act are as under:

i) To facilitate e-commerce;

ii) To give recognition to e-record and digital signatures;

iii) To enable to conclude e-contracts;

iv) To create rights and obligations through electronic medium;

v) To provide regulatory mechanism for issuing Digital Signature Certificates;

vi) To supervise the Supervising Authorities issuing Digital Signature Certificates.

vii) To prevent possible misuse arising out of transactions and dealings carried out and concluded over electronic medium.

viii) To create civil and criminal liabilities for breach or contravention of its provisions.

ix) To facilitate and promote electronic governance.

x) The Act provides for acceptance of electronic and digital signatures in the Government offices and other Private and Public agencies.

xi) The Act lays down the procedure to deal with IT violations, which amount to an offence under the provisions of the Act.

xii) The Act gives recognition and legal shape to electronic fund transfers between the financial Institutions and Banks.

xiii) The Act gives legal sanctity for books of account maintained in the electronic form by the Financial Institutions and Bankers.

xiv) The IT provides for necessary changes in the existing laws and for this purpose amendments in the relevant provisions of the of the following have been made.

a) Indian Penal Code 1860

b) Indian Evidence Act 1872

c) Reserve Bank of India Act 1934

d) Banker's Books of Evidence Act 1891

xv) The provisions of the Act [34] however, do not apply to the following:

a) A negotiable instrument as defined in Section 13 of the Negotiable Instruments Act, 1881 (26 of 1881)

b) A power-of-attorney as defined in Section 1A of the Powers of Attorney Act, 1882 (7 of 1882)

c) A trust as defined in Section 3 of the Indian trusts Act, 1882, (2 of 1882)

d) A will as defined in clause (h) of Section 2 of the Indian Succession Act 1925 (39 of 1925), including any other testamentary disposition by whatever name called.

e) Any contract for the sale of conveyance or immovable property or any interest in such property.

f) Any such class of documents or transactions as may be notified by the Central Government in the official Gazette.

Contraventions under the Act

The IT Act analyses contravention of the provisions of the Act and defines various forms of the offences which attract the provisions of the Act. The contravention under Ss 43 & 44 of the Act are basically of two patterns. The first one falls under the category of damage to the computer, computer system or computer net-work and the second one under the category of failure to furnish information. The Act provides that any one who with out the permission of the owner or any other person who is in charge of the computer, computer system or computer net-work commits any of the violation falling under the first category shall be liable to pay damages by way of compensation not exceeding one crore rupees to the person so effected by such act. The second pattern of violations pertain to failure to furnish information and penalty is provided for each violation.

a) Damage to the Computer and Computer System

If any one with out the permission of the owner or any other person who is the incharge of a computer, computer system or computer network, is liable for an offence under the Act. (S.43), if he:

i) Accesses or secures access to such computer, computer system, or computer net-work; [S. 43(a)]

ii) Down loads copies or extracts of any data, computer data base or any information from such computer, computer system or computer network including information or data held or stored under in any removable storage medium; [S. 43(b)]

iii) Introduces or causes to be introduced any computer virus or containment into any computer, computer system or computer net-work; [S.43 (c)]

iv) Damages or causes to be damaged any computer, computer system or computer network, data, computer data base or any other programmes residing in such computer, computer system or computer net-work; [S.43 (d)]

v) Disrupts or causes disruption of any computer, computer system or computer net-work;

vi) Denies or causes the denial of access to any person authorised to access any computer, computer system or computer net-work;

vii) Provides any assistance to any person to facilitate access to a computer, computer system or computer net-work in contravention of the provisions of this Act; and

viii) Charges the services availed of by a person to the account of any other person by tampering with or manipulating any computer, computer system or computer net-work.

b) Failure to Furnish Information:

i) The Act provides that if any person who is required to furnish any information or document, return or report to the Controller or the certifying authority or any rules there under does not furnish the same shall be liable to a penalty up to rupees one lakh and fifty thousand for every such failure.

ii) The Act provides that any person who fails to file any return or furnish the same within the stipulated time therefore in the regulation, shall be liable to a penalty not exceeding five thousand rupees for every day during which such failure continues.

iii) The Act provides that any person who fails to maintain books of account or records shall be liable to a penalty not exceeding ten thousand rupees for every day during which the failure continues. Further, tampering with computer source document, hacking, publication of obscene information and various other forms of contravention are punishable under the Act.

Penalties under the Act:

The punishment for various types of the offences/ contraventions under the Act are analysed as under:-

S. No	Offence	Punishment
1.	Damage to computer system etc (S.43)	Fine upto rupees one crore.
2.	Failure to furnish information (S.44/a)	Fine upto rupees one lakh and fifty thousand.
3.	Failure to file information within specified time. (S.44/b)	Fine upto fifty thousand for each day.
4.	Failure to maintain books of Accounts/record. (S.4/c)	Fine upto ten thousand rupees each day
5.	Contravention of any rule or regulation, where penalty is not expressly provided (S.45)	Fine upto rupees fifty thousand or upto same amount person concerned
6.	Tampering with the computer source document (S.65)	Imprisonment upto three years or fine upto two lakhs or both.
7.	Hacking with computer system (S.66)	Imprisonment upto three years or fine upto two lakhs or both
8.	Publication of obscene information	
	First Conviction (S.67)	Imprisonment up to five years and fine upto rupees one lakh
	Second Conviction	Just double the punishment prescribed for first conviction
9.	Failure to comply the direction of the Controller of Compliance with the Act (S.68)	Three years imprisonment and a fine upto two lakh or both
10.	Failure by the subscriber in not helping any agency	Imprisonment upto seven years

	to decrypt Information on the direction of the Controller, which may be against the sovereignty or security of the State. (S.69)	years.
11.	Securing or attempt to secure access to a protected system (S.70)	Imprisonment upto ten years and fine
12,	Supression or mis-represetation of the material facts to the authorities (S.71)	Imprisonment upto two years Fine upto rupees one lakh or both
13.	Securing access to any confidential book or record and to pass it on to (S.72)	Imprisonment upto two years or fine upto one lakh or both
14.	Publication of DSC	
	a) with false particulars (S.73)	Imprisonment and fine as prescribed under S.71 and S.72
	b) For fraudulent purpose (S.74)	-do-
15.	Computer or any other material used for contravention of the Act (S.76)	Confiscation
16.	Contravention of a rule or order by a company	
	a) Liability of a person (S. 85/1)	Punishment as per rule
	b) Attributable to any other person (S. 85/2)	Punishment as per rule

>>

Conclusions and Suggestions

The internet, the paradise of the computer world is now a place every where devoid of frontiers. It is growing community of millions of people around the world, which any one can join at his will. (The Brave New World of Cyberspace, Copyrights and Internet: An Interface Nafees Ahmad et al.). Copyright and the the internet is common language which helps computers with different operating systems to communicate with each other, using a standard set of protocols. A protocol is a set of rules which the computers use to communicate with each other. There are now more than 70 million users of the internet world wide, and the number is on increase. (Sharat Jain & B.M.Agarawal, The Internet Chapter One, Mashbra Industries (P) Ltd. New Delhi (2000) 7.

The Internet is a global collection of computer net-works linking millions of computers around the world. The internet is now recognised as an international system, a communication medium that allows any one from any part of the globe with access to internet to freely exchange information and share data. The internet provides on a variety of matters. A computer or device that is attached to internet and has an address which is known as 'Domain Name' [Akhtar, A. Junaid].

India is the 12th country in the world to have comprehensive law with clear definition of crime and punishment. But immediately after the law came into cyber force, a number of incidents of violations came to the surface. The rate of incidents of cyber crimes is on increase. The Act no doubt, covers a number of issues viz. unauthorised access to computer net-works, data bases, viruses, damage to the systems, disruption of services, copying of software, tampering with the computer source documents, pornography and electronic forgery are all covered under the Act. At present, e-banking provides online account information, request and intimation of bill presentation and personalised customer service.

However, there are some uncovered in the Act, that could limit its efficacy. The issues of legality, security and accountability could potentially block the movement forward, in areas like online opening of accounts, electronic funds transfer, electronic cash and virtual banking.

Pramod Rao, VP, ICICI, pointed out that on line opening of account is hampered due to legal requirement of physical proof of residence and identity. T.K. Viswanathan, Member Secretary, Law Commission also concedes that law is not very effective.

The IT Act provides for establishment of Cyber Appellant Tribunal and appointment of adjudication officer for holding enquiries under the Act. There is a special provision under the Act that appeal from the order of an adjudication officer can be made to Cyber Appellate Tribunal only and not to any Civil Court, and appeal from order of Cyber Appellant Tribunal to the High Court.

The Act provides for legal sanction to electronic records, as well as acceptance of contracts by electronic means of communication.

01) Detection of Cyber Crimes

The entire Criminal Justice System is defective, where in it is very difficult to deduct the traditional crime. (Tandoori murder case, Priyadarshini murder case and Jasika Lal murder case). It is very difficult to track, deduct and prove computer related crimes.

02) Professional Agencies:

The professional agencies in India are not well prepared and equipped to handle and investigate the cyber crimes. Most of the police officers are not aware about electronic transactions and digital system.

03) Digital Evidence:

The mafia dons who utilize the services of the experts, know how to manipulate, tamper with or even destroy any type of evidence within the shortest possible time.

04) Money Laundering:

The fast speed of electronic transactions, easy access to each other and lack of face to face contact has promoted money laundering and they are going far

06) Supari Commerce

07) Proper Training:

08) Proper Registration:

a) Subscribers

b) Internet Service Providers

c) Cyber Cafes

09) Proper authentication of the user

Chennai based Myespace has devised Web authentication of the genuineness of the user. Enter Oye Nok Web authentication, it will ensure the genuineness of every transaction of the user. For instance, a person went to a Hotel, gave his credit card to the Receptionist for payment. The Receptionist, before returning the credit card to the Plaintiff noted the number and other details and passed on the information to the Computer Operator and succeeded in making online purchases to the tune of Rs. 42000/-. The Plaintiff received the bill for the said amount.

10) Cyber Task Force

National Information Technology Security Centre (NITSC) as a part of multi-prolonged approach to control crime.

- Intruder attack on many high profile organisations Web sites in India.
- Web defacement of Bhabha Atomic Research Centre
- The theft of telephone numbers related to information from the system of Chief Manager, Department of Telecom in Hyderabad by a haker of Australian origin.
- Web-page defacement of the Department of Electronics by a Pakistani Hacker.

11) Cyber Cell

District/State/Centre

12) Computer Forensic Centres

Power of computer reaching millions

13) Online Purchases

14) Proper Co-ordination

Notes and References:

1) Bigelow: (1973) Computer and the Law, Chap. 9.

2) Cormish; W.R: (1989) Intellectual Property, Sweet & Maxwell.

3) Nafees Ahmad et al: The Brave New World of Cyberspace: Copyrights & Internet: An Interface, Paper submitted in a National Seminar on 'Copyright and Information Technology: Problems and

Prospects' Faculty of Law, Aligarh Mualim University, Aligarh. (May 5-7,2001)

4) Copyright Act 1957 S.9

5) Id. Ss 11 & 12

6) Code of Criminal Procedure 1973 (2 of 1974) Ss. 345 & 346

7) Indian Penal Code 1860 (45 of 1860) Ss. 193 & 228

8) Supra note 3, S.13 (b) (Act 38 Of 1994)

9) Supra note 3, S. 2(ff)

10) Supra note 3, S 2 (0) (ffb), 2(hh) (Act 38 of 1994).

11) Supra note 3, S.17

12) Supra note 3, S. 22

13) Supra note 3, Ss. 22-24

14) Supra note 3, Ss. 25-29

15) Supra note 3, Ss. 18 &19

16) Supra note 3, S.21

17) Supra note 3, S.32

18) Supra note 3, Ss. 37-39-A

19) Supra note 3, Ss. 33-36

20) Supra note 3, Ss.40-43

21) Supra note 3, S. 63

22) Supra note 3, S. 64

23) Supra note 3, Ss.71 and 72/1

24) Supra note 3, S. 72/2

25) Sam Ricketson (1987) The Berne Convention for the protection or literary and Artistic Works, 896.

26) Barton; JH 'Adopting the Intellectual property system to New Technologies. Wallerstein et at. (ets) Global Dimensions of Intellectual Property Rights in Science and Technology. 1993

27) The Berne Convention. Arts 2(1) and 2(5)

28) Ibid

29) The Trips Agreement 1995 Art.9-40

30) John Croome, Reshaping the World Trading System. History of the urguay Round,1996

31) WIPO Copy right Treaty 1996 Art.

32) Id. Art. 8

33) Information Technology Act. (21 of 2000) It came into force on 17th Oct. 2000 vide G.S.R.) dated 17th Oct. 2000

34) Id. S. 1(4)

35) Id. Ss. 43-44

-oo-

04

SURVEY OF INTERNET PAYMENT SYSTEMS

Khavar Meraj Handoo

Abstract

There are several classes of commercial transactions necessary for Internet Commerce. One of the more important of these transaction classes, payment systems, enables consumer-oriented activities such as on-line shopping and bill payment. Payment systems also enable business activities such as invoice payment, cash management, supply chain settlement, and procurement.

The method of payment is one component which is critical to successfully conducting business across a network. There are various payment systems currently available designed to provide payment transactions over the Internet. It is the intent of this survey to assist prospective Internet users, merchants, and service providers in understanding the various Internet payment alternatives. This survey ,of the major electronic payment schemes currently available - from a technical perspective, is meant as a starting place to learn about these payment systems and provide "at-a-glance comparison," of some of the payment systems.

Introduction

The use of the WWW as an electronic marketplace is increasing, and there is a need for a cash payment system that is scaleable, anonymous and secure.

The World Wide Web (www) has potential to become a highly efficient electronic marketplace for goods and services. When payments are effected electronically, there is always a risk that organizations may resort to gathering information relating individuals with the amounts that they have spent, locations involved and types of good purchased. Misuse of such information can give rise to serious breaches of personal privacy. If a payment system for the WWW is to receive widespread support, it must offer its users some form of protection against the gathering of such information. The most effective method of achieving this is to implement a form of electronic cash, where the coins' being spent cannot be linked with their owner. This gives rise to a secondary problem in that since the coin is an electronic quality that is easily duplicated, such a payment system must guard against the coin being spent more than once. It should not be possible for an attacker to bypass the system or to falsely obtain monetary value from it.

At the time of writing, it has been estimated that there may be over 30 million users of the Internet spread across 96 different countries using over 6.6 million host computers, and these figures are rising very rapidly. This means that an effective electronic payment system must be highly scaleable. In practice, the system must support large numbers of buyers and sellers affiliated to many different banks. The problem of detection of double spending is particularly acute, and solutions must be found that allow for large numbers of payments to take place without requiring unreasonably large databases to be maintained.

A digital money transfer is a payment mechanism that empowers the consumer to take possession of the electronic money, from a bank account or credit card, and store the monetary value on a card or piece of hardware (i.e., a PC or personal digital assistant). Once the consumer takes possession of the "electronic cash" he or she is able to transfer the value to another party – a consumer, bank, or vendor - over the Internet.

The following is a list of digital money transfer mechanisms that included in the matrix. This list is divided into two categories, systems that depend on the use of smart cards to provide security and other features; and those that are strictly software based.

1. Smart Cards

Mondex: Mondex uses a smart card to store electronic cash, which can be used to pay for goods and services in the same way as cash. A locking system makes it more secure than cash. Mondex cash can be sent and received across phone and computer lines and between Mondex wallets. Each time the card is used, the chip on the card generates a unique "digital signature" that guarantees that the card is genuine and identifies the card for which the cash is intended, so it is not intercepted.

EMV '96: EMV '96 is a proprietary specification developed by Europay MasterCard and Visa (EMV) that performs electronic payments using cards with embedded integrated circuits. EMV '96 is a set of global specifications for credit and debit applications employing smart card technology. These specifications provide the framework for moving debit and credit cards from magnetic stripe to chip technology to reduce fraud and improve management of credit risk.

2. Electronic Cash

ECash: ECash is digital coinage for on-line transactions developed by Digicash. Using the e-cash client software, a customer withdraws ecash from a bank and stores it on his computer. The bank that mints coins validates existing coins and exchanges real money for ecash. Merchants can accept ecash coins in payment for information or goods. The client software is called a "cyberwallet" and is responsible for withdrawing and depositing coins from a bank and for paying or receiving coins from a merchant. The identity of the payer is not revealed.

Millicent: MilliCent is an Internet payment system for small-scale commercial transactions. The MilliCent Wallet uses electronic tokens called scrip that can be spent on the Web. Scrip is kept safely on the user's PC disk and protected by a personal identification number or password. MilliCent provides a number of authorities, or brokers, to sell scrip – only one broker per customer. Payments can happen in two ways: (1) pay-per-click for just the content needed, as small as 1/10 of a cent, or (2) a subscription can be opened that allows unrestricted access.

Worldpay: Worldpay is a secure multi-currency electronic payment system designed to be used over the Internet. Customers have a WorldPay multi-currency account authorized by a credit or debit card. The accounts are operated centrally; therefore, funds can be accessed from any computer anywhere in the world. WorldPay handles micro-payments over the Internet in over 16 currencies. It transfers funds from the customer's account to the merchant's WorldPay bank account. Unused funds can be returned any time to the original credit/debit card used to fund the account.

Cybercoin: Cybercoin can be used for credit card transactions and, within the U.S., for micro-payments and electronic check transfers. In short, Cybercoin is a software-based electronic cash product. The protocol is a proprietary specification that is currently unpublished. Recently the system has closely aligned itself with SET.

This survey is restricted to the study of two electronic cash systems, requiring no additional hardware such as smart cards, which can be used to make payments for WWW resources have been published.

The first, Ecash, is a fully anonymous electronic cash system, using numbered bank accounts and blind signatures. The second, NetCash, uses identified electronic cash giving a more scaleable but less anonymous system.

Electronic cash is the electronic equivalent of real paper cash, and can be implemented using public-key cryptography, digital signatures, and blind signatures. In an electronic cash system there is usually a bank, responsible for issuing currency, customers who have accounts at the bank and can withdraw and deposit currency, and merchants who will accept currency in exchange for goods or a service. Every customer, merchant, and bank has its own public/private key pair. The keys are used to encrypt, for security, and to digitally sign, for authentication, blocks of data that represent coins. A bank digitally signs coins using its private key. Customers and merchants verify the coins using the bank's widely-available public key. Customers sign bank deposits and withdrawals with their private key, and the bank uses the customer's public key to verify the signature.

Ecash from DigiCash

Ecash is a fully anonymous electronic cash system, from a company called Digicash, whose managing director is David Chaum, the inventor of blind signatures and many electronic cash protocols. It is an on-line software solution which implements fully anonymous electronic cash using blind signature techniques.

The Ecash system consists of three main entities:

- ***Banks*** who mint coins, validate existing coins and exchange real money for Ecash.
- ***Buyers*** who have accounts with a bank, from which they can withdraw and deposit Ecash coins.
- ***Merchants*** who can accept Ecash coins in payment for information, or hard goods. It is also possible for merchants to run a pay-out service where they can pay a client Ecash coins.

Ecash is implemented using public-key cryptography. Every user in the system has their own public/private key pair. Special client and merchant software is required to use the Ecash system. The client software is called a "cyberwallet" and is responsible for withdrawing and depositing coins from a bank, and paying or receiving coins from a merchant.

Withdrawing Ecash Coins

To make a withdrawal from the bank, the user's cyberwallet software calculates how many digital coins of what denominations are needed to withdraw the requested amount. The software then generates random serial numbers for these coins. The serial numbers are large enough so that there is very little chance that anyone else will ever generate the same serial numbers. Using a 100-digit serial number usually guarantees this. The serial numbers are then blinded using the blind signature technique. This is done by multiplying the coins by a random factor. The blinded coins are then packaged into a message, digitally signed with the user's private key, encrypted with the bank's public key, and then sent to the bank. The message cannot be decrypted by anyone but the bank.

When the bank receives the message, it checks the signature. The withdrawal amount can then be debited from the signature owner's account. The bank signs the coins with a private key.

After signing the blind coins, the bank returns them to the user, encrypted with the user's public key. The user can then decrypt the message, and unblind the coins by dividing out the blinding factor. Since the bank couldn't see the serial numbers on the coins it was signing there is no way to now trace these coins back to the user who withdrew them. In this way the cash is fully anonymous.

Spending Ecash

To spend Ecash coins, the user starts up their cyberwallet software and a normal Web client and then browses the Web till they find a merchant shop selling goods. The Ecash software can be used with any existing Web client and Web server software. A merchant shop is simply a HTML document with URLs representing the items for sale. To buy an item the user selects the URL representing that item. The user's Web client sends a HTTP message requesting the URL to the Merchant's normal Web server. This URL will invoke a Common Gateway Interface (CGI) program.

The CGI program invoked will be the merchant Ecash software, and it will be passed details of the item selected encoded in the URL. The location of the buyer's host machine will also be passed in an environment variable from the server to the merchant Ecash software.

The merchant software, now contacts the buyer's wallet using a TCP/IP connection, asking it for payment.

When the cyberwallet receives this request, it will prompt the user, asking them if they wish to make the payment. If they agree, the cyberwallet will gather together the exact amount of coins and send this as payment to the merchant. The coins will be encrypted with the merchant's public key so that only the merchant can decrypt them:

If they disagree or do not have the exact denominations necessary to make a correct payment, the merchant is sent a payment refusal message.

When the merchant receives the coins in payment, he must verify that they are valid coins, and have not been double spent. To do this he must contact the bank, as only the minting bank can tell whether coins have been spent before or not. Thus the merchant packages the coins, signs the message with his private key, encrypts the message with the bank's public key, and sends it to the bank.

The bank validates the coins by checking the serial numbers with the large on-line database of all the serial numbers ever spent and returned to the bank. If the numbers appear in the database then they are not valid, since they have been spent before. If the serial numbers don't appear in the database, and have the bank's signature on them, then they are valid. The value of the coins are credited to the merchant's account. The coins are destroyed, and the serial numbers added to the database of spent coins. Thus coins are good for one transaction only. The bank notifies the merchant of the successful deposit.

Since the deposit was successful, the merchant was paid, and a signed receipt is returned to the buyer's cyberwallet.

The purchased item, or an indication of successful purchase of hard goods, is then sent from the merchant Ecash software to the Web Server.

The Web server forwards this information to the buyer's Web client.

Ecash client and merchant software is available for many platforms. Currently no real money is used in the system, but an Ecash trial with 10,000 participants, each being given 100 "cyberbucks" for free has been running since late 1994. There are many sample Web shops at which to spend cyberbucks.

Advantages and Failings

The strengths of Ecash are its full anonymity and security. The electronic cash used is untraceable, due to the blind signatures used when generating coins. By employing secure protocols using public key cryptography, the Ecash system is safe from eavesdropping, and message tampering. Coins cannot be stolen while they are in transit. However, the protection of coins on the local machine could be strengthened by password protection and encryption. The main problem with Ecash may be the size of the database of spent coins. If a large number of people start using the system, the size of this database could become very large and unmanageable. Keeping a database of the serial number of every coin ever spent in the system is not a scalable solution. Digicash plans to use multiple banks each minting and managing their own currency with interbank clearing to handle the problems of scalability. It seems likely that the bank host machine has an internal scalable structure so that it can be set up not only for a 10,000 user bank, but also for a 1,000,000 user bank. Under the circumstances, the task of maintaining and querying a database of spent coins is probably beyond today's state-of-the-art database systems.

NetCash

NetCash is a framework for electronic cash developed at the Information Sciences Institute of the University of Southern California. Many of the ideas used in PayMe came from the NetCash proposal. It uses identified on-line electronic cash. Although the cash is identified there are mechanisms whereby coins can be exchanged to allow some anonymity. The system is based on distributed currency servers where electronic checks, such as NetCheque can be exchanged for electronic cash. The use of multiple currency servers allows the system to scale well.

The NetCash system consists of buyers, merchants, and currency servers. An organisation wishing to set up and manage a currency server obtains insurance for the new currency from a central certification authority. The currency server generates a public/private key pair. The public key is then certified by being signed by the central authority. This certificate contains a certificate ID, name of the currency server, currency server's public key, issue date and an expiry date, all signed by the central authority:

The currency server mints electronic coins, which consist of: Currency Server Name: Identifies a currency server. Currency

Server Network Address: Where the currency server can be found. If this address is no longer in use, a name server can be queried to find the current address.

Expiry Date: Limits the state that must be maintained by each currency server.

Serial Number: Uniquely identifies the coin. Coin Value: Amount coin is worth.

The coin is signed with the currency server's private key. The currency server keeps track of the serial numbers of all outstanding coins. In this way double spending can be prevented by checking a coin's serial number with the currency server at the time of purchase (or exchange). If the coin's serial number is in the database it has not been spent already and is valid. When the coin is checked the serial number is then removed from the database. The coin is then replaced with a new coin (coin exchange). An electronic cheque can be exchanged with a currency server for electronic coins. The currency server is trusted not to record to whom the coins are issued. To further aid anonymity a holder of coins can go to any currency server and exchange valid coins for new ones. The currency server does not know who is exchanging coins, only the network address of where they are coming from. By performing the exchange and by choosing any currency server to do this with, it becomes difficult to track the path of the coins. If a currency server receives coins that were not minted by it, it will contact the minting currency server to validate those coins. When a buyer uses NetCash coins to purchase an item from a merchant, the buyer remains anonymous since the merchant will only know the network address of where the buyer is coming from. NetCash assumes that the buyer has or can obtain the public key of the merchant, and that the merchant has the public key of the currency server.

Implementation details of how the NetCash protocols might be linked with applications such as the Web are not available, but it could be done in a similar fashion to Ecash using an out-of-band communications channel. The transaction consists of the following four steps, starting from when the buyer attempts to pay the merchant:

The buyer sends the electronic coins in payment, the identifier of the purchased service (S_id), a freshly generated secret key, and a public session key, all encrypted with the Merchant's public key, to the merchant. The message can't be eavesdropped or tampered with. The secret key is used by the merchant to establish a secure channel with the buyer later. The public session key is later used to verify that subsequent requests originate from the buyer who paid for the service.

The Merchant needs to check that the received coins are valid. To do this he sends them to the currency server to be exchanged for new coins or for a cheque. The merchant generates a new symmetric session key SK [Merchant] and sends this along with the coins and the chosen transaction type to the currency server. The whole message is encrypted with the server's public key so that only it can see the contents:

The Currency Server checks that the coins are valid by checking its database. A valid coin is one whose serial number appears in the database. The server will then return new coins or a cheque to the merchant, encrypted with the merchant's session key:

Having received new coins (or a cheque) the merchant knows that he has been properly paid by the buyer. He now returns a receipt, signed with his private key and encrypted with the buyer's secret key. The buyer can then use the transaction identifier and the public session key to obtain the service purchased.

This is the basic purchase protocol used in NetCash. While it prevents double spending it does not protect the buyer from fraud. There is nothing to stop the merchant spending the buyer's coins without providing a receipt.

Extensions to the protocol are more complex but give protection against fraud for both the merchant and buyer. There are also mechanisms to allow the merchant to be fully anonymous to the buyer. Partially off-line protocols where the bank does not need to be contacted during a purchase are also described. These however, rely on the buyer contacting the currency server beforehand, and knowing who the merchant is at that time. They use a time window in which the coins are only valid for certain short lengths of time. Full technical details are given in Appendix-I.

The advantages of NetCash are that it is scalable and secure. It is scalable since multiple currency servers are present and security is provided by the cryptographic protocols used. Possible disadvantages of the system are that it uses many session keys and in particular public key session keys. To generate a public key of suitable length to be secure takes a very large amount of time compared with that involved in generating a symmetric session key. This could compromise the performance of the system as a whole.

NetCash is not fully anonymous, unlike Ecash. It is difficult but not impossible for a currency server to keep records of who it issues coins to and who it receives them back from. The ability to exchange coins and use any or multiple currency servers increases the anonymity of the system.

A NetCash system is currently being implemented, but no details are given as to how it will be linked with applications such as the Web. NetCheque will be used to provide cheques which can be used to buy coins or which can be issued when coins are traded in.

The two payment systems outlined each have their strengths and weaknesses. Ecash is a fully secure system that provides for very strong anonymity. The use of banks within the system reflects current practice in non-electronic payment systems. Successful operation of the Ecash system depends on the maintenance of a central database of all coins ever issued within the system. If it were to become accepted as a global payment system, this would quickly become a major problem.

NetCash uses identified coins with multiple currency servers, and thus, while anonymity is maintained, there is only a requirement to keep track of all currency currently in circulation. This makes for a much more scaleable solution to the payment problem. NetCash is also fully secure, and achieves this using protocols that are quite complex in nature.

The PayMe Protocol Set

In an attempt to combine the best features of the two systems described, a new payment system called the PayMe

Protocol Set was devised. A major goal was to preserve as much of the anonymity provided by Ecash while adopting many of the features of NetCash that allow it to scale to large numbers of users with multiple banks. In the following sections, we will discuss the overall design of the protocol set and work through an example of a network payment. Since this paper concentrates on payment for WWW resources, detailed coverage will be given of both the currency representation and the protocol primitives used during a Web transaction.

The PayMe system and protocol set are now presented. Many of the design ideas are based on a close examination of systems such as NetCash, Ecash and other related systems such as Magic Money and Netbill. In this way PayMe is a collection of the successful parts from existing systems, minus the failings of those systems.

PayMe is an on-line electronic cash system. The entities involved are banks and users. Users can be either buyers or merchants but each has the same functionality. They can make payments, accept payments, or deal with the bank. Each bank mints its own identified electronic cash with serial numbers. Double spending of coins is prevented by the bank maintaining a database of coins in circulation. This scales better than the blind signature electronic cash approach. Any user in the PayMe system can accept payments and make payments. Merchants can receive payments for selling Web goods but they can also make payments to the buyers. This can be used for making refunds or in pay-out services. Both symmetric and public-key cryptography are used. Each entity has its own public/private key pair. It is a stand-alone system which has been tailored for use with the Web.

The PayMe system uses its own secure communications protocol, the PayMe Transfer Protocol (PMTP), to communicate between entities. This provides security and a means of communicating out-of-ba nd, that is, outside the Web's HTTP protocol. This approach was adopted to allow a full prototype to be developed that could eventually be used with any emerging Web security standard.

Conclusions

It has been examined that two existing means of effecting anonymous electronic payment across networks and looked at their strengths and weaknesses. Then the design of PMTP was presented, a hybrid of these two approaches that offers a fully secure, scaleable anonymous payment system. It has been shown how this can be combined with WWW client and server software allowing payment to occur on an out-of-band link as users browse the Web. Only a payment system with these properties will allow the Web to be used as an electronic marketplace without compromising the privacy of its users.

Bibliography

Bos, J. and Chaum, D. Smart Cash: A Practical Electronic Payment System. Technical Report, CWI-Report: CS-R9035.

Chaum, D. Online Cash Checks. In Advances in Cryptology, EuroCrypt Proceedings, Springer-Verlag, Berlin, pages 288-293.

DigiCash. Ecash, http://www.digicash.com.

Gennady Medvinsky and Clifford Neuman, B. Electronic Currency for the Internet. Electronic Markets Vol 3. No. 9/10, pages 23-24.

Network Wizards, Menlo Park, California, http://www.nw.com/. Internet Domain Survey.

Product Cypher. Magic Money Digital Cash System, ftp://ftp.csn.org

---

Appendix I

Description of Technical Terms used

Certificate Authority: A trusted company or organization that will issue keys with some proof of the user's identity, and serve as a repository for digital certificates.

CGI Script: Common Gateway Interface, which is a scripting system that works with HyperText Transfer Protocol web servers. The scripts are used to exchange information between a web server and database.

Digital Certificate: An electronic document, issued by a certificate authority, used to establish a individual's identity by verifying its public key.

Digital Signature: A digital equivalent of a handwritten signature on a document, produced by encrypting the document digest with the sender's private key.

Electronic Wallet: A helper application for a web browser used to pass an encrypted credit card number to a buyer, through the sales merchant, and on to the server maintained by the sponsoring company for authentication and approval.

POS: Point of service.

Public-key: A cryptographic system that uses two keys -- a public key known to everyone and a private or secret key known only to the recipient of the message. For example, when John wants to send a secure message to Jane, he uses Jane's public key to encrypt the message. Jane then uses her private key to decrypt it.

RSA: A public-key cryptosystem for both encryption and authentication supported by RSA Data Security Inc.

SSL: Secure Sockets Layer. An authentication protocol for web servers and browsers that provides data integrity and confidentiality for communications between web servers and browsers.

Symmetric-key: An encryption system in which the sender and receiver of a message share a single, common key that is used to encrypt and decrypt the message. Contrast this with public-key cryptology, which utilizes two keys - a public key to encrypt messages and a private key to decrypt them. Symmetric key cryptology can also be used to perform authentication and provide data integrity.

TCP/IP Protocols: These protocols define how data is subdivided into packets for transmission and how an application can transfer files and send email.

HTML: HyperText Mark Up Language, a simple markup language used to create hypertext documents that are platform independent.

--oo--

Section II: Human Resource Management

05

SOCIAL SECTOR DYNAMICS AND ECONOMIC REFORMS IN INDIA

G. M. Bhat

Abstract

The quality of life depends on the level of social development. All things remaining the same, the level of social development depends on economic condition of the state. First decade of reforms have neglected education and as a result India, by the end year 2001 AD is having 54.81 per cent of world illiterate population in the age group of 15-19 years. Half the Indian adult population continues to be illiterate and two-thirds of women are illiterate. Similarly a lot needs to be done in the dwelling sector of the country. Health facilities in rural areas remain poor. There is serious shortage of community health centres. Secondly, the reforms have not emphasized on the promotion of basic consumption needs including safe drinking water, sanitation and electricity. Over and above Central Government expenditure on social services has shown a very little expansion during the first decade of reforms. On the social front, India's performance is disappointing at the international level. At 128th position, it is ranked among the lowest as far as human development is concerned -much lower than the comparable economies like Mexico (55th), Srilanka (84th) and China (99th).

Apart from people's participation, there should be better coordination of activities of various agencies directly connected with the programmes of social sectors. All these issues of social sector are discussed in this paper.

Introduction

Planners and policy makers have not accepted 'Growth for the sake of growth' approach. A vigorous thrust for social justice is an integral element of our development strategy. Poverty alleviation and raising the average standard of living have been the central aims of economic planning in India. Three distinct phases emege if we review the planning process and growth with social justice objective. During the first phase, the prime emphasis was on growth based on Mahalanobis strategy of heavy industrialisation. The general contention was that growth will automatically take care of the aspect of social justice and it will percolate to the poor. In the second phase, starting from the fifth plan, it was realised that growth has failed to trickle down, so in order to fulfil the objective of social justice, special targeted programmes were framed. In the third and present phase, it is realised that a strategy based on growth or one on equity and poverty alleviation could not be made effective in isolation. A distinction is being made between growth and development. Development was seen as going beyond economic growth and bringing about changes in the structure of the economy. Equitable distribution of benefits of economic growth became an independent goal. Further, the concept of equity was translated into provision to everyone of the 'basic needs', which include the basic requirements of life such as educatsion, safe drinking water, sanitation and health services.

In 1991, India witnessed changes in her economic policy when we adopted the economic reform measures in the wake of acute balance of payment crisis and mounting fiscal deficit. To quote Manmohan Singh,

> *'If we had not attempted fiscal restructuring in 1991-92 we could not have restored confidence in the economy., Our creditors were at our throats, forex reserves had disappeared. If we had continued to mismanage the fiscal system, we would have gone under. I would have had to declare India a debt defaulter and we would have gone the route of the African and Latin American countries. Further we had to mortgage gold to raise even $500 million. Only the IMF was willing to help at that stage, but we had to abide by its conditions. We opened up the economy to foreign direct investment and institutional investors to buy ourselves, some manoeuvarability.'*

'The economic reform process initiated by the Government of India since July 1991 was aimed at decontrolling and de-bureaucratising the economy. Trade policy, exchange rate, capital market and financial sector etc. are broadly covered in the reforms.

Finance Minister Yashwant Sinha in his budget speech 2000-01 stated very clearly that NDA Government intends to carry forward the process of implementation of the Second Generation Reforms. Elaborating on the philosophy of the Second Generation Reforms, he stated: "Growth is not just an end in itself. It is the critical vehicle for increasing employment and raising the living standards of our people especially of the poorest. Sustained broad-based growth, combined with all our programmes for accelerating rural development, building roads, promoting housing, boosting knowledge-based industries and enhancing the quality of human resources, will impart a strong impetus to employment expansion. There can be no better cure for poverty than this in our country".

The "First Generation Reforms" initiated in 1991 were crisis -driven. The crisis in the balance of payments and mounting fiscal deficits prompted the congress Government under the leadership of P. V. Narasimha Rao to initiate economic reforms. Since economic reforms were born out of an economic crisis, the prevailing thinking among the people, the Government and the policy makers was a keen desire to go in for a programme of structural adjustment which should help to strengthen the process of stabilisation to pulling the economy out of the crisis of balance of payments and fiscal deficits. Nearly a decade of the working of economic reforms has brought about a significant stablisation of our economy. The growth rate of Indian economy increased from 5.8 per cent in the Seventh Plan (1985 to 1990) to 6.8 per cent in the Eighth Plan (1992 to 1997). Even during 1999-2000, the GDP growth was estimated to be nearly 6 per cent. Thus, the Indian economy has crossed the barrier of 'Hindu rate of growth' as propagated by Raj Krishna. Secondly, the country has been able to manage its external debt, which stood as US$ 98.2 billion in 1999, but the short-term debt was only of the order of US$ 4.3 billion. Thirdly, the country has been able to build a foreign exchange reserve of the order of US$ 32.4 billion in 1998-99 and thus is not threatened with the problem of paying for her imports. Thus, the country has no fear of defaulting on its external obligations. Fourthly, the average export-import ratio has improved to 87 per cent for the period 1992-93 to 1998-99. This is really a healthy sign. This ratio had slumped to 79 per cent during 1987-88 to 1990-91. Fifthly, wholesale price index during 1995-96 to 1999-2000 has shown a very modest increase of 3.54 percent per annum on the average. During 1999-2000, the economy witnessed whole sale price index (WPI) increasing by only 2.9 percent. Sixthly, the entry of foreign investors in India created a competitive environment. The actual F.D.I flows had jumped from US$ 150 million in 1991-92 to US $3.2 billion in 1996-97. The total portfolio investment has increased from US $ 244 million in 1992-93 to US $ 3312 million in 1996-97. Lastly, on the question of reducing fiscal deficit of the Central Government, performance has not been upto the mark and fiscal deficit which was 6.3 percent of GDP in 1993-94, came down to 4 percent in 1996-97, but again rose gradually to 5.6 percent in 1999-2000 and is expected to be around 4.5 percent during 2000-01. But for the fiscal deficit, which has evaded an effective downtrend, it can be reasonably established that stabilisation of the economy has been achieved as a result of economic reforms and the country should shift gears of the economy from a crisis-driven economic reforms to development-driven economic reforms. Yashwanth Sinha, the

Union finance Minister while presenting the Union Budget for the financial year 2000-01 said: there is need for preparing an agenda and action plan regarding "Second Generation Economic Reforms" to go further in achieving the Liberalisation, Privatisation and Globalisation (LPG) in India. The Finance Minister further asserted "I propose to put India in a sustained, equitable and job creating growth path of 7 to 8 per cent per year to order to banish the scourge of poverty from our land within a decade. The next 10 years will be India's decade of development."

There are many apprehensions that new economic reforms have not succeeded so far in achieving the objectives laid down in the 1991 Industrial Policy statement. Not-withstanding the significant achievements of the Indian economy during the past 50 years admittedly, the performance has fallen short of expectations. Two world Bank economists Ravallion and Subbarao, have argued that in the short run, the adjustment process would affect the poor adversely because the costs would be felt quickly, whereas the benefits would take time to materialise. Therefore, it is the responsibility of the Government to take care of the poor as far as possible by maintaining the social sector expenditure during the adjustment period. Further, there are many dimensions in which performance has lagged behind the expectations. Faster economic growth has not reduced illiteracy and poverty as much as it should have been. According to Sharif and Ghosh, "After 50 years of independence, India spends less than 4 percent of GNP on education and less than half of this amount on elementary education (1.8 percent). Lack of resources cannot be a convincing argument for failing to discharge this national duty. If the Government can find the money to implement the fifth pay commission's recommendations, which will entail additional expenditure to the extent of about 3 percent of GNP, surely the requirement of elementary education can also be met. What is needed is political will and public pressure".

Social Sector and Economic Reforms

There is no conflict between social sector reforms and economic reforms because a country cannot achieve higher level of human development without having high rate of economic growth. There is no trade-off between the two. Both are complimentary to each other. Although it has been established that the theory of trickle down effect has failed in case of India, but what we need is a special drive against poverty; malnutrition, illiteracy, .hunger, deprivation and unemployment. Since economic reforms have their transitional costs which are to be borne more by the vulnerable sections, so we need a special corrective mechanism to plug the loopholes of new economic policy. Recent economic policy contains an important fiscal component, i.e., bringing down the size of the fiscal deficit. Normally, the economic sectors or the commodity sector gets the priority over the social sector spending. Whenever any cut has to be made to reduce the fiscal deficit, it is always the social sector, which has to bear the brunt of deficit reduction.

The problem of poverty and unemployment has to be based on four types of strategy consisting of higher growth, redistribution, basic needs and directed programmes. The development strategy of the 9th plan has, therefore, indicated the following objectives relating to social sector as:

(i) Ensuring food and nutritional security for all, particularly the vulnerable sections of the society;

(ii) Providing basic minimum services of safe drinking water, primary health care facilities, universal primary education, shelter and connectivity to all in a time bound manner;

(iii) Empowerment of women and socially disadvantaged groups such as SCs/STs and other backward classes and minorities as agents of socio-economic change and development.

The 9th plan, therefore, underlines, the need for state intervention in three broad areas to take care of the imperfections of the market forces. These forces are:

i) quality of life of citizens

ii) generation of productive employment, and

iii) regional balance.

To provide primary education, primary health care, safe drinking water, nutrition and sanitation, investment will have to be provided out of public funds, since private initiatives and markets are unlikely to play a significant role. Economic growth is important since it creates more resources and has the potential of creating more space for' the involvement of the poor. Therefore, it is important to source a large part of economic growth in agriculture, in rural non-agricultural activities and in productive expansion of the informal sector which all have high employment statistics.

Growth with social justice and equity sums up the goal set forth before the nation. P.R. Panchmukhi (2000) has analysed the social impact of economic reforms in India. According to him "the human capital revolution of the post 1960's and focus on human development rather than on income growth have brought into a sharp focus the indispensable role played by the components of the social sector in economic development". Education, health and family welfare, water supply, sanitation, housing, rural development, social welfare, nutrition and minimum basic service are the main components of social sector. It is evident from Table 1 that Central Government .expenditure (Plan and Non Plan) on social sector as a ratio to total expenditure increased from 7.7 percent in 1991-92 to 11.4 percent in 1999-2000 only. As a ratio to GDP at current market prices, the Central Government expenditure on social services increased from 1.33 percent in 1991-92 to 1.68 percent in 1999-2000 only.

Similarly, the 9th plan also highlighted that drinking water supply and sanitation facilities are very important and crucial for achieving goal of 'Health for all'. The Government has promised to provide drinking water to every settlement in the country within five years. The Government has also decided to go all out to achieve the goal of expansion and improvement of sanitation facility. The comparative position of such facilities for 1981 and 1991 is shown in Table 2. The census data reveal that the problem of safe drinking water is more acute in the rural areas as compared to the urban areas. Households with electricity in the rural areas comprise only 31.1 % of the population whereas, households with toilet facility form only 8.84% of rural population.

Table 2: Households having drinking water, electricity and toilet facilities (percentage)			
		1991*	1981*
1.	Households with drinking water	63.71	37.91
	• Rural	55.92	26.34
	• Urban	8159	74.13
2.	Households with Electricity	42.98	25.74
	• Rural	31.10	14.29
	• Urban	75.93	61.60
3.	Households with Toilet facility	23.55	NA
	• Rural	08.84	NA
	• Urban	63.58	57.44

* Excluding Assam in 1981 and Jammu & Kashmir in 1991

Source: Statistical Outline of India, 1989-99, Tata Services Ltd., Department of Economics and Statistics

Similarly, a profile of housing census (Table 3) also reveal that 41.6 million persons have pucca houses in comparison to 30.9 million living in semi-pacca houses and 27.4 million live in purely kutcha houses according to 1991 census report. There is enormous shortage in the housing sector and major deficiencies in the housing related infrastructure. The overall shortage is estimated at 185 lack dwellings units-the rural areas account for 140 lack units. Also, about 122 lack units require substantial up gradation to make then habitable. The Government has been progressively adopting the role of an enabler rather than a direct provider. This has necessitated a policy shift to encourage private and co-operative sector to play a major role in housing sector.

Despite Government efforts at universalisation of elementary education, half the Indian adult population continues to be illiterate and two-third of women are illiterate. Although literacy rate increased to 52% in 1991 but the number of illiterates has increased from 301.9 million in 1981 to 328.9 million in 1991. Literacy among females is much lower than males -61% of Indian females are illiterate as against 36 percent males. The primary enrollment (Table 4) which reached an all time high of 101 percent in 1990-91 declined to 89 percent in 1996-97, of which girls enrolment stood at 76.2 percent in 1996-97 as against 85.6 percent in 1990-91. Similarly, middle level enrolment has also declined by 5.2 percentage points to 54.9 percent as against girls enrolment of 44.3 percent in 1996-97. It is only at higher secondary level -that the enrolment figure increased from 19.1 million in 1990-91 to 27 million in 1996-97. At the international level, especially with its peer countries India has done appreciably well with regard to certain economic indicators like GDP growth rate, GDS and GDI rates, external debt and average annual rate of inflation. But as far the social indicators are concerned like education and health and also the overall HDI ranking the performance has not been satisfactory (see Appendix I).

Table 3: A Profile of Housing Census (Million)

		1991	1981
1.	Census Houses	195.0	151.0
2.	Housing Stock	197.2	111.6
3.	Number of Shortage	151.1	118.6
4.	Housing Shortages	18.5	21.1
	• Rural	13.7	16.1
	• Urban	4.8	5.0
5.	Percentage of Households living in		
	• Pucca Houses	51.6	32.7
	• Semi-pucca houses	30.9	33.3
	• Kutcha houses	27.4	34.0

Source: Statistical Outline of India, 1989-99, Tata Services Ltd., Department of Economics and Statistics.

Table 4: Enrolment of Students

Category	1996-97	1990-91	1980-81	1970-71
Primary (Mn.)	110.4 (89.0)	97.4 (101.0)	73.8 (80.5)	57.0 (76.4)
Of which Girls	47.9 (76.2)	40.4 (85.6)	28.5 (64.1)	21.3 (59.3)
Middle (Mn.)	41.1 (54.9)	34.0 (60.1)	20.7 (41.9)	13.3 (34.2)
Of which girls	16.4 (43.3)	12.5 (46.1)	6.3 (28.6)	3.9 (20.8)
High/Higher Secondary (Mn.)	27.0	19.1	11.0	7.6

Figures in parenthesis showing percentage of gross enrolment in classes I-IV (6-11 years) and VI-VII (11-14 years) to total population.

Source: Statistical Outline of India, 1989-99, Tata Services Ltd., Department of Economics and Statistics.

Conclusion

In the light of above facts and figures conclusion is reached that the sustainable growth and development over a longer period of time in the economy can be achieved only by fostering human resources and social development. Therefore, the basic objective of the economic reforms particularly the Second Generation of Reforms before India should be to intensify efforts so as to increase public as well as private investment and spending on key social services. In order to achieve the above objective it is essential to declare social sector as a priority sector and encourage foreign direct investment in social sectors.

References

Bhalla, Sheila (1994): "Globalisation, Growth and Employment", in G. S. Bhalla and Manmohan Agarwal (eds.), World Economy in Transition -An Indian Perspective, Har anand Publications New Delhi.

Chadha, G. K (1999) "Economic Reforms and Emerging Demand Supply Hiatus in India's Rural Labour Market", Conference Volume IEA 82nd Conference, Amritsar

Dhindsa, Paramjeet Kaur (2000), "Second Generation Reforms -Agenda for Social Sector", Conference Volume IEA 83rd Conference, Jammu.

Panchmukhi, P.R (2000) "Social Impact of Economic Reforms in India: A Critical Appraisal", Economic and Political Weekly, Vol.XXXV, No.10.

-OoO-

Table 1: Central Government Expenditure (Plan and Non-Plan)

(in Rupees crores)

Item	1991-92	1992-93	1993-94	1994-95	1995-96	1996-97	1997-98	1998-99	1999-00	Mean value
Y	616700	705918	859220	1009906	1181916	1361952	1515646	1762609	194000	12171.12
X1	5892	6397	8150	9223	11631	13659	16007	20315	22921	12688.33
X2	1755	1878	2378	2799	3630	3988	4983	6733	7138	3920.22
X3	1382	1722	2148	2413	2542	2751	3235	4046	5000	2804.33
X4	934	788	1262	1351	1756	2957	3328	4325	4898	2399.89
X5	417	371	392	479	596	593	928	1028	1109	657.00
X6	419	488	564	744	800	833	692	977	1108	736.11
X7	357	347	526	440	507	587	642	771	908	565.00
X8	628	803	880	997	1800	1750	2209	2435	2760	1606.89
X9	2283	3211	4680	5803	6609	5081	5116	5571	5416	4863.33
X10	-	-	-		-	2466	2873	3684	4043	3266.50
X11	8175	9608	12830	15026	18240	21206	23996	29570	32380	19003.44
X12	11414	122618	141853	160739	178275	201007	232053	279365	303738	192340.20
X13	17.2	16.8	15.9	15.0	14.2	14.0	14.3	14.5	14.7	-
X14	7.7	8.1	9.4	10.0	10.8	11.1	11.1	11.6	11.4	-
X15	1.33	1.36	1.49	1.49	1.54	1.56	1.58	1.68	1.68	-

Where

Y = GDP at market price
X1 = Social Service
X2 = Education, Sports and Youth Affairs
X3 = Health and Family Welfare
X4 = Water Supply, Sanitation, Housing & Urban Dev.
X5 = Information and Broadcasting
X6 = Welfare of SCs/STs & other Backward Classes
X7 = Labour, Employment and Labour Welfare
X8 = Social Welfare and Nutrition
X9 = Rural Development
X10 = Basic Minimum Services including Slum Development
X11 = Social Services, Rural Development and BMS
X12 = Total Govt. Expenditure (Plan and Non Plan)
X13 = Total Central Govt. Expenditure as percentage of GDP at current market prices
X14 = Social Services, Rural Development and BMS as percentage of total Expenditure.
X15 = Social Services, Rural Development and BMS as percentage of GDP at current market prices.

Appendix - I: Selected Economic Indicators of India and Peer

Indicators	India	Signa-pore	China	Pakistan	Sri Lanka	South Africa	Mexico	USA	Japan
Annual GDP Growth Rate (1990-00 in %)	6.1	8.0	10.7	4.0	5.3	1.9	2.7	3.4	1.4
Average Annual Rate of Inf. (1990-98 in %)	8.9	2.1	9.7	11.1	9.7	10.6	19.5	1.9	0.2
Gross Domestic investment % of GDP (1997-99)	23.9	34.5	38.8	15.7	24.8	15.9	24.8	18.5	29.2
Gross Domestic Savings % of GDP (1997-99)	20.3	51.4	42.5	11.2	18.3	17.3	23.8	16.7	30.0
Average Annual Exp. Growth (1990-99)	11.3	-	13.0	2.7	8.4	5.3	14.3	9.3	5.4
External Debt, as % of GNP-1998	23.0	-	16.4	52.8	54.9	18.9	42.0	-	-
Education Expenditure as % of GNP (1994-97)	3.2	3.0	2.3	2.7	3.4	8.0	4.9	5.4	3.6
Expenditure on Health % of GDP (1990-98)	0.6	1.1	2.0	0.9	1.4	3.2	2.8	6.5	5.9
The Rankings									
Human Development Index - 1998	128	24	99	135	84	103	55	3	9
Economic Creativity Index, 2000	38	3	48	-	-	26	35	1	21
Emerging Market Access Index, 2000	46	86	37	-	-	72	68	-	-

Source: The Economic Times, April 25, 2001

06

STRUCTURAL ADJUSTMENT PROGRAMME (SAP) AND CHALLENGES TO UNION FUNCTION

Nazir Ahmad Nazir

Abstract

The present paper deals with the need for structural adjustment programme (SAP) and challenges it posed on Industrial Relations System (IRS) in India especially trade unionism. Further, it analyses the changing role of unions for making them responsive to the needs of the time.

Introduction

Structural Adjustment Programme (SAP) is a product of counter revolution and distortionists' view/approach, the main proponents of which are International Monetary Fund (IMF) and World Bank (WB). As per this school of thought, Government as much as possible should try to delink herself from regulating the business establishments etc. both in manufacturing as well as service sector through privatization and dis-investment. The reason put forth is that state intervention results in inefficiencies arising from rent seeking or directly unproductive profit seeking activities of the labour. In other words, distortionists' hold the view that job, social security, minimum wages, recognition of trade unions actually raise the cost of labour, reduce the labour demand and distort the labour market artificially thereby raising level of wages in the formal sector, while decreasing wages and increasing unemployment in informal sector. Hence, these distortions' lead to inefficient use of human resources.

Institutional view propagated by ILO althrough the past four decades entails that the protection of the interests of lower income group is possible through minimum wages, sound industrial relations is possible through the formation of unions and justice to the larger working group for their role in the production process is ensured by the social security measures. In this context, ILO passed a good number of conventions like Convention of 87, 98, 131, 154 from time to time. These conventions take the formation of unions, comprehensive collective bargaining process to be prevalent in organisations in high priority and esteem. It is, therefore, through these conventions unions got the international recognition. India being a member country of ILO followed suit and therefore, immediately after the formation of ILO, passed the Trade Union Act of 1926, to uphold and meet the ILO commitments. Fact of the matter thus is, that the formation of unions was a systematic and concerted effort on the part of the Government to intervene in the matters of the labour relations with the premise that unions would safeguard the interests of their members, act constructively and collectively try to resolve the disputes, if any, between them and the management without any undue delay and loss of productive days/capacity. This effort was continued through other enactments' like Industrial Dispute Act of 1947, Factories Act of 1948, Standing Employment Orders Act of 1946 etc. as well. It would be appropriate here to highlight the results and impact of these enactments on labour relations in India. As such the following discussion will reveal the objectives of Industrial relations systems and its performance.

Objectives of IRS

As reported by Sunder (1997; 1983), the labour policy should be designed to --

- eliminate disputes, rather than simply resolve them and have industrial harmony as its goal;
- develop a strong, well organised responsible and independent trade union movement;
- have a genuine system of collective bargaining that requires a minimum of state intervention;
- promote industrial democracy

Evaluation of the Performance of IRS

While there are several methods through which the performance of IRS could be examined, however, some of the most prominent and reliable methods (Sunder, 1997) are discussed hereunder:

1) Comparing the strike record of India with that of other countries
2) Studying trends in strikes over time during the interventionist era.

The handling of strike data is problematic both at conceptual and as well as empirical level, especially, when international comparisons of such data are proposed. For there are differences in the definitions of strikes and in data collection system in countries which significantly effects the comparability of strike data (Fisher, 1973; Walsh, 1983). However, with some assumptions strike data could be managed for comparability purposes/reasons.

As reported by Edward (1981: 29), workdays lost measure is least affected by the differences in data collection system and hence, is the most ideal measure for international comparisons. Table 1 and 2 provide the statistics on working days lost in India in comparison to other countries and industrial conflicts in India alongwith the number of workers involved and working days lost in India between 1950 and 1997 on period comparison basis respectively.

Table 1: Average Number of Workdays lost, per year, per employee (WDL/E) in the manufacturing sector in Selected countries.

Country	WDL/E 1972-81	WDL/E 1982-92
India	4.070	5.736
Indonesia	0.004	0.010
Thailand	0.108	0.039
Malaysia	-	0.004
Korea	0.005	0.216
Singapore	0.010	0.000
Pakistan	-	0.039
Sri Lanka	0.070	1.088
Philippines	0.160	0.646
Japan	0.137	0.009
France	1.333	0.168
Australia	1.286	0.365
UK	1.068	0.240
USA	0.819	0.163

Source: Agrawal (1997, Table 3, p. 160).

Table 2: Industrial conflict (1950-1997)

Year	Number of disputes			No. of workers involved in disputes (000's)			No. of work days lost in disputes (000's)		
	Strikes	Lock outs	Total	Strikes	Lock outs	Total	Strikes	Lock outs	Total
The first phase (1950 to mid-1960s)									
1950	-	-	814	-	-	720	-	-	12807
1951	-	-	1071	-	-	691	-	-	3819
1952	-	-	963	-	-	809	-	-	3337
1953	-	-	772	-	-	467	-	-	3383
1954	-	-	840	-	-	477	-	-	3373
1955	-	-	1166	-	-	528	-	-	5698
1956	-	-	1203	-	-	715	-	-	6992
1957	-	-	1630	-	-	889	-	-	6429
1958	-	-	1524	-	-	929	-	-	7798
1959	-	-	1531	-	-	694	-	--	5633
1960	-	-	1583	-	-	986	-	-	6537
1961	1240	117	1357	432	80	512	2969	1950	4919

1962	1396	95	1491	575	130	705	5059	1062	6121
1963	1364	107	1471	491	72	563	2229	1040	3269
1964	1981	170	2151	876	127	1003	5724	2001	7725
1965	1697	138	1835	889	102	991	4617	1853	6470
The second phase (mid-1960s to 1979)									
1966	2353	203	2556	1262	148	1410	10377	3469	13846
1967	2433	382	2815	1340	151	1491	10565	6583	17148
1968	2651	325	2776	1465	204	1669	11078	6166	17244
1969	2344	283	2627	1687	140	1827	15477	3571	19048
1970	2598	291	2889	1552	276	1828	14749	5814	20563
1971	2478	274	2752	1476	139	1615	11803	4743	16546
1972	2857	386	3243	1475	262	1737	13748	6796	20544
1973	2958	421	3370	2358	187	2546	13862	6764	20626
1974	2501	428	2929	2710	145	2855	33643	6619	40262
1975	1644	299	1943	1033	111	1144	16706	5195	21901
1976	1241	218	1459	550	186	737	2799	9947	12746
1977	2691	426	3117	1912	281	2193	13410	11910	25320
1978	2762	425	3187	1690	226	1916	15423	12917	28340
1979	2709	339	3048	2714	159	2873	35804	8050	43854
The third phase (1980 to 1991)									
1980	2501	355	2856	1661	239	1900	12018	9907	21925
1981	2245	344	2589	1261	327	1588	21208	15375	36583
1982	2029	454	2483	-	-	1469	-	-	74615
1983	1993	495	2488	-	-	1461	-	-	46858
1984	1689	405	2094	-	-	1949	-	-	56025
1985	1355	400	1755	878	201	1079	11487	17753	29240
1986	1458	434	1892	1444	200	1644	18824	13925	32749
1987	1348	451	1799	1495	275	1770	14026	21332	35358
1988	1304	441	1745	937	254	1191	12530	21417	33947
1989	1397	389	1786	1158	206	1364	10695	21968	32663
1990	1459	366	1825	1162	146	1308	10640	13446	24086
1991	1278	532	1810	872	470	1342	12428	14000	26428
The fourth phase (1992 to 2000)									
1992	1011	703	1714	767	485	1252	15132	16127	31259
1993	914	479	1393	672	282	954	5615	14686	20301
1994	808	393	1201	626	220	846	6651	14332	20983
1995	732	334	1066	683	307	990	5720	10570	16290
1996	-	-	1166	-	-	939	-	-	20285
1997	-	-	1305	-	-	981	-	-	17033

Source: Various issues of *Indian Labour Yearbook*, Labour Bureau; *Indian Labour Statistics*, Labour Bureau; *Indian Labour Journal*, Labour Bureau.

From the above, it is clear that India has been the most strike prone country in comparison to other countries shown in Table 1. Similarly, Table 2 reveals that though the number of disputes have gone up from 814 in 1950 to 1305 in 1997, but the increase is still marginal compared to other years in the middle. As in 1979, disputes had shooted up beyond 3000 with all time high, 3 crore workers being affected and about 4.5 crore workdays lost. However, workdays lost and number of workers hit has been again high in 1997 compared with the corresponding figures of 1950. This indicates that on the whole, number of disputes and the number of workers involved and workdays lost in these disputes during the selected period have not come down but have substantially increased in the middle years, thus defeating the very purpose of industrial relations system which not only aimed at resolving the disputes but eliminating them from the very scene as stated earlier.

A more comprehensive data regarding strikes and lockouts in India is presented in Table 3 below:-

Table 3: Strikes and Lockouts in India, 1958-90

Period	WS/N= 000*	WDL/B = 1000	WI/WS	WDL/ WI	WDL/ WS
1958-62	39.3	1628	511	8.1	4142
1963-67	47.0	2108	504	8.9	4481
1968-72	57.3	3763	607	10.8	6572
1973-77	43.9	4159	739	12.8	9481
1978-82	40.5	5866	688	21.1	14497
1983-87	26.1	5206	968	20.6	19967
1988-90	21.7	3678	721	23.5	16934
% change					
1988-90 over 1958-62	-44.8	125.9	41.0	190.1	308.8

*Note: WS/N = No. of work stoppages per one lakh employees in organized sector; WDL/N - Workdays lost per one thousand employees.

Source: Sunder (1997: Table 1, p. 86)

While the relative strike frequency has come down in last two sub periods, the workdays lost per work stoppage have been high by about 126 percent in comparison to 1958-62. Further duration of strikes has increased by about 190 percent which is from around eight days in 1958-62 to about twenty four days in 1988-90. Therefore, the decline in frequency of strikes is badly eclipsed by the prolongation of work stoppages. This indicates that strikes once begun do not end easily, hence reflecting inefficiency of intervention machinery.

From the given data, it seems that IRS could not yield as expected. It could not form the sound basis of industrial relations. It could not instill a sense of commitment, accountability and responsibility in the labour force. It rather paved the way for dilatory mechanism in resolving the disputes (NCL, 1969; Patil, 1976; Saini, 1992). And, indeed created a dependency kind of culture in the organisations where the unions and managements feel and find the Government intervention as a first resort rather than a last resort. It was on account of the failure of the interventionist and protectionist regime, that the Government embraced the Western thought of free market economy, the main agenda/focus of which is that the fate of an economy, industry, company would be determined by the interplay of market forces, thereby leaving little scope for the unions to come up with unreasonable and unwarranted demands. Therefore, SAP has a tremendous bearing on the trade union movement. Infact, with the onset of globalisation in early eighties, there has been a widespread orchestration of the "Distortionist's View" by the World Bank, IMF as pointed out earlier that trade unions distort wages, create hurdles in the production process, deter investment, thereby reduce growth and also resist change. Though it is hard to prove these propositions, the depiction of unions, minimum wages legislation's, other labour interventions as obstacles to growth have become part of the SAP strategy. The ideological hype thus created poses a serious threat and challenge to trade unions as a labour institution with a large social purpose" (Reddy, 2000: p. 211). Further, Tulpule (1999) commenting on the influence of National Economic Policy (NEP or SAP), observed, "Under NEP, industrial labour is viewed as excessively protected, the labour market as excessively rigid, and TU's as primarily responsible for these conditions. This, in effect questions the very *raison detre* of TU's. There is pressure for making the labour market flexible, which is a emphemison for making it easier for employees to freely hire and fire workers as and when they feel it profitable. There also proposals are made for revoking some of the statutory benefits available, especially to workers in small industries in the name of making them more competitive. Clearly, the earlier view that workers are the weaker and vulnerable side in the employer-worker interaction, and, therefore, needs state protection, has gone over board in NEP."

An overview of trade union movement made by Thomas (1994a) in the light of SAP reveals highly unfavourable trends in Asia, Africa and Latin America. The World Labour Report 1997-98, observed, "It is generally agreed that the trade union movement has fallen on hard times. The extent of its difficulties may sometimes of course, be exaggerated by overemphasizing adverse national situations, sometimes for ideological norms, or for the sake of convenience. Nonetheless, workers organizations are losing members. Some even have doubts about their future. The 1980's it seems were particularly bad" (p.6). Thus, the unlimited effort of the ideological onslaught on the one hand, the policy package of SAP, on the trade union movement has been devastating. However, considering the collectivist nature of the society and a long cherished dependency proven culture which the worker in India enjoyed althrough, the role of unions cannot be outrightly rejected or undermined. In fact, unions need to be made effective, constructive, provided some pertinent issues both external like politicisation of unions, multiplicity of unions, external leadership, non recognition of unions by management and internal like over-centralisation of unions, lack of enthusiasm in young workers to take up the union activities and non-fulfilment of social obligations on the part of unions etc. are addressed seriously by the parties involved. This needs a lot of concerted effort/work on the part of Government especially to change the labour laws to suit the present business environment without compromising on the cultural fundamentals etc. It is thus, expected that unions can play major developmental role by focussing on communication, motivation, counselling, education, training, welfare, research, family, vocational guidance. This can enable them to evolve beyond their traditional roles of bargainers, negotiators, agitators, blackmailers and leaders (Khandelwal, 1998).

References

Edwards, P. K. (1981). Strikes in the United States, 1881-1974. New York: St. Martin's Press.

Fisher, M. (1973). Measurement of Labor Disputes and their Economic Effects. Paris: OECD.

National Commission Labor (NCL) (1969) The Report, Government of India.

Patil, B. R. (1976). "Collective Bargaining and Conciliation in India", Journal of Industrial Relations, Vol. 12, 41-60.

Reddy, Y. R. K. (2000). "Structural Change, Structural Adjustment and the Challenge to Union Function". The Indian Journal of Labour Economics, Vol. 43, No. 2.

Saini, Debi, S. (1992). "Failure of Conciliation: Perceptions, Realities". Indian Journal of Industrial Relations, Vol. 28.

Shyam Sundar, K. R. (1997). "Structural Adjustment and Industrial Relations in India". Management, Change, Vol. 1, No. 2.

Thomas, Henk (ed.) (1994a). Globalization and Third World Trade Unions: The Challenge of Rapid Economic Change, Zed Books.

Tulpule, B. (1999). Trade Unions on the Threshold of 21st century; paper presented at the Seminar on Trade Union Movement on the Threshold of 21st century, Shramika Pratishthan, Mumbai, August, 1-2.

Walsh, K. (1983). Strike in Europe: The United States - Measurement: Incidence, Francis Printer Publishers.

07

BUSINESS STRATEGY AND HRD IN THE NEW CENTURY

Riyaz A. Rainaya

Abstract

Globalization, the new economic creed, organizations world-wide shall have to deal with stiff competition, turbulent economic scenario and state of the art technology. The new century's clarion call, therefore, will be new strategic initiatives. The "strategic advantage" in 2k will be only ephemeral. Reinvention of business will be name of the game. Naturally, then, enterprises will have to operate differently. Organizational designs will have few strict rules; managers will have to speak transparently about the doings of the organization; organizations will have to go beyond customer surveys; entrepreneurship and venture teams will have to be created to buoy up the organization out of the traditional box. Attitudes towards customer needs and emerging markets will have to be changed. Ahead in the 21st century when all business will face stiff competitive environment, the key to winning, among these initiatives, will be effective development of human resources. Technology belongs to everybody, but the genial core of an organization is its own singular property - the human resources. HRD is directly related to strategic goals of the organization. Authorities agree and stress upon the connection between HRD, business strategy and other business processes. This paper focuses on the much needed HRD initiative --- team building; intellectual capital; multi-rater 360-degree feedback; pay for performance — all of which will combine to win the competitive battles in the new century.

Introduction

All pointers incline to indicate that the new century shall have to deal with three prime factors – namely, bigger, stronger more agile competition; mixed economic growth; cutting edge of technology. And accordingly, the new century is bound to cry for new strategic initiatives that go beyond current management thinking, imbibe new radical technologies, and jump into new entrepreneurial horizons.

Indications are that Michael Porter's 80s' Five Forces Model as well as Hamel and Prahalads' 90s' Core Competency Model being done away with, the new century may have to adopt Brown and Eisenhardts Competing on the Edge Model instead. Both these management thinkers in their C*ompeting on the Edge* suggest that all companies in the new century will have to go by new ways of thinking, after accepting the hard truth that today's distinctive core competencies may be of little value in tomorrow's markets. They also believe that the strategic advantage in 2000s will be only temporary. Strategy not being a single approach, but a complex of loosely knit semi-coherent moves in a strategic direction, reinvention of business will be name of the game.

Naturally then, all enterprises will have to organize and operate differently. In organizational design, companies may have to live by making structures with few strict rules and minimal bureaucracy. Firms may have to reach into future in the very present itself, launching more experimental products and services, align strategically with focus on new technologies and markets, and all the time innovate futuristically. The organizational design very likely to be virtual and of network form, sharing authority and responsibility and resources, among the people and also among the frequently cooperating divisions, will begin to replace traditional hierarchical structures. The virtual organizations may well multiply their capabilities by pooling their individual talents, expertise, finances, etc., towards a specific project. Even sworn competitors, adopting flexibility, may become temporary partners in a project, change their team members in the conglomerates as and when required, these members may never come face to face but communicate electronically, with the sole purpose of completing a specific project, after which they may again separate to compete. The new century thus, will have to see some new things advancing up- such as, recombinant work teams, co-destiny (of the several firms), networks and webs, virtual offices, probabilities, contingent (disposable) workers, temporary staffers, corporate downsizing, and so on (Wilson and Pearson, 1996; Nadler and Tushman, 1999; Lei, et al., 1999). As an instance, Corning Inc. uses 23 strategic alliance to compete in a variety of high technology markets.

Further, adoption of new designs will have managers intermittently changing their strategies, freshly relating their organizations to upcoming opportunities, and making such new articulations as candidly speak to everyone involved about the doings of the organizations. This style of thinking, Five Forces Model and Core Competency Model aside, meets one of the major strategic initiatives needed for the next century, namely, to proactively and continually adjust to an ever-changing environment.

Beyond Customer Dictates

The new century will compel the organizations go beyond the old way of doing things. The scenario till now was that the company focussed on its customer base. The customers were pleased with what the company provided, which flourished upon such roots. To take just a few instances, IBM, Montgomery Ward, Digital Equipment touched pinnacle of the market share and financial success, which later doomed them to their fall. Success in fact led them to speculation, complacency, dogma, ritual, etc.;

they were unwilling to forego current profitable products; they got tied to a particular box of thinking. Against that, upstart or second tier firms, giving up this accepted line of doing things, considered the customer surveys not as they existed in the living present but as they would in future. Further, they made innovations, introduced new products with the belief that customers would prefer them to the older ones. This did happen and in fact the newly emerging firms elbowed out the older ones.

What follows is clear: the new century will not be dictated wholly by the customer, but the company will mould the customer to its new visions and products. At the same time, managers shouldn't afford being blinded by the competitors that offer new goods and services, nor by a customer base that may not yet have bloomed forth. Two steps are important: Firstly, managers must continually monitor the environment and take every development not as a threat but as a guiding lesson; Secondly, they must clearly realize that their present customers, stakeholders (owners, employees, suppliers, communities), and the existing state of their technology can be limiting or inhibiting factors in determining their future plans and actions. Further, they must at no cost allow the existing stakeholders and technologies impose the maintenance of the *status quo*, but, instead, take new bold decisions and concrete steps toward dominance in the emerging new environment (Hodgets et al. 1999).

Entrepreneurship; Venture Teams

Very large MNCs dominating the scene no doubt, the economic growth of any country is directly related to small upstart firms and also to the venture teams in large concerns. Indications are that such entrepreneural strategic initiatives will play a major role in the new century. Further, newly emerging technologies aside, venture teams and focus on the newly emerging markets, will critically matter in their own ways.

The venture team, comprising two or more people of the organization, and dedicated to the creation of the spirit of entrepreneurship, is in fact a mini-organization within the parent one. Exercising great autonomy, the venture team is no slave of structure and formalities, formulates its own aims and objectives, plans its own budget, and decides how to proceed. As such, this is distinctly qualified to deal with change. Its members not given to a concrete *status quo*, it buoys up the organization out of the traditional box. It often offers new goods and services to newly emerging customer groups, thereby dominating the scene. It doesn't totally discard the existing niches, but imaginatively creates new niches, not unoften with singular success. It must be noted , however, that a firm straightly devoted only to a particular emerging customer group shall be severely threatened (Gingrich,1999). The point, therefore, is that a firm has to simultaneously look to two aspects – how to satisfy the existing customers? and second, how to satisfy the emerging groups of customers? Chrestinsen in *Innovators Dilemma,* is very right that the rightful approach is the establishment of venture groups, and the division of responsibilities between the older establishment burdened with current strategy for current customers and the younger venture group burdened with customer groups emerging in future, and neither encroaching upon the other. Chrestinsen thus laid the foundation of a new entrepreneural thinking very likely to dominate the new century

Attitudes

The new century demands new attitudes: managers shall have to modify their old approaches, mainly in three ways. Firstly, organizations shall have to tailor–make their products to particular needs of their customers. Dell Computers is a model case. This company makes computers basically designed to meet the exact needs of each and every customer. Auxiliary firms, making components of highest computer industry standards, have of their own accord tied up with Dell, making parts and components Dell needs, the result is complex of organizations naturally under Dell, earning themselves great individual customer satisfaction and rich dividends. If Dell soared so high, it was only because it tailor-made what every customer needed, infact with the help of several organizations subservient to it.

Secondly, emerging markets shall have to be allotted more funds. The traditional way of granting highest budget allocations to better paying products/markets, by the yardstick of return on investment forecasts, and ignoring thereby the latent potential of emerging markets and hence according them smaller budget allocations, shall have to be changed. By such a change the emerging products/markets may well prove better than those established.

Thirdly, organizations well treading on established markets, shall have to move further out into the concealed /emerging markets. That is a job quite challenging and requiring new initiatives. Brazil provides a good illustration; here, "sack ladies" go from door to door in poorer neighborhoods and their efforts once amounted to 20 percent of the total sales in cosmetics. In US, direct sales forces do much of the total sale – in fact they almost put out Revlon Inc. simply because the company depended on traditional methods of sale. And here "First come, first served" is the golden rule- late movers may not reap what early ones do (Hodgets et al. op cit).

Human Resource Development

Human Resource Development (HRD) is no smaller a factor in today's and tomorrow's organizations. The 4 Ms (Material, Money, Methods, Man) having had almost an equal importance throughout, infotech indeed has accorded pivotal importance to Man in the very dawn of the 21st century. Organizations will go for innovation, hi-tech manufacturing facilities, customer facing, and latest management techniques, but they shall have to pay keenest attention to the men who are at the helm of affairs. Belief goes that the infotech may ultimately put men out of scene, just as machines were once believed to shunt out all workers. The truth seems otherwise. To quote just one instance, the need and importance of human resources only increased in a model organization that is Dell. Information technology tools such as their premier pages (small web pages, linked to large customers intranets that let their employees configure their PCs on-line, pay for them, and track the delivery status) can greatly reduce costs and ordering errors, and also free up the Dell's sales representatives to do more and better customer service and serious selling.

Dell is a typical instance and Jeff Pfeiffer in *Competitive Advantage Through People* and *Human Equation* certifies that human resources can provide the unchangeable competitive edge in the new century. The hard truth is that technology belongs to everybody, but the genial core of an organization is its own singular property. Skills, ideas, efforts, behavior, etc., of a company's men make it distinct and render it above all the rest. In other words, it is the *men* who matter, their brains that count. To sum up, importance will, over the coming years, shift from all other factors to the human factor. It will be a progression , with no retrogation at all.

HRD, as contended by Swanson and Arnold (1997), certainly is directly related to strategic goals of the organization. Garavan (1991) rightly says that HRD, "is best seen as the strategic management of training, development and of professional education interventions, so as to achieve the objectives of organization while at the same time ensuring full utilization of knowledge in detail and skills of individual employees. It is connected with the management of employee learning for the long term, keeping in mind the explicit corporate business strategy". Twigg and Albon (1992) agree and stress upon the connection between HRD and business strategy, and other business processes. They associate a number of aspects of HRM with HRD itself. They suggest that HRD is a chain of processes for developing people at work , which should be linked to business strategy and integrated with other major business processes such as supplier management or purchasing. All these management thinkers are convinced that HRD will play a more distinct and important part in the decades ahead. One simply can't disagree. Agreeing with the above and going far ahead, Plott (1995) gave his "wake up call". Plott assured that there is a ferment in the profession and a new richness in the complexity of offerings, recognizes that learning and technology are not enough, the new links between knowledge and learning and performance need to be established and in that great change HRD professionals have to play the pivotal role. Plott clearly saw that HRD in US was in a historical transition. In the past HRD focussed on classroom training and education of individual employees, and now it focuses on workplace learning and enhancement of performance. This in turn was leading to knowledge creation at the macro-organizational level and contribution toward sustainable competitive advantage in the global marketplace.

Plott advised the HRD professionals to recognize and act according to four basic factors: Firstly, organizations have changed their systems and processes, HRD professionals have to consider themselves as architects of that change; Secondly, HRD professionals' primary aim should be not training individuals but creating shared learning through operating at organizational level; Thirdly, they must encourage them according to change in perspective; and Fourthly, they must initiate and encourage line managers and other key organizational players also thinking in terms of emerging new perspectives. Noel Tichy advocated for an HRD global agenda. That was at WFMPA World Congress in Sydney in 1988. Proceeding upon a summer symposium held in France, which was attended by experts from US, Europe and Japan, Tichy strongly advocated for development of three aspects: Firstly, leaders of companies shall have to go beyond their particular national boundaries and cultures, and work in a multi-national and multi-cultural frame.

Secondly, they shall have to accept a global industrial culture sure to be born of the global business. They shall have to transmit this change down throughout the whole establishment. Thirdly, organizational forms shall have to be metamorphosed from national to multi-national kind. In doing so, distribution of tasks, defining of roles, authority relationships, and centers of power shall have to be identified and defined afresh, and appropriate drastic steps shall have to be taken towards new global accomplishments. All such change shall have to be, unavoidably, global. All recruiting, selecting, developing, rotating, and managing shall have to be done on similar lines.

Team Building

HRD unfolds team building also. Team building always is a diverse exercise encompassing self- managed teams on factory floor, senior – management outdoor teams and quality circles. Self managing teams, as pointed out by Dumaine (1990), have been experimenting upon one half of US' large companies. Team working, again, has been a hub of production and service delivery methods in UK, as found out by the University of Bath (Purcell, 1996). Team work, says Purcell (1996), is the fulcrum of most of the organizations. All are agreed that team-work improves decision making, reduces response time, provides social cohesion, improves employee satisfaction, enhances organizational culture, builds up commitment and sincerity, extols the identity of the firm, and is therefore decidedly the great way of doing things. In fact project teams, self-managing teams, semi-autonomous work groups have been mushrooming up everywhere, and each of them is a posse of experts, and all teams together shoulder the company responsibilities (Hackman and Oldham, 1980). These teams need autonomy which is related to job motivation; job motivation is related to team process; and team process is related to team effectiveness. But in reality no work teams enjoy complete autonomy, are interlinked with other teams, and are therefore only interdependent (Sunderstrom et al. 1990). Autonomy or independence, the new century, will have the concept of team work only more and more materializing out. And in future, every organization shall be considered as a company of work teams rather than of individuals.

Intellectual capital

HRD, then, succinctly envisages that no firm possibly in future can survive without its individual intellectual capital. The merger of Price Waterhouse with Coopers & Lybrand laid a glorious example in the creation of Director of HRD and Intellectual Capital. The intellectual capital, including distinct individual skills and expertise evolved by a firm's workers, is sometimes called the "Knowledge Theory of the Firm". That theory visualizes that knowledge is the key to value addition as well as to strategic advantage and advance (Grant,1997). Tom Peters put forth the simple concept of Knowledge Management structure (KMS) wherein he advised the companies to do away with bureaucracy in order to generate knowledge, cultivate skills, and enhance the power in the workplace. Illustrious examples were laid down by Dow Chemicals, Enderson Consulting, Polaroid, Skandia, ICL, each installing a Director/Vice President of Knowledge/Intellectual capital, under whom they took great strides in explicit knowledge. Naturally, HRD people had a new major role with innovation the key word. Innovation gave each of them a competitive edge and innovation was mothered by knowledge. These competencies made strides in knowledge, gave them strides in competition also. They made it abundantly clear that a company in order to survive and progress in the new century shall have to advance both in explicit and implicit knowledge[1] composing its distinct intellectual capital. This intellectual capital should not simply be a sum- up of the inherited past knowledge but must include also the intellectual gains made in the living present and to be passed down to the running company. Trainers in the company, thus, have to be learners themselves. This concept beautifully materialized in a UK government Green Paper titled the "Learning Age". Herein a number of organizations, well established over centuries though, were called *learning* organizations. Trainer himself being a learner now, HRD terminology changed such as from "Training and Development" to "Learning and Development Services" (Walton, 1999). And thus emerges a new challenge- how to carve out a *learning* organization? And at the same time, deliver results and value to shareholders? For any company to transform itself into a *learning* organization, it is important to put the following critical success factors in place- a clear mission statement, long term approach, a comprehensive business plan, result orientation, right organizational structure, team work, individual drive, customer focus and focus beyond survival. Today, money is everywhere, but brains are scarce. Capital markets will value this scarcity, so they will learn to put new value on intellectual capital. New ways to trade human capital will develop and blend into global risk market. Job markets will morph into human capital markets, trading a variety of wealth- creating activities from job creation and placement to rationing scarce talen.

Multirater 360- Degree Feedback

A distinction of the new century very likely may be the performance of an executive being assessed not just by supervisor but by multirater 360 degree feedback. This feedback has been studied from upstarts of a few dozen people to Fortune 500 firms and industry from hi-tech manufacturing to professional services firms. Self-estimation and estimation by others is not unoften widely different and the differences certainly are educating; also, multiple anonymous feedback about performance are certainly highly educative. Estimation by, say, one single boss

[1] By *explicit* is meant the branch of knowledge generally used for routine tasks; and by *implicit* that which is creatively applied to a particular business problem or opportunity (Hansen and Oetinger, 2001)

can never be as valuable. Self estimation or estimation by a boss is quite often deceptive; whereas that by superiors, subordinates, peers, even outside customers is often informative, educative and indeed precious. It has revolutionized performance management for the better. No surprise then that AT&T, Bank of America, Exxon, GE, etc., have been depending on 360 degree feedback for a long time now, both for individual and collective performance. This feedback is not just for employee measurement, development, feedback and behavior change- it also can improve employee performance at the company (Peters, 2000). However, there has been concern about the complexities of the 360 degree approach in terms of psychometric (measurements) properties and implications, of the ratings, especially the relationship between self and others ratings of compensation and promotional issues. Also, personal leanings and other minor factors tend to influence estimations, as, for example, peers tend to be more lenient in public sector organizations than private sector organizations. All that standing, it remains that multirater 360 degree feedback system shall be more and more used in the new century.

Pay for Performance

All know that appropriate compensation helps establish and enhance a company's culture by enhancing its employees' values and behavior. Teamwork and cooperation degenerate unless there is a group based component in their compensation system. Many organizations are often for team work and team performance, but reward only the individuals and individual outputs (Maury, 2001). Exhibits I and II sum-up the merits and demerits of the individual and the team appraisals.

I

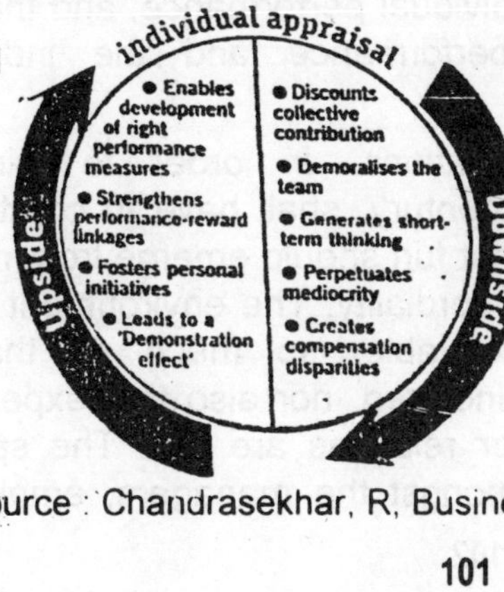

II

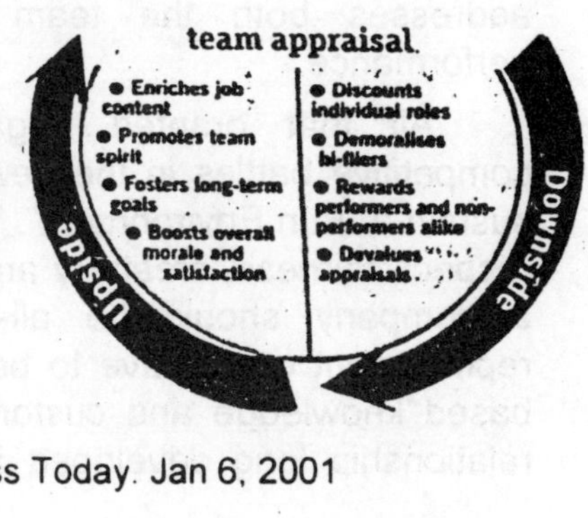

Source : Chandrasekhar, R, Business Today. Jan 6, 2001

Taylor, at the end of this century, led the scientific management movement, where pay was straightly related to performance. For years, many companies rewarded employees including managers for their individual performance. Such initiatives released new energies in old workers, new drives, new dedication and devotion, all combining to extol the company to new heights. According to "Fortune 1000" the percentage of companies going by individual performance of its employees rose from 38 to 50, in the last part of the previous century . And again, the percentage of sales people working on commission basis (individual performance) went up to 14 (quoted by Hodgets et al. op cit) Still, pay according to individual performance has its own shortcomings (Business Today,2001). Fortune, again reported that 50 percent of the employees declaimed this system as neither fair nor sensible, and the same percentage held that this system didn't in any way help the company instead. It undermined teamwork, made employees myopic, and made them believe that personality and diplomatic skills amount to performance (Hodgets,1991 op cit). That was why Dr. Deming and other quality gurus disqualified this method arguing that it kills much of the management time and resources and leaves almost all dissatisfied. They add the new century is not going to accept this mode of payment. In view of the focus on customers, leadership, associates knowledge and skills and competence, they outrightly discard this traditional view. They uphold that the doctrine of pay for performance calls not only for traditional productivity but also for improvement in customer satisfaction, employee satisfaction, cycle time, and the ability in demonstration of skills. Going by such dictates, General Mills accords half of its bonus to business unit results, and the other half to individual performance, and this way addresses both the team performance and the individual performance.

All that granted, organizations, in order to win the competitive battles in the new century, shall have to create and sustain a "Fun Environment". That fun should emerge from mutual respect, fairness, creativity and cordiality. The environment within a company should be all-enjoyable, so much so that no replacement costs have to be incurred, nor also that experience based knowledge and customer relations are lost. The spiritual relationship long developed amongst the managers, employees and customer base must always be nourished environmentally (Luthans and Stajkovic, 1999; Hodgets et al., op cit).

References

Chandrasekhar, R., (2001). "The case of team reward", Business Today. Jan 6.

David Lei; John Slocum Jr. and Robert Pitts, (1999) "Designing Organisations for Competitive Advantage, The power of Unlearning and Learning" Organisation Dynamics (winter).

Dumaine, B. "Who Needs a Boss" Fortune, May 7, 1990.

Garavan, T N. (1991) "Strategic Human Resource Development" Journal of European Industrial Training, Vol. 15(1).

Gingrich, J A. (1999) "Five Rules for Winning Emerging Market Consumers", Strategy and Business, Second Quarter.

Grant, R. M. (1997) "Strategy at the Leading Edge– The Knowledge – based View of the Firm: Implications for Management Practice", Long Range Planning, Vol.30(3),June.

Hackman, J.R. and Oldham, G.R. (1990) Work Redesign. Readings, M.A: Addison Wesely.

John Walton (1999) Strategic Human Resource Development. Prentice Hall.

Luthans, F. and Stajkovi, A.D. (1999) "Reinforce for Performance : The Need to Go Beyond Pay or Even Rewards", Academy of Management Executive, Vol.13(2).

Maury A Peiprl. (2001) "Getting 360 feedback Right" Harvard Business Review, Jan.

Morten T Hansen and Bolko von oetinger (2001) "Introducing T-Shaped Management" .Harvard Business Review, Vol.79(3), March.

Nadler, D.A. and Tushman M.L. (1999) "The Organisation of the Future : Principles of Design for the 21st Century",Organisation Dynamics(summer).

Paul F.Wilson and Richard D.Pearson. (1996) Performance- Bsased Assessment Tools for Total Quality Management. Tata Mc Graw Hill.

Petrers Carvey (2001) "Designing a 360 Feedback System to Improve Employee Performance" HR Focus, Sept.

Pfeffer Jeffery (1994) Competitive Advantage through People – Unleashing the Power of the Workforce. Boston M A : Harvard Business School Press.

Pfeffer Jeffery (1998) The Human Equation : Building Profits and putting the People First, Boston, M A : Harvard Business School Press.

Plott, Curtis (1998) Introductory Address to Conference of ASTD. Dalls.

Purcell, J. (1999) "People Management Implications of Learner Ways of Working" Quoted in John, Walton. Strategic Human Resource development, Prentice Hall.

Richard M Hoggetts; Freud Luthans and Johan W Slocum Jr. (1999) "Strategy and HRM Initiatives for '00s Environemt," Organisational Dynamics.

Sunderstrom E; De Muse K.P and Futrell D. (1990) "Work teams : Applications and Effectiveness," American Psychologist, 45.

Swanson, R.A and Arnold, D E. (1997) "The Purpose of HRD to Improve Performance," Proceedings of Academy of HRD, Atlanta.

Tichy Noel, Quoted in Micheal V P. (1995) Human Resource management and Human Relations. Himaliya publishing House.

Twigg G and Albon P, (1992) Human Resource Development and Business Strategy. In M Armstrong (ed.) Strategies for HRM – A Total Business Approach," London. Kogan Page.

--O--

08

EMERGING ISSUES IN HUMAN RESOURCE DEVELOPMENT

Parvez A. Shah

Abstract

The HRD arena has been totally transformed over the last two decades especially while being in the midst of an engulfing globalisation, the diversification of the financial forces, the topsy-turvy turbulent economic liberalisation and the rumblings of the mammoth high-tech multi-nationals beyond the boundaries of national economies. Against this backdrop of gigantic growth & impending stiff & fierce competition, the introduction & propagation of the philosophy of HRD becomes indispensable in order to bring about the excellence in the performance of the organisation. But this cannot be done, unless it is ensured that the issues like, whether organisations have been in a position to adapt themselves with the emerging changes in the changing environment, or are they by nature, learning and humanised organisations with a coping stance to meet present days technological onslaught, globalisation challenges viz-a-viz its organisational strategy committed from line and top management etc. The present paper as such is a moderate attempt in this direction.

Introduction:

Over the last two decades, organisations world-over have increasingly become aware of the importance of the human resources. This awareness in a sub-system is a critical dimension in the organisational effectiveness. The real experiences substantiate the assumption that no matter how sophisticated and modern the business activities of the organisation may become, it will find it extremely difficulty to sustain its growth & effectiveness unless its human resources are complementary to its operations. Some more than 25 years ago Herbst (1975) observed that the product of work is people. The world is becoming far more competitive and volatile than ever before causing organisations to gain competitive advantage whenever & wherever possible in todays globalised and informationalised world. Organisational survival & success will invariably depend on how they respond these challenges. For effective management response, organisations have to evolve internal capabilities for enhancing speed, quality, learning & building employee competencies. HRD is fundamental to generating & effecting these capabilities.

The field of HRD defies definition & boundaries. It is difficult to put in a box. It has become so large, extensive & inclusive that it is now greater than all outdoors. And the field keeps growing not just domestically but internationally as well (Blake, 1999, Mufeed, 2001). Whatever the specifics, the general category & focus of HRD seems to centre on human betterment, wherever & in whatever domain of life.

Our age has been called the age of "Progress Through People". Despite the splashy entrance of the computer onto the management scene, and perhaps because of it many people now believe that the human dimension is the key to an organisation's future. High tech has made the need for high touch apparent.

Developing & motivating people have become even more pressing needs because of the current obsession with technology.

Not too long ago, human resource people were the last to know of important organisational changes. They found it hard to be effective when their main source of information was the company newspaper. But times are changing, and HRD professionals are being given much greater responsibility. For better or worse, HRD has become the latest 'panacea'. During the past 25 years HRD professionals have been conducting needs analyses, designing programs, evaluating behaviour change & measuring results. They have charged into the fray with the battle cry, "Seek ye first operational excellence and all else shall follow ".

Spotting problems, putting out fires and running top-notch departments are important, given management's emphasis on bottom-line results for training and development efforts. But an excessively operational focus shortchanges the future. Too much attention has been paid to how well the organisations accomplish present goals and not enough methods for accomplishing future goals. To correct this myopia, HRD professionals must learn to put operational excellence in the service of clear strategic thinking.

The approach of the management in recent past towards its employees has undergone a drastic change. By the 1970's a shift in professional values was discernible with a development status "impressing with sophistication". During the period major emphasis was laid on regulatory conformance and imposition of standards on other functions. It shifted from a concern for welfare to a focus on efficiency. During the period 1980' s -1990' s, professionals began to talk about new technologies, human resource management challenges and human resource development, when the emphasis was on human values, productivity through people. The output of these decade changes is a growing awareness of the importance of the human side of organisations as a vital factor in over all progress.

Emerging Issues in Human Resource Development

Human resource issues are like a double-edged sword as these issues can represent an opportunity for improvement or a chance to gain competitive advantage. (Walker, 1992). In the negative sense, they also represent problems or shortcomings that must be resolved. The organisations are required to build new capabilities & competencies to resolve these issues. Some of the issues that HRD professionals are beset with are :

i) HRD & Changing Environment

ii) HRD & Learning Organisation

iii) HRD & Technological onslaught

iv) HRD & Globalization

v) HRD & Organisational Strategy

vi) HRD & Humanisation

vii) HRD & Low Commitment from Management

HRD & Changing Environment

Change is endemic in our society, perhaps the only factor that remains continuously present in our system is change. This aspect has led many organisations and individuals to look at themselves with anticipation and ask what the future would look like. The global managers of tomorrow are therefore, becoming pro-active for future requirements, perhaps they are now more aware of what lies ahead of them. Changes sometimes call for drastic changes in structures & strategies. Recent times in India we have witnessed the dramatic transformation of some organsiations that have managed to cross the boundaries of time-worn traditions & practices in order to assume vibrant new identities. Flexibility that is adoptiveness to rapid changes, has replaced stability, quality, the Japanese mantra, has invaded every aspect of organisation from management to product. HRD will be expected to playa key role in translating these words from paper into action. HRD professionals being the architects of change, have to learn to change faster and more comfortably and have to deal with questions like:

i. how do we honour the past & adopt to the future?

ii. how do we change every one to change?

iii. how do we change & learn more rapidly?

iv. how do we unlearn what we have learned

(Ulrich, 1997)

HRD & Learning Orgnanisation

One of the features of recent years has been a greater emphasis on the term "learning", in organisational and indeed national vocabularies. Individuals are enjoined to engage in continuous life-long learning. The UK Govt., in February, 1998, produced a green paper entitled "The Learning Age". A number of organisations are referred to in their brochures & literature as "Learning Organisations". As a parallel trend there has been a shift in HRD terminology from training & development towards learning & development. The swing towards learning has been followed by an interest in knowledge as a means of developing human and intellectual capital as a source of sustainable competitive advantage in a post-industrial Revolution; Information Age. Technology global markets, customer expectations & competition have all contributed to the view that learning is the only strategy to cope with change. There has been a growing emphasis on viewing an organisation as a total learning system & finding its 'Core Competencies' which reveal its 'Collective Learning'. (Prahalad & Hamel, 1990). Learning is not just an acquisition of new knowledge, it is collaborative process of observation, experimentation and experience which can be mobilised to deal with new opportunities and threats. The learning organisations also require their members to have a corresponding learning mode, a change proneness, a willingness to try new ideas and so on.

HRD and Technological Onslaught

New technologies have changed the life of organisations and individuals. From video-conferencing to the Internet, technology has made our world small and being termed as global village. Ideas & massive amounts of information are in constant movement through fax, e-mail, internet and other electronic devices which ensure transformation of communications on the spur of the moment. The Challenges for managers is to make sense & good use of what this technology offers. Not all technology adds value. So, in coming years managers will need to figure out how to make technology a viable productive part of the work setting. (Ulrich, 1997). The HR professionals need to have some skill to cope these challenges such as, they must be dexterious in managing strategy, planning, change & development

& managing integration. In other words, it has accentuated the need to upgrade the employees' skills & competencies. All these changes are already producing a profound impact on how organisations work, how will they will restructure themselves, what services they can provide, & which among the employees, they will retain, re-skill & deploy or retrench.

HRD & Globalisation

Gone are the days when companies created products at home & shipped them abroad "as is". With the rapid expansion of global market, managers are struggling to balance the paradoxical demand to think globally & act locally. That imperative requires them to more people, ideas & information around the world to meet local needs. In future human resource professionals will need to create models and processes for attaining global agility, effectiveness and competitiveness. In short globalisation requires that organisations increase their ability to learn and collaborate and to manage diversity, complexity & uncertainty.

HRD & Organisational Strategy

Strategy is managements' vision of what organisation should be, not how the organization will get there. The how's are the operational plans & activities, but there also must be an outline that guide choices about the organisations nature & direction. This is Strategy. Strategic approach required a learning mode in the organisation. It takes an organisation beyond a concern for operational effectiveness, which involves incremental improvements in all critical activities over their own previous, or their rival's performance. The new techniques used are TQM, benchmarking, outsourcing, reengineering & so forth. Strategic approach takes an integrated view to guide the organisation in undertaking these new activities. (Porter, 1985). It involves identifying the organisation mission, developing a vision, setting specific goals, designing systems & procedures. But while integrating these all, HR people will have to keep the human beings the centre.

HRD & Humanization

It is all the more important issue, for HRD people to see as to how are employees who might be spending say 30-40 years of their life in the organisation throughout their long service and remain motivated and productive and simultaneously maintaining a reasonable level of job satisfaction? Many organisations in the country have yet to examine this issue satisfactorily. A linkage problem is another serious humanistic issue in HRD. If the employee does not get a good feedback about the development needs, he remains non-involved in his own development & becomes potentially complacent. This issue needs to be examined by our HRD managers more closely: Similarly, existence of a continuous optimal challenge keeps human growth & effectiveness such a challenge is provided to some members in the organisation through promotion to higher levels. Such opportunities are limited to other members because Pyramid narrows down at the top. An effective human resource planning & development will therefore concentrate on developing career paths; systems of job rotation, changing assignments & other job moves.

Low Commitment from Management

HRD efforts are not likely to succeed unless top management is highly committed to HRD. But the line-managers are comparatively more non-serious towards HRD. In an essay on "how managers sabotage their own development", one of the authors had already warned if HRD does not succeed, it may be more because of line managers themselves. (Roa, 1981, Roa & Abraham, 1987). The changing role of line management at Xerox is well depicted in the following table:

Administrative Role	Democratic Role
One-to-one Supervisor	Team Leader
Telling	Teacher
Planning	Facilitator
Controlling	Workers assume Responsibility
	Trained to function as a work group

Similarly, delegating HRD to line managers has the problems. Even the best-motivated line manager cannot give the strategic attention to HRD issues that a specialist function would offer. The another apprehension is that they may interpret learning issues in a way that is particular to their own specialisation or operational interest. The HRD specialists realise that top management obstructs HRD to flourish on expected lines. The more a manager climbs up the executive leader, the less he gets to hear of the happenings to human resources down below. Hence, a prime HRD strategy is to ensure a free flow of information & cultivate empathy.

The other issues of HRD that need a serious consideration from the HRD professionals are as under:-

i. Innovative ways of compensation attractive to employees, yet economical to the company.

ii. Training programs are specific & based on individual & organisational needs perhaps more towards the enhancement of skills -than of concepts.

iii. To bring about a sense of autonomy and sense of identity among people.

iv. Ways of attracting and retaining talent, measuring competence & securing intellectual capital.

v. The HRD professional must understand organisational strategy, driving force and develop an HRD strategy accordingly.

Conclusion

HRD issues if addressed properly and with adequate strategies will help solve real-life organisational problems and bring about flexibility, resilience and business success for the organisations. This will constitute a new shift for the HRD function in general and for HRD professionals in particular- a shift that is necessary to prevent it becoming redundant in the changing business scenario of the 21st century making it an accountable and proactive function. When major change is needed HRD practitioners must think creatively -and may have to transform the HRD effort into something utterly different what... has been in the past.

References

Dave Ulrich (1998), "The Future Calls for Change", Workforce, January.

Dave Ulrich (1998), "A new Mandate for Human Resources", HBR, Vol. 76, January-February.

Herbst, P.G. (1975), "The Product of Work is People", National Labour Institute Bulletin, Vol. 1(4).

Mufeed, S.A. (2001), "Human Resource Development in Universities: A Fresh Look", The Business Review, Vol.7 (2-3), March-April.

Prahalad, C. K. & Hamel, K. (1990), "The Core Competence of the Corporation ", HBR, May-June.

Porter, M (1985), "Competitive Strategy", New York. The Free Press

Roa, T. V. (1987), "Planningfor Human Resource Development', Vikalpa, Vol. 12(3), July-September.

Roa, T. V. & Abraham, E. (1987), "Human Resource Development Practices in Indian Industries -A Trend Report ", Management & Labour Studies, Vol.II (2).

Roa, T. V. (1981), "How Managers Can Sabotage Their Own Development", Indian Management, Vol. 20(12).

OOO

09

ROLE STRESS IN INDIAN BANKING INDUSTRY - A STUDY OF SELECTED BANKS

Farooq A. Shah

Abstract

With the growing recognition of the 'Human Relations Approach' in the management of organizations, the discomforts and dishonour associated with work are apparently missing today but the intangible vulnerability and hazards in the shape of stress, strain and anxiety are still ingrained in it. This intrinsic and hidden susceptibility, which is more precarious and has been covertly taking the toll on working people, is a fallout of the worker and work environment misfit. Consequently, job stress has been a fascinating field of research during the recent years. However, the studies have mostly focused on its few dimensions only thereby ignoring the other equally potent constructs. The present study has been undertaken to provide an adequate explanation of stress; its nature, dimensions, causes, manifestations and coping up strategies. The study, conducted in the banking industry in Kashmir, reveals that most of the employees experience medium to high level of stress at work. Role stagnation, inadequacy of role authority and role erosion are, comparatively, high rated dimensions of job stress. The study further reveals that employees belonging to the clerical cadre, relatively, experience more stress on most of the dimensions. The available literature on the subject has been critically reviewed and various measures to effectively manage stress experience at the job have been suggested.

Introduction

Around 40 percent of the sampled executives say that they frequently lie awake at night or wake up thinking about work problems, while another 33 percent report that they often feel incapable of relaxing at home because of stress". This is the crux of a survey conducted by the *Wall Street Journal* (1982), which so ingeniously conveys that how latently, and relentlessly job stress takes the toll on working people.

Stress has probably been associated even with the life of prehistoric man and is there to stay in every socio-economic setting. The stress level is on the continuous rise because of the increasing competition and attempts at trying to keep pace with the advancement in one's field together with constant threat of falling short of one's own and those of others' expectations.

The term stress has been borrowed from physical sciences where it is used to mean force, pressure or strain applied on an organism, which resists these forces and struggles to maintain its original position. It was Hans Selye who introduced the concept of stress in life sciences more than five decades ago. Selye (1946) observed the reactions of his animal subjects to a variety of stimuli and proposed three stages in the *'General Adaptation Syndrome'* (GAS) model, to explain the stress phenomenon; *Alarm Reaction Stage, Resistance Stage, and Exhaustion Stage*.

Ever since Selye's pioneering work on stress, researchers of various academic fields to meet their specific requirements have used the term variously. Even the psychologists and behaviouralists have been using the term differently. One group of researchers, viewing stress as a stimulus phenomenon, regard it as an external force operating on an individual which is perceived as a threat, the other group believes that stress should be conceived as an organism's response to internal and external processes that go beyond the limits of physical, psycho-physiological and integrative capacities. There is, however, still another group of analysts who feels that stress is the outcome of the transaction between the stimulus and the response. Most of the behavioral scientists belong to the third category and believe that stress is a situation created by the interaction between the stimulus or the external force upon the individual and the deviation or the changes made by the individuals in response to that external force. Stress, therefore, is a dynamic condition in which an individual is confronted with an opportunity, constraint or demand related to what the individual desires and for which the outcome is perceived to be both uncertain and important. Hence, stress involves an interaction between the person and the environment, it begins with the environmental demand or opportunity for a person to behave and ends with the person's response to that opportunity or demand. These demands and influences combine and continuously pressurize an individual until stress develops. However, stress is essentially a psychological and internal phenomenon and its level is subservient to many factors like perception of the individual vis-à-vis his capacity to deal with the situation and the importance of the possible outcome thereof etc.

The common connotation which the term 'stress' has acquired is a negative one; something, which should be avoided. Nonetheless, the researchers have, of late, started feeling that a moderate amount of stress is not only essential but also desirable for effectiveness and improvement. They feel that it is natural and healthy to maintain optimal level of stress and believe that success, achievement and high productivity call for optimum amount of stress. A reasonable level of stress is positively related to job satisfaction and involvement and a high level of stress (hyperstress) is found to be responsible for poor performance and physical and psycho-physiological disorders. Similarly, too little stress (hypostress) is as undesirable as too high stress. Thus, somewhere between these two extremes is the moderate level of stress where performance is optimal.

Stress is known to have two dimensions. It can be an individual's best friend or his worst enemy. In case it assumes the role of the latter, it tears one down in a number of subtle ways and hits at his physical, mental and behavioral faculties. This is truer under the modern belief according to which illness is considered as physiologically and chemically founded and socially and culturally conditioned. This social and cultural contribution to illness is, to a great extent, stress causation. Given the implications, the literature on stress and health has been accumulating in magnitude ever since the stress conceptualisation came into being. Research has been conducted on all the aspects of stress, particularly its physiological, psychological and behavioral ill effects. The common manifestations observed due to stress are, anxiety, depression, cardio-vascular failures, headaches and muscular aches, allergies, sexual dysfunction, gastric and peptic ulcers, malignancies, bronchial asthma, insomnia, increased smoking/drinking and over or under eating and so on.

Stress has been a part of every civilization and as such people cannot imagine of a stress free life. Nevertheless, given the physical, psychological and behavioral repercussions, individuals and organizations cannot afford to live in the continuous state of tension and anxiety. The researchers have, therefore, been trying to find out the ways and means to counteract stress. In general, two different strategies of coping with stress have been advocated, '*avoider*' and '*coper*'. The avoider solves the stress problems simply by denying them, diverting attention, taking time off from routine preoccupations and developing hobbies etc. (Sharma 1983). Contrary to it, the '*coper*' seeks out stress situations so as to learn how to cope with them. Similarly, Pareek (1983) suggests that effective coping strategies are '*approach*' strategies; to confront the problem of stress as a challenge and to enhance the capability of dealing with it and the ineffective and unpleasant strategies are '*avoidance*' or '*escape*' strategies; to reduce the feeling of stress by resorting to escapism;

denying the reality of stress through use of alcohol, drugs and smoking, for example. Numerous studies have suggested that social support moderates the negative effects of stress on personal well-being. Some researchers believe that organisational stress can best be managed by creating a person-work environment fit (Agrawal, 1985). Calling this synthesis as a *'job-characteristics approach'*, he has empirically found that linking the individual to the job characteristics yields the results of low absenteeism and turnover and high worker satisfaction. Investigating the impact of yoga and meditation on stress experience has been yet another field of fascination for researchers. Despite the voluminous research on stress management, no panaceous therapy has so far been evolved for effectively managing stress that has been covertly taking its toll. Moreover, the thrust has unevenly been on 'coping' and the preventive antidote, as a potent method of mitigating the impact of this inevitable phenomenon, has been largely overlooked.

Due to its far-reaching consequences for organisational health and member well-being stress phenomenon has, globally, emerged as a focal theme of research. Banking sector has been no exception to this general tendency and a number of studies have been conducted to explore stress situation in the Indian banking industry as well. The studies conducted by Ananthrama and Begum (1982), Bhatnagar and Bose (1985), Singh and Nath (1987), Achmamba and Gopikumar (1990), and Rajeshwari (1992), are but to name a few.

In view of the fact that most of these studies are descriptive, non-specific and generic in nature and far from empirical and pragmatic basis, the stress scenario in the banking industry has, largely, remained unexplored. This limitation is of serious concern especially in view of certain peculiar characteristics, particularly tight time schedule, work overload and inherent risk attached to the banking job. Besides, the industry witnessed a significant growth during the last few decades. The sizeable increase in the volume of banking business along with the inherent characteristics of the job described above, has given rise to a large-scale feeling of stress and anxiety among banking personnel. Such a feeling has been on the continuous rise and has impinged upon the performance of the banks. The industry, therefore, should be regarded as a priority sector for such type of research as the stress experience in the industry is harmful not only for the members and the organisation but for the customers as well, and its repercussions are most likely to reflect, in the long run, on the national economy which is by all counts undesirable for any country. Moreover, not much studies, aimed at exploring the ways and means of improving the quality and climate of work life with a view to alleviate the stress borne organisational work settings, have been conducted and the dictum that 'prevention is better than cure' has remained, more or less, unattended. The available research on organisational stress is largely biased towards role, while other equally crucial constituents of organisational climate like decision making practices, leadership style, communication pattern and reward system etc., as potent sources of job stress, have been overlooked. Above all, no study has, so far, even been attempted on the subject in Kashmir. It is in this backdrop that the present study has been undertaken to fill in this vital gap in the existing research.

Objectives of the Study

The study has been undertaken with the following objectives in view:

- To assess the nature, level and sources of job stress,
- To examine how the stress level varies with the nature of the job of employees,
- To suggest, on the basis of the results of the study, the workable stress managing strategies, and
- To highlight the implications of the study results for employees, management, policy makers and academicians.

Methodology

For an in-depth investigation, the study has been confined to three large banking organizations operating in Kashmir. The selection of the banks has been done on the basis of a well set criteria. Of the three two of the organisations belong to the nationalized sector and employ, in aggregate, 3745 employees, which constitutes the universe for the study. The total sample size was restricted to 125. Using the stratified sampling technique, the population was stratified as (i) officers and (ii) clerks. The clerks for the sample included cashier-cum-clerks, clerk-cum-typists, assistant cashiers and special assistants etc. Likewise, the officers for the sample constituted the top management, the middle management, the functional heads and the management level 1 in the organisational hierarchy.

With a view to ensure adequate representation to all the three organisations, the total sample size was divided among the organisations using the proportionate representative sampling technique. The individual samples thus arrived at, for each organization, was further stratified using geographical location and scatteredness as stratifying factor so as to give sufficient representation to the domain of the study.

Besides discussions and deliberations with the management personnel and employees, their personal interview through a properly designed comprehensive questionnaire constitutes the primary source of data for the study. The questionnaire consisted of two parts. Part I was designed to elicit the socio-economic background of the respondents and part II pertained to stress experience at their job. Ten specific dimensions of job stress with the help of four statements each were individually assessed. Since the statements in the questionnaire were qualitative, they were quantified on a five-point scale using Likert type technique. The respondents were asked to tick mark the appropriate score on a five point continuum *(1= True to Almost No Extent, and 5= True to a Very Great Extent)*. Besides averages, standard deviation and regression etc., the statistical tools like $\chi 2$ test, *t* test and inter-correlation were made use of.

Findings

Overall Stress Experience

With a view to measure the overall stress experience of employees in terms of severity, the total stress scores on all the dimensions by the respondents were pooled together so as to classify them into 'low', 'medium' and 'high' categories. The results contained in Tale 1 signify that most of the employees experience medium intensity stress at work. An incredible majority of over 72% employees faces medium degree of stress and the number of employees confronting high intensity stress is more than the employees experiencing stress of low intensity.

Table 1: Index of the Level of Job Stress			
Scores	**Level of Stress**	**Frequency**	**Percentage**
120 and above	High	19	15.20
81 - 119	Medium	91	72.80
Upto 80	Low	15	12.00
Total		**125**	**100.00**

The magnitude of stress experience on various dimensions is evident from the results obtained by each dimension on the ranking progression in Table 2. An analysis of the data in the table reveals that employees confront various forms of stress with varying degrees. Role Stagnation, being on the top in the ranking pattern, is the manifestation of how terribly people experience the fear of being stranded in their present role within the organisation. Inadequacy of Role Authority, with the average rating of 57.1%, ranks second. Thus, there is a vast gap between authority and responsibility and employees frequently find themselves inadequately harnessed with authority in order to carry out effectively the responsibilities assigned to them. Role Erosion, Role Overload and Personal/Resource Inadequacy are the other potent sources of stress with the average rating of more than 50%. As such, the employees feel that they are doing less important things than they can do on their jobs, there is a great scope for enrichment of their jobs and that they are overburdened with the quantity of work they have to perform within the available time and other resources.

Table 2: Means, Standard Deviations and Ranks of Stress Dimensions					
S. No.	**Dimensions of Job Stress**	**Mean Score**	**S.D.**	**Mean in %age**	**Rank**
1.	Self Role Distance	8.38	2.86	41.90	9
2.	Role Stagnation	12.22	3.22	61.10	1
3.	Role Ambiguity	7.93	2.46	39.65	10
4.	Role Conflict	8.89	2.79	44.45	7
5.	Role Overload	10.66	3.23	53.30	4
6.	Role Erosion	11.29	2.83	56.45	3
7.	Lack of Group Cohesiveness & Supervisory Support	8.96	2.69	44.80	6
8.	Personal/Resource Inadequacy	10.13	3.19	50.65	5
9.	Constraint of Change	8.62	2.76	43.10	8
10.	Inadequacy of Role Authority	11.42	3.19	57.10	2

Interestingly, Role Ambiguity and Self-Role Distance, probably the most widely researched dimensions of stress, emerged as the feeblest constituent of organisational stress in this study. This important revelation suggests that the bank employees suffer least for want of sufficient information relating to their jobs and the job demands are hardly contradictory to their values and beliefs. Constraint of Change, with the eighth rank on the continuum, is the other least important source of job stress, which means that the organisational members do not confront much stress on account of technological and procedural changes. However, the employees are moderately stressful due to Lack of Group Cohesiveness/Supervisory Support, and Role Conflict, the average scores being 44.8% and 44.45% respectively. This implies that inter-group and superior-subordinate relationship at work is not too unpleasant and the employees do not suffer much due to incompatible orders and conflicting expectations from different quarters.

Summing up the above discussion, it can be inferred that the members of the banking organisations are stressful, in order of severity, due to poor growth prospects, non-compatible authority with responsibility, shrinkage and dissipation of role importance, too much work with too little resources, clashing demands from various interests, frequent changes in regulations and policy matters and lack of clarity about the requirements of the job etc.

Stress Experience of Officers and Clerks

Numerous studies have been conducted to examine the relationship between stress level and the level of management. However, the results have often been inconsistent probably because there are always other interacting factors that also play their role. In spite of this unconformity, it is interesting to study the nature and magnitude of association existing between stress experience and hierarchical position of employees.

Table 3: Overall Stress Experience of Officers and Clerks		
	Hierarchical Position of Employees	
	Officers (N=44)	Clerks (N=81)
Mean Scores	95.64	100.06
Standard Deviation	16.80	14.70
t Value	1.46*	
χ^2 Value	1.52*	

*Non-significant.

A perusal of the data in Table 3 suggests that the overall stress situation is, comparatively, better with officers. Nevertheless, the difference in the stress feeling of two groups is neither significant (t=1.46), nor is there any association between stress experience and nature of the job of employees (χ^2 = 1.52).

Keeping in view the vagueness of Table 3 results, it is worthwhile to go for some more specific analysis. Accordingly the relevant data have been plotted in Table 4 which indicates that 11.36% and 15.91% of the total officers have a high and a low stress sensation respectively. Similarly, 17.28% of the clerks experience a high and 9.88% of them experience a low level of stress. The analysis further reveals that the percentage of officers and clerical cadre employees does not vary much on the medium stress level.

Table 4: Hierarchical Placement of Employees and Level of Stress						
Level of Stress	Level of Placement of Employees					
	Officers		Clerks		Total	
	F	%	F	%	F	%
High	5	11.36	14	17.28	19	15.20
Medium	32	73.73	59	72.84	91	70.80
Low	7	15.91	8	9.88	15	12.00
Total	44	100.00	81	100.00	125	100.00

In order to go for still more specific investigation, the dimension-wise comparative profile of stress as experienced by officers and clerks has been examined (see table 5). Role Stagnation and Role Overload are found to be the foremost constituents of stress where clerks suffer significantly, *t* values for the two components being 4.57 and 4.16 respectively which are significant beyond 1% level of significance. This manifests that the lower level employees feel extremely upset by being stuck into their positions for long. This is probably true of the banking industry, more so in the Indian context, which in the absence of large scale mechanization and computerization, continues to be labour intensive. Obviously, the higher positions do not fall frequently vacant as a result of which the promotion prospects attached to a lower level job are poor.

Table 5: Dimension-wise Job Stress Experience of Officers and Clerks

S. No	Dimensions of Stress	Officers (N=44)		Clerks (N=81)		t
		Mean	S.D.	Mean	S.D.	
1.	Self Role Distance	8.83	2.84	8.14	2.87	1.30
2.	Role Stagnation	10.55	3.12	13.14	2.91	-4.57**
3.	Role Ambiguity	7.37	2.98	8.23	2.85	-1.56
4.	Role Conflict	9.23	2.58	8.70	2.74	1.07
5.	Role Overload	9.12	2.84	11.49	3.39	-4.16**
6.	Role Erosion	10.59	2.90	11.67	2.66	-2.06*
7.	Lack of Group Cohesiveness & Supervisory Support	8.59	3.12	9.16	2.44	-1.94*
8.	Personal/Resource Inadequacy	9.22	3.06	10.62	2.88	-2.49**
9.	Constraint of Change	9.30	2.96	8.26	2.51	1.98*
10.	Inadequacy of Role Authority	12.85	3.29	10.65	3.13	3.63**

* *p* < 0.5 ; ** *p* < 0.1.

On Role Overload also the clerks scored significantly high. This result is in the expected direction because a bank job is time-wise tightly scheduled as the routine work can in no case be deferred. Consequently, the operative staff which is concerned with carrying out, within the time frame, work of routine nature is, relatively, overburdened. The other dimensions where clerical employees experience high stress are Role Erosion, Lack of Group Cohesiveness/Supervisory Support and Personal/Resource Inadequacy. The time, a crucial factor in a banking job, at the disposal of a clerk is terribly limited. Further, a clerk finds his job highly eroded and monotonous as it is strictly confined to routine operational tasks. Given these characteristics, lack of understanding and proper adaptation between supervisory and subordinate staff is but natural.

Inadequacy of Role Authority and Constraint of Change are, nevertheless, the two dimensions of stress where the officers scored significantly higher. Thus, apart from frequent and severe procedural, regulatory and conceptual changes, the officers are more stressful than the lower level personnel for want of adequate authority needed to carry out their assignments more effectively and independently. These results are on the expected lines as both these unwanted situations concern the officers and the clerks are least affected by such predicaments.

The results of the preceding few sections reveal that though there is some prominent quantitative variation in the stress experience of officers and clerks, yet the quality of such experience is more or less similar. A perusal of Table 6 indicates that the ranking pattern of the total sample vis-à-vis the sample of the sub-group (officers and clerks) is, to a great extent, alike. The rank order correlation between the total sample and its sub-group ranges between 0.92 and 0.72 which is highly significant ($p<.01$). Similarly the correlation coefficient between officers and clerks is 0.61 ($p<.02$). The results further indicate that Role Stagnation and Inadequacy of Role Authority are consistently high rated components of job stress while as, Role Ambiguity and Self-role Distance are invariably its low rated dimensions. All these observations make it clear that, by and large, the experience of stress among all the categories of employees is identical by quality and the difference, if any, is only quantitative.

Table 6: Percentage Mean Scores and Ranks of Various Dimensions of Job Stress: Overall in the Industry and Employee Position-wise

Dimensions of Stress	Total Sample (N=125)		Hierarchical position of Employees: Officers (N=44)		Clerks (N=81)	
	X%	R	X%	R	X%	R
Self Role Distance	41.90	9	44.15	8	40.70	10
Role Stagnation	61.10	1	52.75	3	65.70	1
Role Ambiguity	39.65	10	36.85	10	41.15	9
Role Conflict	44.45	7	46.15	5	43.50	7
Role overload	53.30	4	45.60	7	57.45	3
Role Erosion	56.45	3	52.95	2	58.35	2
Lack of Group Cohesiveness & Supervisory Support	44.80	6	42.95	9	45.80	6
Personal/ Resource Inadequacy	50.45	5	46.10	6	53.10	5
Constraint of change	43.10	8	46.50	4	41.30	8
Inadequacy of Role Authority	57.10	2	64.25	1	53.25	4

a) The Rank Order Correlation between Total Sample and:

i) Officers = 0.72

ii) Clerks = 0.92

b) The Rank Order Correlation between: Officers and Clerks = 0.61

Conclusions and Suggestions

The study reveals that Role Stagnation, Inadequacy of Role Authority, Role Erosion and Role Overload are the premier constructs of stresses confronting employees. This shows that the banking employees find their career development opportunities bleak along with inadequate authority to carry out their responsibilities efficiently. Moreover, there is a widespread feeling that they are asked to discharge less important duties than what their abilities warrant and are overburdened with the amount of work within the given resources and time.

As per the study results, most of the employees experience medium to high level of stress. A large majority of around 73% employees face moderate level stress and the percentage of workers facing high intensity stress is slightly greater than those reporting low on it. So the people are generally concentrated on the medium stress level. The dimension-wise analysis indicates that different ingredients of work stress encounter employees with varying vigor and gravity. Workers suffer least for want of job related information, the job demands are more or less in tune with their values and expectations, and the technological and operational changes in the industry are not so stressful. The study further reveals that the inter-group and superior-subordinate relationship at work is not so distasteful and the employees are not much disturbed on account of conflicting orders and expectations from various quarters.

Studying the nature and degree of relationship existing between stress experience and job nature of officials, it was found that the situation is relatively better with officers. A component-wise comparative analysis signifies that clerks confront high stress on a majority of variables including role stagnation and role overload. Once an organisation is in the post-developing stage it reaches saturation, whereafter, the personnel, especially the lower rung, have bleak growth chances thus, confronting a feeling of being stagnant for long at their present positions. Further, the clerks are generally entrusted with the work of routine nature which, more so in a banking organisation, can not be put off and is to be performed within the given time schedule which is always tight. The study results indicate that the officers suffer more than their clerical counterparts on account of inadequate authority and rapid administrative, regulatory and conceptual changes. This is obviously because the exercise of authority and adaptation to change is generally the game-play of officers. The findings also indicate that while as, the stress experience in the banking industry differs with the position of employees in the organisational hierarchy, the nature and essence of stress prevailing in the industry is, more or less, same.

Since the important revelation of the study is that Role Stagnation, Inadequacy of Role authority, Role Erosion and Role Overload are the key components of job stress in the banking industry, it is imperative that steps be taken to improve the overall stress situation on these fronts.

The seventies and eighties have been the decades of rapid growth in the banking industry and the consequent quick promotions, which often resulted in serious skill gaps at certain levels. It has obviously raised the expectation level of lower cadre employees who joined lately. However, the present sluggish growth has greatly deterred the proportionate promotion opportunities to higher levels. This has obviously created organisational frustration and stress. With a view to make the aggrieved employees committed, dedicated and satisfied, it is, therefore, highly essential that specific structural and behavioral remedies are adopted so that this unpleasant state of affairs is mitigated. It may, however, be noted that such an arrangement should be both inspiring for the employees as well as financially viable for the organisations.

Considering the fact that banking is basically a labour intensive industry, much needs to be done in so far as work scheduling is concerned. Since, the employees have to work under strict time deadlines, it is essential that physical and mental comfort at work is ensured. Such an arrangement can weaken the intrinsic strain attached to the job. For example, providing air conditioning and central heating facilities during appropriate seasons and operating a music channel at a modest volume in the premises after the banking hours can go a long way in this regard.

Mechanization and computerization can reduce the strain of employees caused due to work overload. Apart from stretching the faculties of work force, the manual methods of work adversely affect customer service and increase operational costs. Further, due to heavy demands on employees' time, the records and books are often not maintained up to date which ultimately affects the quality of decision making at all levels. With a view to provide quick and error free service to customers, reduce operational costs, improve productivity and quality of decision making and above all make employees get rid of routine and lengthy operational processes, mechanization and computerization is indispensable.

Last but not least the industry, at the organisational level, should undertake a periodic stress audit, studying systematically the dominant stresses prevalent in the organisation, its departments and divisions. It should include data gathering on the climate of organisation, satisfaction, frustrations and role stresses of employees. Stress management programmes should be encouraged and the organisation should disperse information about the fundamentals of stress and its managing tactics like exercises, meditation and dietetics etc.

References

Achmamba, B. and Gopikumar, K. (1990), "Locus of Control and Job Involvement among Men and Women Bank Employees", *Indian Journal of Applied Psychology*, 27(1): 6-9.

Agrawala, M. (1985), *A Study of Stresses Among University Students*. Ph.D. thesis, University of Allahabad, Allahabad.

Anantharam, R. N. and Begum, K. S. (1982), "Job Involvement Among Bank Employees", *Indian Journal of Applied Psychology*, 19 (11): 11-13.

Batnagar, R. and Bose, K. (1985), "Organisational Role Stress and Branch Managers", *Pranjana Journal of Social and Management Sciences*, XIV(4):349-360.

Pareek, U. (1983), "Organisational Role Stress". In. L. D. Goodstein and J. N. Pfeiffer (Eds.), *The 1983 Manual for Facilitators, Trainers and Consultants*. San Diego, California: University Associates.

Rajeshwari, T.R. (1992), "Employee Stress: A Study with reference to Bank Employees", *Indian Journal of Industrial Relations*, 27:47-57.

Selye, H. (1946), "The General Adaptation Syndrome and the Diseases of Adaptation", *Journal of Clinical Endrocrinology*, 6:117.

Sharma, B.R. (1983), *Administrative Stress*. New Delhi: IIPA.

Singh, A. P. and Nath, K. (1987), "Effects of Organisational Role Stress and Locus of Control on Job Involvement of Banking Personnel", *Indian Journal of Industrial Relations*, 27 (2): 63 -76.

10

HUMAN RESOURCE DEVELOPMENT IN BANKING INDUSTRY: A BOON FOR SUSTAINED COMPETITIVE ADVANTAGE

Nisar Ahmad Yatoo

Abstract

With the opening up of the economy of the country, human resource development in Banking sector calls for indepth study to suggest ways and means for better customer service and profitability. Many banks in the country have established their Human Resource Development Cells to upgrade the professional competence of their employees. The mission of the banks at present is among other things, to develop professionally qualified and competent bankers through a process of training, evaluation and continuing professional development programmes for employees. Banks have now understood the practicing of HRD concept in a better way.

In this paper, an attempt has been made to indicate what actually HRD concept signifies? The paper also aims at highlighting the practices which the banks adopt to create an environment where employees can contribute their, best for the recognition of good work, generate their sense of competitiveness and upgrade their human and technical skill. The paper also reveals that HRD concept is "An Ideal Ideology " and is quite cumbersome to be pragmatised but can go a long way in attaining an objective for competitive advantage. Nevertheless, HRD concept is in vogue in Indian Banks, but there remains much to be done in pursuit of competitive advantage.

Introduction

Prosperity of a nation is not as much dependent on capital, as on quality of human resource. Researches reveal that about 60% of the affluence is the contribution of human element. Undoubtedly, the prime importance of human resource among other factors of production is an established and accepted fact (Khandelwal, 1999). In India, importance attached to human element is increasing at a faster rate. Right from independence, India has felt that the man is more important than 3 Ms i.e. money, machinery, and materials. Against this context, the decision taken by the Govt. of India to create Ministry for Human Resource Development (HRD) is a step in the right direction.

In operational terms HRD means building three Cs: Capabilities, commitment and culture. Capability building needs enlarging knowledge, imparting skills. Capability has to be supported by commitment. The commitment comes through desire to excel. Positive attitude to work and towards life; awareness of one's potentialities; concern for one' s ownself and society; involvement; participation; co-operation and team work, besides capability and commitment building culture is the most important factor for HRD. Culture is a way of life, a guide to human behaviour and expression of values; and ideals and what one would like to standing culture includes creating an awareness of what is ideal and real; what is desirable and feasible, moving from competition to cooperation; moving from concern for self to concern for others, organization and society.

HRD in Banks:

The HRD approaches assume relatively greater importance in banking industry because of the following:

a) It is essentially an industry in which considerations of personalized customer service are paramount. In fact, rendering of efficient customer service depends on the quality work attitude and performance of the employees.

b) Following recent growth and diversification of the banking industry, it has to consider adoption of appropriate changes in work technology, particularly by way of computers and mechanization of important banking practices.

c) Being an industry which provides wide-ranging services, both financial and non- financial it requires appropriate training programmes to develop requisite type of professional skills among its employees.

d) With emphasis on a vision for the future, banks have to adopt long term planning and performance budgeting as an effective tool of management.

Being a unique creation, human being is a mixture of Psycho-Social-Physical traits. From the view point of physical and social traits, any person joining the banks is considered developed. The bank can hardly influence these traits, but have enough chances to direct the psychological traits. Banks adopt proper and purpose-oriented, activity-based, environment-based training, logical and rational placement, development of healthier attitudes, objective appraisal system, better leadership and development of higher individual group morale for the development of the human resource at their command.

All Indian Banks now have a separate cell on human resource development. State Bank of India has emerged as a leader. Deregulation and changing environment of banking makes managing banks-a complex exercise. People becoming more and more important in banking sector makes an HRD an indispensable segment of the management. But the attempt to implement the mm concept must be with firm determination.

HRD in practice:

Banks have now understood in a better way about the practicing of HRD concept. This can be gauged through their Annual Reports. The Punjab National Bank has gone a long way in creating an endwonrnent where employees are at liberty to contribute their best for the recognition of their good work thereby inculcating in them the sense of competitiveness. Employees are made to receive specialised training to upgrade their technical, human and conceptual skills.

Executive Development Programmes were also organised in the area of rural oriented banking, export finance and behavioural sciences. The Canara Bank also reviewed its policy and switched over from Administrative outlook to developmental outlook. Rural Branch Managers are now called change agents rather than target achievers. The employees feel to be highly involved in policy matters, thus, they feel proud.

Career planning in Indian Banks is introduced for its employees. The Banks make SWOT (Strengths, Weaknesses, Opportunities, and Threats) Analysis prognosis of future plans for HRD (Yattoo, 2001).

The Punjab and Sind Bank reviewed performance appraisal systems and introduced self-evaluation for its employees. The State Bank of India opened five more Staff Training Centers. The Bank of Patiala published "HRD News Letter" to make aware the employees and public about the HRD philosophy. Vijaya Bank sent some of its officers abroad for training on areas of rural and semi-urban managing. Some other Banks like Indian Overseas Bank, State Bank of Bikaner & Jaipur, State Bank of Indore also contributed into the HRD efforts. The Jammu & Kashmir Bank has become conscious and is engaged in sharpening techniques and developing skills of the employees at various levels, to enable them to gain confidence and to cope up with emerging challenges of banking. The Bank besides imparting training to its staff in its Staff Training Colleges at Srinagar and Jammu has been deputing its officials to different training colleges of repute within and outside the country. During the year 1999-

2000, 51 training programmes were conducted and 1062 officials were imparted training in Bank's own training colleges which include 405 officers, 594 non-subordinate and 63 subordinate staff. In addition 681 officers were deputed to other banking training institutes. In order to recognise and promote the talent, Certificate of Merit and Excellence has been introduced in the Bank for the first time.

State Bank of India one of the premier Bank in the Indian Banking Industry feels that the success of the Bank's operations ultimately depends on the quality of its human resources. The bank has made huge investments in training infrastructure to continuously upgrade the knowledge and skills of its employees and reorient their attitudes to enable them to meet the emerging challenges in the years ahead. During the year 1996-97 (48,000),1997-98 (51,000), 1998-99 (60,000) employees were exposed to 2400, 2500 and 2730 training programmes respectively conducted by the bank at its various training centres. To motivate and enthuse the employees for superior performance, a Multiple Reward and Recognition Scheme was introduced in 1996-97.

It is deduced that the keen interest taken by the management of Indian Bank's in the application of HRD programmes has resulted in better customer service in general and profitability in particular. Thus, HRD in Banking hldustry has proved a boon for the Sustained Competitive Advantage

Conclusion

It is, of course, in1portant to achieve competitive advantage to thwart any forthcoming competition which would, otherwise, deplete the profitability of the organization and at the same time the inception of HRD programme is essential for the development of an individual, the organization, society and the nation. HRD concept is "An Ideal Ideology" and is quite, difficult to be practiced but can serve as an objective to be achieved for competitive advantage. So far as the service industry is concerned, HRD concept needs to be introduced and is very essential for the banks. But, HRD concept which is practiced in Indian Banks is yet to find ways to achieve Sustained Competitive Advantage.

References

Annual Report (1999-2000) The J&K Bank Ltd.

Annual Report (1998-99 & 99-00) The State Bank of India.

Annual Report (1998-99) The Punjab National Bank Ltd.

Khandelwal, P. N. (1999). HRD in New Millennium

Yatoo, N.A. (2001) "Executive Development in Banking Sector" (Sarup & Sons, New Delhi)

-oOo-

Section III: Corporate Governance

11

CORPORATE CRIMINAL LIABILITY UNDER THE INDIAN ENVIRONMENTAL LAWS: MYTH OR REALITY

M. Ayub Dar

Abstract

The American and English legal systems have developed newer concepts of corporate criminal liability. The Indian archaic legal system continues to follow the traditional legal systems in this behalf. The vice continues and has infected the growing body of environmental laws. These new laws, like their older counterparts operating in socio-economic field, sing louder tunes of failure in holding corporations liable for their criminal activities. Bhopal Tragedy whose tears are difficult to be dried up from human history was a beginning of the legal failure to hold companies liable for their criminal negligence relating to environment. After liberalization MNC's have developed new appetite to exploit the environment in the developing countries. The concern for India in such a scenario should not be limited to a mere encouragement and increase in foreign direct investment but also improve, reform and update its corporate liability concepts so that companies tune their activities with the requirements of environmental protection.

Introduction

Business corporations wield enormous economic power and represent a distinct and powerful force at regional, national and global level with a potential to influence the lives of human beings, socially, politically and economically. Of all business corporations, a corporation with a limited liability is considered ideal for carrying on business activities of a large magnitude. This is due to the fact that it is legally distinct from the individuals who compose it, has legal personality in itself and can accordingly sue and be sued. But the device of incorporation under law meant to facilitate business has turned out a shell and shelter to commit offences. Though traditional criminal law has been pressed into service to regulate corporate behavior in socio-economic field in India and corporate criminal liability principle has taken firm roots, legislators have in some cases failed to provide a clear mode of punishment for corporations. The vice continues and has more recently infected the growing body of environmental laws in India. The deterrent sanctions have been provided, overlooking the corporate veil, to curb environmentally damaging behavior. The sanctions apply to individual decision makers as well as companies, but as sociological research indicates that certainty of punishment deters much more effectively than the severity of punishment, the adequacy, effectiveness and certainty of sentencing scheme warrants close examination.[1] Given the unlimited exploitative tendencies of corporations especially MNC's in the modern era of globalisation, a closer examination of sentencing provisions in anti-pollution legislations cannot be neglected to allow corporations to operate in a legal vacuum where individualism has free reign. It is argued here that corporate criminal liability principle in environmental laws in India is frustrated because of unclear and uncertain sentencing policy which needs a general restructuring so that companies that do not take seriously their responsibilities to environment are adequately punished.[2]

Corporate Criminal Liability and the Criminal Law

The traditional criminal Jurisprudence has developed without company being in mind and is equipped with conceptual tools to regulate individual behavior and fix responsibility on them. The rapid growth of corporate activity has left the legislators with no option but to utilize the existing criminal law without suitable alternatives to cope with and regulate the offensive corporate behavior. The inevitable result is the stress and strain when a company attempts to squeeze corporate square pegs into the round holes of criminal law doctrines.[3] The earliest Anglo-Indian Code recognising corporate criminality is the Penal Code which defines the word person as including a company, association or body of persons whether incorporated or not.[4] Courts have however recognized certain limitations while dealing with corporate criminal liability e.g., certain offences like murder, rape, treason and perjury can be committed by individual human beings only and that in certain other offences which necessarily entail the consequences of corporeal punishment or imprisonment, prosecution of a company would only result in the court stultifying itself by embarking on a trial in which if a verdict of guilty is returned, no effective order by way of sentence can be passed.[5] In adopting these limitations courts in India seem to have been over-influenced by English legal system.[6]

In England the approach of humanizing companies has been adopted by the application of identification doctrine, which states that in every corporation there are certain people who control and direct its activities and who are considered, when they act on the company's business, to be the embodiment of the company, their acts and states of mind are thus the corporations' acts and states of mind and it is held liable not for the acts of its servants, but for what are deemed to be its own acts.[7]

But there has been a growing realization over the past more than a decade that this doctrine does not reflect the modern corporate practices especially in larger companies. The identification doctrine, it is said, ignores the reality of modern corporate decision making which is often the product of corporate policies and procedures rather than individual decisions.[8] Accordingly to circumvent the rigours of identification doctrine, courts have started the alternative device of vicarious liability.[9] For instance in National Rivers Authority v. Alfred M. C Alpine Homes East,[10] at the trial of the company and two of its employees- the site manager and the site agent who accepted the responsibility for causing wet cement to enter the controlled waters contrary to Sec. 85(1) of the Water Resources Act, the company was acquitted on the ground that it could not be directly liable under the identification doctrine of Tesco v. Nattraas,[11] On appeal however looking at the purpose of pollution legislation providing for a strict liability offence the Divisional Court held that the best way of enforcing such legislation, where pollution will often be caused by persons of low position in the corporate hierarchy, was by imposing vicarious liability on the company.[12]

Simply for being metaphysical entities we cannot say that corporations cannot be culpability bearing agents as their rules. policies and operational procedures can exhibit the requisite degree of mens rea and can be accordingly blamed. therefor. Application of the same tests of criminal liability to both individuals and companies will show the corporate offences are no more treated as 'poor cousins of crimes committed by individuals'. "Kicking a few more corporate bodies and damning a few more corporate souls can stimulate the development of a few more consciences in these companies that have the lives and safety of their workers in their hands, and who operate in spheres that pose serious threat to the people and the environment".[13]

In U.S.A., the scope of corporate criminal liability is very broad and a corporation may be liable for almost any crime except those requiring commission by natural persons such as rape and murder. The liability is based on the imputation of an agent's conduct to a corporation through application of the doctrine of *Respondeat Superior*.[14] Under this doctrine the three pre-requisites to impose liability on a corporation are: (i) Commission of an illegal act by corporate agent with the requisite state of mind (mens rea), regardless of his rank in corporation, which can be attributed to the corporation. mens rea can alternatively be shown on the basis of collective knowledge of the employees as a group, even though no single employee is shown to possess sufficient information to know that the crime is being committed; (ii) The agent must have acted within the scope of his employment and (iii) must have intended to benefit the corporation though neither actual receipt of the benefit by the corporation nor exclusive purpose of benefiting the corporations are stressed by courts.[15] While under the English alter ego doctrine an agent must be high up in the corporate hierarchy,[16] the American *Respondeat Superior doctrine* does not base imputation of liability upon the rank of the corporate agent who possesses intention.[17]

The American Courts have evolved broader principles in fixing corporate liability.[18] In legislation with a deterrent purpose it has been held that to deny the possibility of corporate responsibility for the acts of minor employees is to immunize the offender who really benefits and thus open a wide door for evasion.

Placing an agent with enough of authority and responsibility to act for and on behalf of the corporation in handling the particular corporate business, operation or project in which the agent was engaged at the time of the commission of the criminal act is sufficient to convict the corporation.[19] Recognising the difficulty of finding requisite culpable intention in a single individual, the Court of Appeal of the First Federal Circuit in *United States v. Bank of New England* held "collective knowledge instruction is entirely appropriate in the context of corporate criminal liability. Corporations compartmentalize knowledge, sub-dividing the elements of specific duties and operations into smaller components. The aggregate of those components constitutes the corporation's knowledge of a particular operation."[20]

In the environmental sphere, the U.S. environmental laws permit criminal convictions without regard to intent to violate the law or forseeability of environmental damage.[21] Courts have not only imputed employees knowledge to corporation but have also provided a method for convicting persons for environmental crimes when the mens rea required to be convicted for common law crimes is not present.[22] The move of lowering the mental state requirements for environmental crimes by courts seems to be an irreversible judicial trend and is consistent with the belief that polluting is wrong and should be punished.[23]

Unlike USA and England where courts have, with a view to protect the environment, initiated newer efforts to control increasing corporate activities traditionally enjoying immunity from the clutches of criminal law, the Indian Courts at times in the past seem to have shut eyes to the fact that great majority of the business activities conducted by the companies are posing unknown threats which need innovative techniques of control to 'protect the society from the evils of devastating character, While the Apex Court had initially shown no interest in curbing the Bhopal type corporate neligience[24] through the archaic legal system, the government still continues to be without a clear policy to deal with the cases of criminal negligence of top corporate executives especially of multi-national corporations.[25]

Widening horizons of Corporate Behaviour and the need for an efficient criminal liability regime

The device of deeming corporations as persons so as to fit them into the pre-existing system for control of rnis-conduct sings louder failure tunes in the context of growing influence of transnational corporations (TNCs).[26] Assisted by recent regional and global free trade agreements, TNC expansion has become increasingly focused on the exploitation of the natural and human resources of the developing countries.[27] These corporations export hazardous processes by establishing highly polluting industries outside home countries creating thereby potential problems with pollution control, disposal of hazardous wastes, workers health and safety, and the risk of major accidents.[28] In developing countries such corporations maintain corporate secrecy and take full advantage of local public ignorance, about their hazardous processes, are reluctant to provide better technical information to regulators and obtain benefit of legal uncertainties concerning the liability for their affiliate's activities.[29] The voluntary private codes of environmental conduct proliferating through out the developing world are not being followed by multinational corporations in the developing nations.[30] The new and the most significant concerns emerging in 1990's are the raiding and appropriating India's biodiversity and acquisition of intellectual property rights to products derived from plants or animals found in developing countries.[31]

Thus the economic exploitation of biodiversity through the growth of new industries such as biotechnology and the expansion of established industries such as pesticides and pharmaceuticals, the double standard practices and above all the appetite of TNC's to operate in a legal and moral vacuum taking full advantage of ineffective and uncertain domestic laws in poorer countries[32] present a whole range of new issues that need to be addressed by environmental law policy makers stringently.[33] India in such a scenario and especially after having learnt crude lessons in the past should not aim merely at making foreign direct investment conditions more attractive to improve its economy at the cost of pollution heavens and hazards but should at the same time develop and implement more stringent environmental legislation where MNC's have no scope to flee regulations and take undue advantage of imperfect and uncertain liability standards.

Duality of criminal liability under the Environmental Laws

In almost all environmental statutes a dual liability structure has been created where under, in the case of offences committed by a company, every person who, at the time the offence was committed was, (directly) in charge of, and was responsible to the company for the conduct of. the business of the company,[34] as well as company, shall be deemed to be guilty of the offence and shall be liable to be proceeded against and punished accordingly.[35] The word 'company' has been used to mean anybody corporate including a firm or other association of individuals.[36]

The legislative policy of deeming the companies guilty of offences has been adopted in certain other socio-economic enactments in India. Under the Code of Criminal Procedure 1973, the offences under the environmental statutes are to be tried in accordance with the procedure laid down in the Code.[38] Where, therefore, both the company and the persons responsible to it for the conduct of its business are the accused, summons on the company will have to be served separately.[39] A corporation may in such cases appoint a representative for the purpose of inquiry or trial and where such representative appears, any requirement of the Code of Criminal Procedure that anything shall be done in the presence of the accused or shall be read or stated or explained to the accused shall be construed as a requirement that the thing is to be done in the presence of the representative or read or stated or explained to the representative and any requirement that the accused shall be examined is to be construed as a requirement that the representative is to be examined.[40] Where, however a representative does not appear, the requirements referred above shall not apply.[41]

The deterrence value of the corporate criminal liability under the Indian environmental statutes is augmented by the capability of these statutes to reach individual corporate officials. Even if a straight economic analysis leads a corporation to violate a statute and risk punishment, an executive's knowledge that he would be personally subject to criminal prosecution and possibly a prison sentence might induce him to think at other than corporate level and in other than economic terms.[42] Given the threat of imprisonment and fines under the environmental laws. the corporate officials have viewed their prosecutions seriously during the last couple of years and have tried to make extensive use of legal technicalities to thwart their prosecution. A bulk of motions have been brought before the High Courts under section 482 of Cr.P.C .asking Courts for exercise of inherent powers to quash criminal proceedings before magistrates against them.[43] Many Courts have, however, rejected[44] these motions stressing the Apex Court principle that it would be 'travesty of justice if the big business houses are allowed to defeat the prosecutions launched and avoid facing trials on technical flaws[45] and that prosecution of polluters inflicting injury on public health at large should not be dealt in casual and routine manner.[46]

Even if the pollution prevention agencies may be in a position to overcome some of the above difficulties through the current judicial vigour to curb environmental pollution there are still some procedural difficulties inherent in the legal web which will keep the success rate of bringing the polluters to book at a very low level. The corporate officers and employees have wide doors of exoneration if they show that the offence was committed without their knowledge or that they exercised due diligence to prevent it or that they were neither incharge nor responsible to the firm for the conduct of its business.[47] Coupled with it the heavy standard of proof on agencies to prove allegations beyond reasonable doubt, the technical nature of evidence involved and a long line of safeguards traditionally associated with the criminal justice system furnish opportunities to corporate power to influence and manipulate the system of regulation raising thereby serious doubts about the practical utility of the criminal liability regime in corporate sector.[48] Keeping in view the unique difficulties associated with detecting. investigating and proving corporate criminality, reliance on criminal procedural protections makes obtaining of convictions more difficult and costly, thereby weakening deterrence and increasing costs for society without any significant countervailing benefits.[49]

Sentencing options in Environmental Statutes

Criminal sanctions enable the courts to shape the punishment to the crime and their severity can induce the polluters to think twice before they violate the laws.[50] Once the corporation is convicted of an offence the enabling legislation ought to equip the judge with a suitable and effective sentencing option which can act as a deterrent to a corporation to repeat the crime. The legislature in India has chosen two types of sentencing options to punish environmental crimes viz. (i) Imprisonment or fine and (ii) Imprisonment with fine. While imprisonment or fine is the main option available under Environment (Protection) Act.1986[51] both types of options have been retained in other important statutes to deal with particular criminal situations; but the option 'imprisonment' and fine is the only mode of punishment to deal with the environmentally serious transgressions prescribed in these statutes. The whole punishment scheme of 'imprisonment and fine' can be explained in conjunction with the nature of offences in the tables 1, 2, 3, 4 & 5.

Imprisonment and Fine: The Judicial Approach

Courts in India have been confronted with hurdles in convicting a company for offences for which imprisonment and fine is a mandatory punishment. After all a company cannot be imprisoned. In several cases the courts have held that a company cannot be convicted of an offence where both imprisonment and fine is the mode of punishment because legislature could not have contemplated imprisonment of a company on being found guilty of an offence.[55] Fine, therefore, remains the only effective mode of punishment in such cases, but again the Supreme Court has long.

Table 1: Water (Prevention and Control of Pollution) Act, 1974				
S. No	Sec.	Nature of Offence	Sec.	Nature of punishment
1.	Sec 32(1) (c)	Failure to comply with orders immediately res-tricting or prohibiting the persons concerned from discharging any poison-ous, noxious or polluting matter into a stream or well or on land or from making unsanitary use of a stream or a well.		Imprisonment for a term which shall not be less than one year and six months but which may extend to six years and with fine
	Sec. 32 (2)	Failure to comply with any direction issued by a court including an order restraining disposal or likely disposal of any matter into stream, well or in any sewer. (52)	41 (2)	Same as for S.No. 1
3.		Continued failure to comply referred to in S.No. 1 or 2 (above) which runs beyond a period of one year after the date of conviction.	41(3)	Imprisonment for not less than two years but may extend to seven years and with fine
4.	24(1) (a)	Knowingly causing or permitting any poisonous, noxious or polluting matter (determined as per SPCB standards) to enter directly or indirectly into any stream or well or sewer or on land	43	Imprisonment for not less than one year and six months but which may extend to six years and with fine
	24(1) (b)	Knowingly causing or permitting to enter into any stream any matter, which may lead either directly or in combination with similar matters, to impede the proper flow of the water of the same stream in a manner leading to or likely to lead to a substantial aggravation of pollution due to other causes or of its consequences	43	Same as above

5.	33A	Failure to comply with any direction given by a Pollution Control Board	41	Same as for S. No. 4
6.	Sec. 25(a), (b) and (c)	Without previous consent of SPCB: a) Establish or take any steps to establish any industry, operation or process or any treat-ment & disposal system or an exten-sion or addition thereto, which is likely to discharge sewage or trade effluent into a stream or well or sewer or on land or b) bring into use any new or altered outlet for the discharge of sewage; or c) begin to make any new discharge of sewage	d) 44	Imprisonment for not less than one year and six months but which may extend to six years and with fine
7.		Any subsequent office (committed within two years from the date of first conviction) of the nature specified in S. No. 1-4 above.		Imprisonment for not less than two years but which may extend to seven years and with fine

Table 2: Air (Prevention and Control of Pollution) Act, 1981				
S. No.	Section	Nature of Offences	Section	Nature of punishment
1.	21	Without previous consent of SPCB, establish or operate any industrial plant in an air pollution control area	37(1)	Imprisonment not less than one year and six months which may extent to six years and with fine.
2.	22	In an air pollution control area, discharging or causing or permitting to be discharged from an industrial plant air emissions in excess of SPCB standards.	31(1)	Same as for S.No. 1
3.	31A	Failure to comply with any direction given by a PCB	37(1)	Same as for S.No. 1
4.		Continued failure to comply with what is referred to in S. No. 1 to 3 (above) which runs beyond a period of one year after date of conviction	37(2)	Imprisonment which shall not be less than two years which may extend to seven years

Table 3: The Environment (Protection) Act, 1986				
S. No	Section	Nature of offences	Section	Nature of punishment
1.		Continued failure to comply with or contravention of any of the provisions of the Act or the rules or orders or directions issued thereunder.[53] which runs beyond a period of one year after date of conviction	15(2)	Imprisonment which may extend to seven years

Table 4: Public Liability Insurance Act, 1991

S. No	Sec.	Nature of offences	Sec.	Nature of punishment
1.		After conviction for the first offence or any offence subsequent to the second offence, handling any hazardous substance	14(2)	Imprisonment for a term which shall not be less than two years but which may extend to seven years & with fine which shall not be less than one lakh rupees
	4(1)	a) without taking one or moreinsurance policy/ ies or fine which shall not be less than one lakh rupees		Same as above
		b) without renewal of insurance policy/ policies before the expiry of the period of validity thereof or		Same as above
	2(2a) and 4(2c)	c) with insurance policy/ policies taken or renewal for an amount less than the amount of paid-up capital of the under-taking and more than the amount not exceeding fifty crores rupees or without crediting alongwith the premium amount of insurance to the insurer, for being credited to the Relief Fund, such further sum not exceeding the sum equivalent to the amount of premium		Same as above
	12	d) after a direction prohibiting or regulating the said handling		Same as above

Table 5: The Wildlife (Protection) Act, 1972

S. No	Section	Nature of offence	Section	Nature of punishment
1.		Contravention of any provision of the Act (except Chapter VA and Section 38J) or any rule or order made there-under relating to any animal specified in Schedule I or Part II of Schedule II or meat of any such animal or animal article, trophy or uncured trophy derived from such animal or relating to hunting in, or altering the boundaries of a sanitary or a National Park	51 (1)	Imprisonment for a term which shall not be less than one year but may extend to six years and also with fine which shall not be less than five thousand rupees
2.		Any second or subsequent offence of the nature specified above in S. No. 1	51 (1)	Imprisonment not less than two years but which may extend to six years and the amount of fine shall not be less than ten thousand rupees
3.		Contravention of any of the provisions of Chapter VA	51(1A)	Imprisonment which shall not be less than one year but which may extend to seven years and also with fine which shall not be less than five thousand rupees
4.		Attempt or abatement or contravene any of the provisions of the Act or of any rule or order of the type referred to in Serial No. 1 & 3 above	52	Same as for S.No.3 above

back settled the principle that where imprisonment and fine is made mandatory by a statute, courts are bound to impose the punishment of imprisomnent.[56] The courts have in numerous cases shown reluctance to impose a sentence of fine alone on the ground that it amounts to usurpation of the legislative function. A contrary approach has no doubt been adopted by some courts by holding that a company cannot be exempted and can be sentenced to the punishment of fine only,[57] the sanctity of such an approach fails to answer the principle laid down by the Supreme Court in *State of Maharashtra v. Jugmantar Lal*.[58]

Conclusion and Suggestions

Stronger Sanctions to deter polluters are a recent development in Indian environmental law.[59] It has been observed that many polluters ignore the regulations and accept the meager amount of consequent fines or civil penalties as a cost of doing business[60] or merely pass them on to the consumer.[61] Often a polluter will save more by his violations than he pays in penalties if caught and if at all fined.[62] The firms fear the criminal law if the sanctions are deterrent and imposed deterrently. Prosecution for the crime in the suites can be more effective than it is for the crime in streets. Deterrence works best with the people who have not contact with criminal justice and for whom prosecution or even investigation will have severe consequences.[63] Despite theoretical possibility of making companies specifically liable under the environmental statutes there has been no serious legislative attempt to provide for an appropriate punishment, which could be imposed on the corporations as well.[64] Prosecution of individual corporate officials is pointless and inappropriate as it ignores the corporate pressures that might have been placed upon them by the corporate structure. Court may simply punish the officer responsible by sending him to jail and the institutional pressures and practices may continue. Even with small close-held companies there is a strong case for criminal liability and removing any illegal profits, as in such companies the directors are usually the shareholders and so will be penalized by a loss of profit[65] and encouraged to correct the practices that led to wrong doing. The case for appropriate punishment of larger corporations including MNC'S is stronger. On the one hand such corporations have complex structures which makes it difficult for outsiders to ascertain who is responsible for a particular decision. On the other hand MNC's have grown beyond the control of national governments and operate in a legal and moral vacuum, exploiting the natural and human resources of especially the developing countries, which need progressive development, implementation and strengthening of more stringent environmental legislation, rather than more attractive investment conditions.[66] Besides, punishing such companies can trigger the most appropriate institutional response, in that these companies are in the best position to identify and discipline their employees. Monitoring the activities of each individual within a polluting organization is costly and raises practical enforcement difficulties. The duality of corporate and individual criminal liability principle enunciated in environmental laws in India has the potential to transfer to a polluting corporation the responsibility of policing itself. But the co-existence of this corporate and individual criminal liability cannot be translated into practice by merely carrying the traditional modes of punishment from traditional criminal law, which is largely obsessed with individualistic approach. It is, therefore, suggested that the legislature should immediately address to the task of how to punish the corporations for their environmentally damaging behavior. As an interim measure the word' and' in provisions providing punishment for environmental offences can be substituted by the word 'or' and the quantum of fines to be imposed on corporations can be linked with the magnitude of the harm and the business of a polluting company by providing for the minimum and maximum amount of fines as an alternative to imprisonment.[67]

Publication of the names of convicted corporate employees for polluting activities though a novel method of punishment has not been generalized nor does the concerned polluting company fall within the ambit of the scheme.[68] Since it is the company that deserves the stigma and shame associated with the adverse publicity attached to a criminal conviction, this mode of punishment can be adopted in all the environmental statutes with the convicted company also to fall within its ambit so as to ensure that the sanction does not fall upon tools or scape goats alone. Another critical aspect of the existing scheme of sanctions in environmental laws is that it focuses more on the firm manager and ignores to motivate a firm to foster its internal discipline. To attain this, scholars have suggested corporate probation in especially environmental matters through which a committee of independent professionals can be invited by courts to comment on the proposed probation and asked to monitor corporate compliance during the period of probation.[69] Besides disqualification of convicted corporate personnel from serving on corporate boards "requiring executives to engage in cleanup activity or other community services and debarring a polluting company from important governmental assignments or contracts are other sentencing choices which can, as part of the existing modes, increase appreciation of environmental concerns by corporations.

Notes and References

1. Upendra Baxi, Environment Protection Act: An Agenda For Implementation, ILI (1987) PP 42,45-46, while appreciating section 16 of the Environment (Protection) Act. 1986, on the ground that it adequately Pierces the corporate veil, the experts have with a view to manage sanctions and realize fully their deterrent potential, recommended a close examination of the relevant aspects of the company and labour laws as well as of the constitutive laws of statutory public corporations, cooperative and other registered Societies

2. Shyam Diwan, Armin Rosencranz, Environmental Law and Policy in India, 2001 (2nd ed.) PP 189-193, after a review of case law on corporate criminal liability the authors conclude that Pollution Control Boards have generally achieved little success in bringing to book violators under pollution control laws and raise several questions to find out the reasons for this failure e.g.. does the fault lie with the boards, the laws, the courts or some other factor? And what systematic changes might improve the success rate? This paper is a humble attempt in the said direction.

3. James Gobert, Corporate Criminality: New Crimes For The Times, (1994) Crim.L.R. at 724

4. Indian Penal Code, 1860, Sec.11, See also the definition of company under the environmental statutes viz. the Water (Prevention and Control of Pollution) Act, 1974 ,Sec. 47(2), The Air (Prevention and Control of Pollution) Act. 1981, Sec.40(2), The Environment (Protection) Act. 1986, Sec. 16(2). The Wild Life (Protection) Act, 1972, Sec.58 (2), The Public Liability Insurance Act, 1991, Sec. 16(2).

5. *State of Maharashtra v. Syndicate Bank Transport Co.* AIR 1964 Bom.195 at 197. The court held that the phrase (unless there is anything repugnant in the subject or context) must always be understood in the context of the definition given in the I.P .C. and despite generality of the word person in Sec. 11, a Corporate body or a company shall not be indictable for offences which can be committed only by a natural person or for offences involving a punishrnent of imprisonment. See also *Esso V Udhararn Bhagvandass* (1975) 45 Compo Cas. 16 (Bomb.)".
6. Id. at 198, the court for instance reflects this influence by quoting Stable Justice in *Rex. V. I. C. R Haulage Ltd.* 1944-1 KB 551
7. Smith and Hogan, Criminal (1989 6th ed). at p 171
8. C.M.V. Clarkson, Kicking Corporate Bodies and Damning Their Souls, (1996) 59 MLR.557-72 at P. 561; See also Celia Wells, 'Corporations: Culture, Risk and Criminal Liability (1993) Crim.L.R 551-66 at PP 565-66 arguing that tile current rules of liability are contingent and of chance nature and that individuals can both be scape goats and can hide behind the corporation.
9. C.M.V. Clarkson, supra note 8 at p. 561.
10. (1994)Crim.L.R 760.
11. (1972) A.C. 153.
12. Supra note 10 at 761, the Queen's Bench Divisional Court citing *Alphacell Ltd. v. Woodward* [1972] A.C. 824 as a similar case of vicarious liability of the company held that an employer was liable for pollution resulting from its own operations carried out under its essential control save only where some third party acted in such a way as to interrupt the chain of causation. Even if those in company's head office had no direct part in detennining the precise system of construction which allowed the cement to wash into the stream, it was sufficient that those immediately responsible on site were employees of the company and acting apparently within the course and scope of that employment.
13. See Supra note 8 at P. 572; see also Stewart Field, Corporate Liability and Man Slaughter: Should we be going Dutch, (1991) Crim.L. R. 156 at p. 159 arguing that for the purposes of moral responsibility on a company its policies, standing orders, regulations and institutionalized practices are the aims, intentions and the knowledge that are not reducible to the aims, intentions and knowledge of individuals within the company, having emerged from a decision making process and thus being authoritative these are evidence of the corporate capacity to differentiate right from wrong,

to think ethically of the consequences of corporate actions for others and to give reasoned explanations to the outside world.

14. See "Developments in the Law- Corporate Crime: Regulating Corporate Behavior Through Criminal Sanctions" (1979) 92. Harv.L.Rev at 1247.
15. Id. at 1250.
16. See John C. Coffee Jr., Emerging Issues In Corporate Criminal Policy, Forward to Richard S. Gruner, Corporate Crimes and sentencing at xix (1994).
17. Supra note 14 at 1247-48, See also *U.S. v. George Fish Inc.* 154 F. 2d 798 (1946) where a corporation was held liable even for the acts of its employees very low in hierarchy.
18. Id; *U.S. v. George Fish Inc.*, Supra note 17
19. *Common Wealth v. Beneficial Insurance Co.* 275 N.E. 2d 33 (1971).
20. 821 F. 2rd 844, Court of Appeals, (First Circuit) 1987.The precedent cited was *U.S v..T.I..M.E.D.*, 381 F .Supp.73.0 (W. D. Va. 1974), Where though no single employee possessed sufficient information to know that crime (requiring knowledge) was being committed, the corporation was convicted on the basis of collective knowledge.
21. See Donald A. Carr, Prosecutors out of control, ECO, June 1993, at 56; see also Environmental Crimes' in 28 Am. Crim. L. Rev. (1991) 427-71 at 432-33.
22. Ruth A. Weidel et a1., The Erosion of Mens Rea in Environmental Criminal Prosecutions, 21 Seton Hall L. Rev. 1100, 1124 (1991). The legal scholars seem to have taken note of this trend -see Jeffrey S. Parker, The Economics of. Mens rea, 79 VA.L.Rev. 741 (1993); Goseph G. Block & Nancy A Voison, The Responsible Corporate Officer Doctrine -Can You Go To Jail For What You Don't Know, 22 ENVTL. L. 1347 (1992); Ronal M Broudy, Note, RCRA and The Responsible Corporate Officer Doctrine: Getting Tough On Corporate Offenders by Side Stepping The Mens Rea Requirement, 80 KY. L. J. 1055(1992)
23. David B Spence, Paradox Lost: Logic, Morality and the Foundations of Environmental law in 21st. Century, Columbia Journal of Environmental Law Vol. 20 : 145 (1995) at 174.
24. The Supreme Court had ordered termination of all the Civil, Criminal and Contempt Proceedings that had arisen out of the Bhopal disaster- See *Union Carbide Corporation V. Union of India*, AIR 1990 SC 273. However through petitions seeking review of the settlement the Supreme Court, while upholding rest of the settlement reinstated

the criminal charges against top executives at Union Carbide including its C.E.O., Warren Anderson. See *Union Carbide Corporation v. Union of India,* AIR 1992 SC 248.

25. The Central Government is reported to have closed the file linked with the extradition of the former Union Carbide chief, Mr. Warren Anderson, one of the main accused in the Bhopal Gas disaster. See The Hindu, August 25,2001 at p. 13.
26. See Christopher D. Stone, The Place of Enterprise Liability in the Control of Corporate Conduct, 90 Yale L. J. 1 (1980).
27. Deborah C. POff, Reconciling the Irreconcilable: The Global Economy and Environment, 13 J. Bus. Ethics 439, 442 (1994).
28. David L. McFadden, A Selected Bibliography on Hazardous Activities, Technology and the Law: Bhopal and Beyond, 19 INTL. Law 1459 (1985), see also U.N. DEP'T of Eco. Social Dev., World Investment Report 1992: Transnational Corporations and Engines of Growth 231, U.N. Doc. ST/CTC/130 (1992).
29. Thomas N. Gladwin, Environment, Development and Multinational Enterprises, in Multinational Corporations, Environment and the Third World: Business Matters 10-12 (Charles S. Pearson ed., 1987); See also World Investment Report 1992, supra note 28 at 226-27.
30. Michel S. Beram, Multinational Corporations, Private Codes And Technology Transfer For Sustainable Development, 24 EnvT'L 33-65 (1994).
31. Karnataka Farmers Target Cargill Again, Down To Earth, Aug. 31, 1993 at 16; Fred Pearce, Pesticide Patent Angers Indian Farmers, New Scientist Oct. 9, 1993, at 7; See also S.K. Verma, Access to Biological And Genetic Resources And their protection, 43JILI [2001] 1- 24 highlighting the unwarranted exploitation of biological and genetic resources and the absence as well as need of clear modalities of access to such resources at the hands of the developed world.
32. Robert J. Fowler, International Environmental Standards For Transnational Corporations, 25 ENVTL. L.1-30 (1995).
33. Gaetan Verhoosel, Foreign Direct Investment And Legal Constraints on Domestic Environmental Policies: Striking A "Reasonable" Balance Between Stability And Change. Law & Po1'y INTL. BUS. 29: 1998 P.P 451- 79 at 452.
34. The word 'directly' has been used in Sec. 40(1) of the Air Act,198l, Sec. 16(1) of Public Liability Insurance Act. 1991; Sec. 26(1) of the

National Tribunal Act. 1995 and Sec. 20(1) of the National Environmental Appellate Authority Act. 1997

35. Ibid. See also Sec. 47(1) of Water (P&C of P) Act, 1974, Sec. 16(1) of Environment (Protection) Act, 1986 and Sec. 8 of Wild Life(Protection Act), 1972.

36. See the explanation appended to Sub. Sec. 2 of the respective Sections and Acts named in supra note 34 and 35

37. See the Drugs and Cosmetics Act. 1940, Sec. 34; The Prevention of Food Adulteration Act 1954 as amended after Amending Act 34 of 1976, Sec. 17; The Essential Commodities Act, 1955, Sec. 10; The Income Tax Act, 1961, Sec. 278B and Foreign Exchange Regulation Act 1973, Sec. 56.

38. Sec. 4(2) of the Code of Criminal Procedure, 1973 lays down that the offences under laws other than the Penal Code shall be investigated, inquired into, tried and otherwise dealt with in accordance with the provisions of the Code of Criminal Procedure, though subject to any enac1ment for the time being in force regulating the manner or place of investigation, inquiring into, trying, or otherwise dealing with such offences. The environmental laws however provide their own manner of investigation and inquiry but no special manner of trial is provided for except the manner in which the court can take cognizance of offences, See Sec. 49 of the Water Act, 1974; Sec. 43 of the Air Act, 1981, Sec 19 of the Environment (Protection) Act, 1986; Sec. 18 of The Public Liability Insurance Act, 199l and Sec. 55 of the Wild [Life) Protection Act, 1972.

39. Under Sec. 63 of the Code Service of Summons on a corporation may be effected by serving it on the secretary, local manager or other principal officer of the corporation or by letter sent by registered post, addressed ro the chief officer of the corporation in India in which case the service shall be deemed to have been effected when the letter would arrive in ordinary course of post.

40. The Code of Criminal Procedure, 1973. Sec 305.

41. Id. Sec 305(5).

42. Cf Comment, Criminal sanctions for environmental crimes and the knowledge requirement: United States V. Hayes International. 786 F.2d 1499 11th CIR,1986.25 Am.Crim. L. Rev. 1988 p. 539.

43. See for example *Medwin Hospitals v. State of A.P.* 1999 (2) Andhra L.T 471; *Industrial Chemical Works vs. Dahyavhai K. Solanki* 1993(2) Guj. L.R. 1318; *Trans Asia Carpets Ltd. v. State of U.P.* 1992 All. L. J. 357;1992 Cri. L. J. 673; *Gujrat Pollution Control Board v. Indian Chemical Manufacturers* 1990 (2) Guj. L. R. 1306; *J.S. Huja*

v. State 1990 All. L.J. 41; 1989 Cri.L.J 1334; *Mahmtd Ah v. State of Bihar* AIR 1986 PAT.133; *Z. Kotasek v. State of Bihar* 1984 Cri.L.J. I 683 and *K.K. Nandi v. Amitabha Banerjee* 1983 Cri.L.J. 1479 I

44. See the verdicts cited in supra note 43 above.

45. *Uttar Pradesh Pollution Control Board v. Modi Distillery*, AIR 1988 S.C 1128.

46. *U.P. Pollution Control Board v. Mohan Meakins Ltd.* 2000(2) SCALE 532.

47. Even in the single reported case of Haryana State Board V. Jai Bharat Woolen Finishing Works 1993. For. L.T. 101, where a board successfully prosecuted a polluting firm for discharging untreated trade affluent without obtaining the consent, the Court, in the absence of proof that the partner was in charge of or responsible to the firm for the conduct of its business, could not convict him and imposed a paltry amount of fine of Rupees 3000 on the firm and Rs. 2500 on the manager; See also Sec. 44read with Sec. 25(a) of the Water Act, 1974 where the nonnal punishment for such an offence is impiisonment for a term, which shall not be less than six months but may extend to six years and with fine.

48. V.S. Khanna. Corporate Criminal Liability: What purpose does it serve? [1996] 109 HARV. L. Rev. 1477-1534, the author argues that from a deterrence perspective the imposition of criminal rather than civil liability on Corporations serves almost no purpose; See also Sara D. Himmelhoch. Environmental Crimes: Recent Effort To Develop A Role For The Traditional Criminal Law In The Environmental Protection Effort, 22 ENVTL.L 1451-1507(1992), arguing.that initial interest in the use of traditional criminal law was premature and the most promising route is to adopt and enforce criminal statutes particularly directed at environmentally damaging behavior.

49. Id. Khanna at p. 1520.

50. Cf Comment, Criminal sanctions for corporations: Alternative Fining Mechanisms, 73 CALIF .L.R. 443, 447 -48[1 985],stating that corporate offenders perform cost-benefit analysis in deciding whether to engage in potentially criminal activity, see also Glenn, The Crime of Pollution :The Role of

    Federal Water Pollution Control Sanctions, IIAM. CRIM.L. REV. 835, 858 (1973), arguing that weaker sanctions fail to prevent pollution practices that are creating a serious national problem, see also supra note 42 at 537-39.

51. See Sec. 15(1) of the Act, but sec. 15(2) again fails to maintain this option as it mandates the punishment of imprisonment only for offences continued beyond a year after the date of conviction.
52. Linking the subsequent conviction with previous conviction of the company makes the punishment all the more a fallacy.
53. For a detailed discussion on nature of duties, contraventions and directions, see sections 5, 7, 8, 10(2) and (3) of the Environment (Protection) Act, 1986 and the obligations imposed under different sets of rules framed thereunder, especially rule 6 and 8 of the Noise Pollution (Regulation and Control) Rules, 2000.
54. *P.V. Pai v. R.L. Rainawma*, (1993) 77 Compo Cas. 179 (Kar); *A.K. Khosla v. T.S. Venkatesan*, 1992 Cr.L.J 1448(Ca1); *Adding Machines India (P) Ltd. v The State*, (1988) 63 Compo Cas. 588 (Cal); *D.C. Goel v. B.L. Verma*, (1974) 93 I.T.R 63 Del.
55. *Kusum Products Ltd. v. S.K. Sinha*, (1980) 126 I.T.R 804 (Cal); *Modi Industries Ltd. v. B.C. Goel* (1983) 4 Compo Cas. 835 (All.)
56. *State of Maharashtra v. Jugmantar La!*, AIR 1966 S.C 940, at P. 942, the Court has further held that the conjunction of word 'and' cannot be construed to mean the opposite that is , to mean 'or.'
57. *Municipal Corporation of Delhi v. J.B. Bottling Co.*, 1975 Cr.L.J. 1148(Del.) and *Manian Transpoters v. Krishna Murthy*, I.T.O. (1991) 72 Comp Cas.745 (Mad.)
58. Supra note 56 above.
59. The Environment (Protection) Act, 1986, Section 15 in particular and the nature of sanctions in other Acts referred to in Tables 1, 2, 4 and 5.
60. M.Clinard & P. Yeager, Corporate Crime 280 (1980).
61. J.Conklin, Illegal But Not Criminal 103 (1977).
62 Id.
63. Dimento Joseph F. Environmental Law and American Business-Dilemmas of Compliance, 1986 (Plenum Press New York) at p.p 42,43; See also Part Q of the Federal Sentencing Guidelines Manual (West 1991) issued by the U.S. Sentencing Commission pursuant to the Comprehensive Crime Control Act, 1984 imposing stiffer penalties on individuals guilty of violating environmental laws. The Sentencing Commission is looking into creative ways to punish corporations since unlike individuals corporations cannot be incarcerated. The Sentencing Guidelines have resulted in increase in the number of trials, as well as stiffer penalties for environmental

violations. See Environmental Crimes in 28 Am. Crim. L. Rev. (1991) 427-71 at 431-32.

64. The Environmental Laws (Amendment) Bill, 1999, provides a comprehensive chapter III-A on offences and penalties but ignores to provide a workable punishment scheme for companies in secs. 15(2), 15 A (1) & (2) and 15 B (2); See also ' Strengthening Environmental Legislation in India' (1999), Report prepared by the Center for Environmental Law, WWF- India for the Asian Development Bank (Manila) and The Ministry of Environment and Forests Government of India, the Draft Environment (Protection) Bill. 2000(Annexure I to the Report) fails to provide a suitable scheme of punishment of companies by recommending in sec. 50(2) the punishment of imprisonment only for failures or contravention extending beyond a year.

65. Cartwright, 'Defendants in Consumer Protection Statutes: A search for consistency' (1996) 59 MLR 225,235.

66. Fowler, Robert J. International Environmental Standards for Transnational Corporations, 25: I). Envtl.L. 30 (1995) at p. 2: See also Gaeton Verhoosal, Foreign Direct Investment and Legal Constraints on domestic Environmental Policies: Striking A Reasonable Balance Between Stability and Change, Law & Pol'y INTL Bus. [Vol. 29 1998) pp 451-479 at p. 452.

67. The Protection of Plant Varieties and Farmers' Rights Bill, 2000 [now Act No.53 of 2001] and providing for corporate and individual criminal liability in Clause 77 is the only legislation providing punishment scheme in Clauses 70-73 in the recommended direction, however, there are still some other workable forms of punishment which this legislation too has ignored.

68. Sec. 46 of the Water (Prevention & control of Pollution) Act, 1974 is the only environmental Act that allows such publication of the names of corporate employees on their second or subsequent conviction. Though the section applies to any person convicted twice or more under the Act, the words used like 'place of residence of the offender indicate that the legislature has restricted its operation to natural persons only.

69. John C. Coffee, Jr., No Soul to Damn: No Body to Kick:" An unscandalised inquiry into the problem of corporate punishment (1981) 79 Michigan L. Rev. 386 at 448-55.

-o-

12

ROLE OF DIRECTORS IN THE ERA OF CORPORATE GOVERNANCE

Arif A. Shah

Abstract

In view of the huge responsibilities cast upon their shoulders, because of being the top decision making body, the Directors of a company are expected to act in the most prudent and logical way. But to hope, that the directors of a company are fool proof and angles, is only being idealistic. In this paper an attempt has been made to highlight the role of the directors in the era of corporate governance especially in the light of recent developments which have taken place in the new corporate scenario in India.

Introduction:

The origin of corporate governances owes to the separation of ownership and control. Because of agency theory, the management has direct involvement in business, there is a greater chance that the erosion of the rights of shareholders may take place. as *defacto* control of the company is in the hands of management. There are two identifiable strands of thinking on what constitutes corporate governance. From one school of thought, corporate governance is referred to as the system, procedures and institutions that ensures that the management acts in the best interest of the shareholders. The other school of thought believes that management has to act in the best interest of all stakeholders, which may include customers, employees, suppliers, creditors, and the society at large, of which the company is a part.

In this way the role of directors for governing a company becomes two pronged as shown in the figure 1

In the figure 1, it is shown that the Board of Directors (B. O. D) in a modem company perform responsibilities towards the company as well as society. The responsibility towards the company involve:-

- Overseeing and evaluating executive management;
- Setting long-term mission, objectives and strategies;
- Removing non-performing top management;
- Advising the management on various strategic issues;
- Corporate compliance with laws of the land;
- Ensuring ethical behavior of executive management;

While as the responsibilities towards society include:-

- Value addition to business for shareholders;
- Compensation to employees welfare;
- Repayment of principal and payment of interest to creditors;
- Regular payments to suppliers;
- Quality products to consumers at reasonable price;
- Payment of taxes and levies to govt.;
- Social welfare and healthy environment for general public.

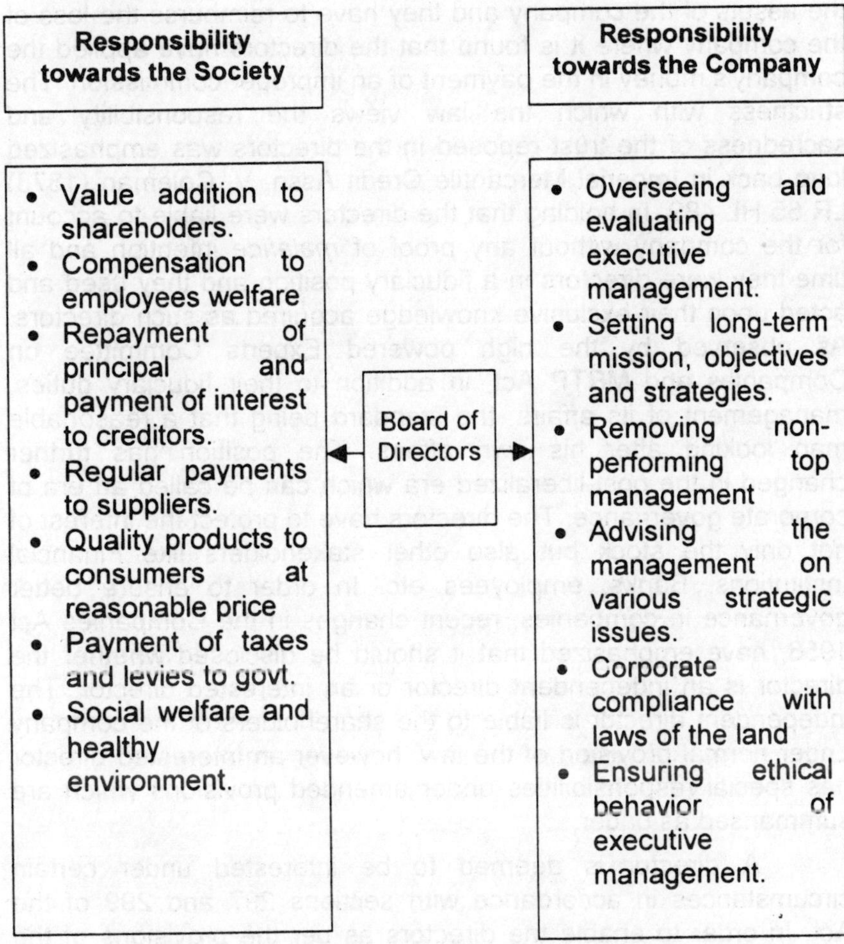

Figure 1: Responsibilities of Board of Directors of a company
Source: Sangmi, Mohi-ud-Din (2000), "Corporate Governance in India: A 21st Century Perspective", The Business Review, Vol. 6(1&2): 57.

Changing Position of Directors

The directors of a company are the custodians of the interest of the shareholders. The supreme court, in Nandlal Zaveri vs. Bombay Life Insurance Co. Ltd.(AIR 1950 SC 172) has clearly laid down that the directors of a company are in a fiduciary position vis-à-vis the company. The directors must exercise their powers for the benefit of the company. They are the guardians of the assets of the company and they have to reimburse the loss of the company where it is found that the directors have applied the company's money in the payment of an improper commission. The strictness with which the law views the responsibility and sacredness of the trust reposed in the directors was emphasized long back in Imperial Mercantile Credit Assn. V. Coleman (1873) LR 65 HL 489. In holding that the directors were liable to account for the company without any proof of *malafide* intention and all time they were directors in a fiduciary position and they used and acted upon their exclusive knowledge acquired as such directors. As observed by the high powered Experts Committee on Companies and MRTP Act, in addition to their fiduciary duties, management of its affairs, the standard being that a reasonable man looking after his own affairs. The position has further changed in the post-liberalized era which can be called an era of corporate governance. The directors have to protect the interest of not only the stock but also other stakeholders like Financial Institutions, Banks, employees etc. In order to ensure better governance in companies, recent changes in the Companies Act 1956, have emphasized that it should be disclosed whether the director is an independent director or an interested director. The independent director is liable to the shareholders of the company under normal provision of the law, however an interested director has special responsibilities under amended provisions which are summarised as under.

A director is deemed to be interested under certain circumstances in accordance with sections 297 and 299 of the Act. In order to enable the directors as per the provisions of the act and also for the interest of director, it is necessary that the director live up to expectation of the provisions of the Act and furnish the following information.

i) List of relatives of the directors;

ii) Names of companies in which the director holds shares, number of shares held in each of their companies and paid up capital of each company;

iii) Names of companies in which a relative of the director holds shares and the number of shares held in each of their companies;

iv) Names of the companies in which the relative of the director is a director;

v) List of firms in which the director or his relative is a partner and the names of other partners in those firms.

For the purpose of proper compliance of the provisions of the Act, the following requirements have to be met by the company.

i) Compile proper database for each director;

ii) Shareholding of each director must be made note of;

iii) Note whether the director is interested within the meaning of Sec 297 and 299 of the act. Similarly whether the director is interested for the purposes of the section 300 of the Act;

iv) As a matter of abundant caution, where in a case, some data (e.g. paid up capital figure) for a company is not available, the director may be shown to be interested;

v) Make entries in Register of contracts wherever a contract of arrangement attracts sec 297 or sec 299;

vi) Keep record of the companies in which any of the directors is interested under sec 297 or 299;

vii) Keep ready another list of companies along with the names of interested director where the latter cannot discuss and vote owing to sec. 300;

viii) Whenever a contract with such a company come up before the Board, make sure that the interested Director does not discuss and vote;

ix) Furnish a dictation about the fact that the company in which a person is a director has;

   a. filed the annual accounts and annual returns for all the financial/ calendar years from the date of incorporation of such companies and,

   b. not failed at any time to repay its deposits or interest there on due date or redeem its debentures on due date or pay dividend and such failure continues for one year or more.

Thus, the recent amendments in the Companies Act have made it clear that the director's interests, intentions, investments should be transparent. When the law requires them to make the above disclosures, their intention of decision-making can be clear, so that the parent company's interests do not clash with the directors personal interests in other companies.

Director's responsibility statement

The companies Amendment) Act 2000 has introduced a unique provision in sec 217 (2AA) of the Act as per which the directors have to sign statement, which will form part of the report of the Board of Directors. The Statement should indicate the following:-

i) Annual Accounts have been prepared in consonance of the applicable accounting standards.

ii) Accounting policies of the company are consistent and prudent so as to give a true and fair view of the accounts of the company.

iii) Proper and sufficient care has been taken by them for maintenance of proper accounting records in accordance with the provisions of the companies Act, 1956, for safeguarding the assets of the company and for checking frauds and irregularities.

These provisions have highlighted the functions of the company which otherwise are the 'suo-motto' functions of the directors. By giving a statement that they act prudently and the accounting policies are prudently designed and implemented, they are made doubly accountable.

Accounting Standards

It is obligatory that financial statements drawn by a company shall comply with .the accounting standards. As per section 211(BB) of the Companies Act where the profit and loss account and the balance sheet do not comply with the accounting standards, such companies shall disclose in their profit and loss account and the balance sheet the following:

i) Deviation from the accounting standards

ii) Reasons for deviation.

iii) Financial implication of such a deviation.

This suggests that not only for managing the internal operations of the company the directors are responsible but also for following accounting standards. Since in view of integrating the Indian economy with the world, the accounting standards are mandatory, no company can afford to prepare the accounts of the company as per its sweet will, but it has to follow the country's Generally Accepted Accounting Principles (GAAP). These GAAPs are prepared by the country's apex accounting body (National Advisory Board on Accounting), their follow up is obligatory for all the companies in the country.

Conclusion

From the above description, it may be concluded that a company has transformed from a managed corporation to a governed corporation, where the directors have responsibilities towards the company as well as towards the society. Thus time has come for directors to understand their new responsibilities. They have themselves to shoulder these responsibilities as responsive, responsible and proactive visionaries of the company in a better way, so that they are in a position to discharge their duties as per new demands of the business. Time has come for directors, (whether they are whole time directors or not), to be sure of what they sign. Gone are the days when directors acted merely as rubber stamps/instruments of promoters. Now the only silver lining is the remote possibility of law enforcing agencies initiating actions for non-compliance with the express provisions of law.

-oOo-

Section IV: Marketing & International Trade

13

SOME REFLECTIONS ON THE CHALLENGES OF GLOBAL MARKETING

M. R. Sofi

Abstract

In this paper, an attempt has been made to study the onslaught of globalization on the developing countries. The author argues that the developed world is creating impediments for the third world countries and identifies some challenges which the developing world has to face in the era of globalization.

The failure of the Marxian Economic edifice in the erstwhile U.S.S.R; resulting in the historical collapse of the close public enterprise economy in late 80's of the 20th century,sent shock waves across all such East European, South Asian and Sub-continental countries, as had become habitual of imitating and emulating the so-called giant Marxian model for resolution of their socio-economic issues. Consequently measures were initiated for ushering in a new era of economic reforms, under the guiding umbrella of the GATT and the Dunkel proposals. Initially with a bit hesitation, and some amount of reservation, about the efficacy of the proposed reforms, eventually in countries like India, Pakistan, Bangladesh, Nepal and Maldives, economic reforms were undertaken with an overwhelming enthusiasm and hope. Whereas the myriadfold activity of their economy was touched by these reforms and from consumption to distribution every segment of the activity was affected, however, the new economic policy, in particular, had a bearing upon their inter-regional and international trade. For collapse of the public enterprise mechanism prompted opening of the door to, what once Adam Smith called, "Laissez Faire" or private enterprise based on the enlightened self interest. Consequently the local economy of India became an integral part of the global economic system.

Substantially equipped with revolutionary advances in the infotech devices viz the Internet, E-mail and E-Commerce, and greatly assisted by the newfound marketing and managerial tools and skills, the local Indian market, as part of the global marketing organisation, has now become a complex phenomenon; signifying both hope and despair; optimism as well as pessimism. Notwithstanding the world having been reduced to a global village, wherein remote distances have been conquered by time saving devices and hazardous and arduous labour saved by labour saving techniques, nevertheless, the ever-growing competition poses the real challenge to those for whom the neo-smithian traits of the open market, viz privatisation and globalisation, came as the heavenly boon for plenty and prosperity, and especially for those who want to reap the harvest of the globalised economic venture.

A careful and keen observation of privatisation and globalisation of the Indian market, in particular, and that of other sub-continental countries, in general. reveals that key elements in decision making; whether to go international, which markets to enter, and how to enter, have been baffled partly by the political, cultural and legal environmental factors of the country and partly by the big brotherly attitude of the global trade giants such as the USA, the UK, Germany, France. These colossal commercial powers, coupled with the Japanese wonderful marketing skills, have reduced the free market of India and Pakistan to, what once Myrdal called, "The Asian Drama" wherein despite establishment of regional free trade zones like ASEAN and SAARC, the issue continues to main globalisation versus safeguard of economic interest of domestic farmers, small manufacturers and petty traders. For the outcome of unrestricted imports and exports results in a "spread effect" for the techno-economically advanced countries of the west and merely "back-wash effect" for the underdeveloped and developing countries wherein NAFTA and EEU seem to be devouring up the slice due to SAARC and ASEAN in the south east Asian region.

The economic concerns and business ventures of the under-developed and developing countries, that decide to go global, are confronted by several major challenges:-

a) High debt, inflation and un-employment in the domestic sector.
b) Unstable political governance and currencies.
c) Governmental regulation on foreign firms, requiring their joint ownership with their domestic partners and mandating the hiring of the domestic nationals and setting a limit on profits.
d) The governmental imposition of high tariffs and trade barriers so as to protect the domestic industries on the basis of the protectionist rationale called, "Infant Industry Argument", "defence Argument" and above all the myopic and chauvinistic" Patriotic Argument' viz "Be Indian, Buy Indian", etc.
e) Rampant corruption in the developing countries

For example, in countries like India and Pakistan, a particular import or export business may not be awarded to the best bidder but to the highest briber. On 21st of August, 2001, chairman of the APEDA (the Agricultural and processed food products export development authority) said that the united states patent and trade mark office (USPTO), ruling upholding the patent claims of Ricetect incorporation did not hit the Indian "interests so far as export of the basmati rice is concerned. In his opinion, Ricetec Incorporations' patent applies to a rain artificially developed In the USA. The patent gave it no, rights over he basmati rice strains naturally occurring in India. But despite these assurances of Mr.Anil Swroop, Chairman of the Apeda, the fact remains that "Jasmati" or" Texmati" of the US ricetec incorporation are bound to endanger the future export potential of India in regard to the Basmati trade. The world famous delicious and Maharaji apples of Kashmir now face a terrible and economically devastating competition from the possible arrival of their Bulgarian counterpart in the domestic market. The Bulgarian horticulture is techno-based, capital intensive, labour scarce, per czentra, Kashmir horticulture is labour intensive and capital scarce and ill equipped to compete with the Bulgarian rival. In the sphere of FMCG (Fast moving consumer goods)unhindered liberalisation of global trade is likely to unleash "an era of what may be termed, import on-slaught on India and Pakistan whereby the domestic markets are likely to be flcoded with sophisticated foreign goods---necessities, comforts and luxuries, cosmetics, Toiletries, beauties, textiles, electronic and house-hold gadgets and what not" As long as the domestic industries, firms and business corporations remain ill equipped to face this challenge, only their western adversaries are bound to reap the fruit of the highly competitive global marketing system.

While bracing the shock of the challenges of the global marketing and braving the struggle for competition, the Indo-Pak business ventures have to learn a lesson from the Japanese experience. Reduced to mere shambles in 1945 and brought miserably down by the politico-militaric defeat they suffered at the hands of the Allies the industrious and visionary Japanese succeeded in raising a super structure of a techno economically sound and financially stable edifice on the debris of the pre-war structure, verily, they performed an economic miracle, rose from an economic ruin to the global market leadership in automobiles, motorcycles, electronics, optical instruments, ship building, chemicals, computers and even clothes, cosmetics and food. Why? Simply because they strived hard to identify global markets for their product, endeavoured strenuously to know how to enter, where to enter and build and protect their market share. This is exactly what our business leaders are expected to do. But their endeavours are bound to meet a few challenges as follows:

a) *Product Adaptation*: This implies that they have to mould their product to suit the socio-economic requirements of the country it is exported to

b) *Communication Adaptation*: This implies that brand name and patent name of the product is to be made communicable and acceptable to the consumers of diverse races, creeds and colours, languages customers and taboos.

c) The International Trade is subservient to international peace and harmony: Business communities across the globe have to use their good offices in prevailing upon the billigerent and hostile countries to bury their hatchet over disputed territories so that regions like Kashmir and Palestine, which have hither-to- become zones of conflict, can become buffer zones of free trade, peace and amity between India and Pakistan, Israel and Arabs respectively.

d) *Attitude of international customer*: Our potential business ventures have to understand and appreciate attitudes of the international customers towards buying of the foreign product. For instance, the Chinese are slightly allergic to Pepsi, the Indians take time in seeing eye to eye with consumer's of deaf sticks and MC-donald burgers. Some fundamentallst and chauvinistic consumers raise alarm at the opening of Kentucky Chicken restaurants in India, nevertheless it is a matter of solace that Coca-Cola, which was irritably bothered with Protectionist restriction in 1977 once again holds sway over the soft drinks market in India.

e) *Political Changes*: In countries like Pakistan and Bangladesh, Governments sometimes change violently and, in response to popular feelings, confiscate foreign company's property and currency holdings, which block the free and favourable flow of international trade.

f) *TRIPS*: While a realistic to dismiss the undue and unwarranted criticism of the Dunkel draft by the protagonists of protectionism, nevertheless, he is not disinclined to castigate the adverse impact of this draft upon the global trade potential of developing countries in terms of Arther Dunkel's ever emphasis on trade related intellectual property rights abbreviated to, "TRIPS" which, in our opinion, stands as a big stumbling block to favourable flow of inter-regional and international trade from the South Asia to the west and the vice-versa.

g) *Environmental Degradation*: The deforestation, soil erosion, noise, water and air pollution is not only the concern of the west, but the worry of the south east Asian countries also. That is why the heads of these nations subscribed positively to the deliberations of Environmental Conferences in Rio-De-Jenero of Brazil. The South East Asian Countries are committed to restoration of environmental balance via measures aimed at environmental preservation and protection. However, that doesn't imply the commercially advanced and technologically superior western powers dictation that International trade be linked with environmental issues. On the one hand, it is the socio-cultural and moral responsibility of the South East Asian countries to leave no stone unturned in preserving and promoting their environmental balance and harmony, on the other, it is unjust on the part of the seemingly bossing west to link our trade and marketing activities with the environmental issues.

h) *Controversy*: Last, but not the least, is the controversy related to international trade versus the human rights violation in the South East Asian region. Verily, it would be intellectually an act of cowardice and dishonesty to refute and deny committing of human rights violation in the South East Asian countries, especially by the belligerent among them, whose forces commit gross violation of these rights particularly in the disputed territories. The business communities and commercial concerns of these countries reserve their right to prevail upon their governments to shun the path of violence and improve their human rights record, but simultaneously, they reserve their right to warn the Western agencies against exploiting the human rights issue for their own commercial advantage and to the detriment of our economic interest. The potential business ventures of the subcontinent have to keep these factors in their mind while responding to the challenges of global marketing.

-oOo-

14

TECHNOLOGY EXPORTS: A THRUST AREA FOR INDIAN EXPORTERS

Zahoor Ahmad Chatt

Abstract

Technology plays a key role in the creation of wealth and its accumulation at an exponential rate. While product exports have inherent limitations, technology exports have a tremendous potential, especially in the era of globalization. With the advent of technological advancement, India has entered the world market as a small player in the technology exports but over the years it has made a dent in this field. An attempt has been made in the present paper to evaluate India's performance on this account vis-à-vis world leaders. The suggestions have been offered to strengthen the India's position in respect of such exports.

Introduction

Enterprises in developing countries and economies in transition can no longer consider exports as just an option to sales in the domestic market. The decrease of tariff and non-tariff barriers, the abatement of transport and communication costs, and the international scattering of operations such as purchasing, production, assembling and marketing by multinational businesses have exposed companies to global competition and challenged their competitive edge, even in their home markets. For long term viability in the new global environment these companies must monitor their competitive position and consider entering international markets to enlarge the scope of their activities and gain market shares against foreign competitors.

Technology exports are increasingly becoming important in the matrix of world commercial transactions. Technologies and technological capabilities are crucial to industrial competitiveness, exports and foreign direct investments which are of major national concern. Sustainable increased exports through export of technologies, higher value added products, projects and related services besides other exports, are the need of the day. The recent experiences of advanced developing countries have shown that technology exports and outward investments enhance domestic technological and industrial capabilities and competitiveness. Thus, there is a need to encourage exports of technologies in various forms such as export of know-how through technology transfer agreements, setting up of technology intensive joint ventures abroad, undertaking turn key projects and providing consultancy services and so on. Taking this into cognizance, the objective of the present study is to evaluate India's performance on account of technology exports viz-a-viz world leaders; and offer suggestions to strengthen her position towards technology exports.

Technology Life Cycle

The life span of technologies can be conveniently identified as consisting of four distinct stages – innovation, syndication, diffusion and substitution. The innovation stage represents the birth of a new product, material or process resulting from R&D activities. The syndication stage represents the domestication (pilot production) and commercialization of a new technology

(Product, material or process) with potential for immediate utilization. The diffusion stage represents the market penetration of a new technology through acceptance of the innovation of potential users of the technology. The substitution stage represents decline in the use and eventual extinction of a technology due to replacement by another technology.

Technology exports vis-à-vis Product Exports

Technology export is being increasingly recognized as an important channel for enhancing national exports and promoting technical cooperation at international levels. With the establishment of the World Trade Organization (WTO) in 1991 and alongwith it, strengthening of Intellectual Property Regime, technology is being increasingly traded as a commodity by many nations. Technology export is quite different from product export in many ways, such as:

(a) the price of product is fixed but technology can be priced depending upon its commercialization potential in a given set of conditions and circumstances, negotiating power of the technology supplier and customer and urgency of need of the customer;

(b) in contrast to product export, technology export is quite often accompanied with export of associated capital goods, materials and services;

(c) a single instance of technology export yields repeated returns for a certain period of time by way of royalty, dividends, additional exports of machinery, raw-materials and training of personnel;

(d) technology exports call for a sound R&D backup to upgrade the know how exported and maintain competitiveness; and

(e) technology export cannot take place unless the technology has been successfully commercialized within the indigenous market. In order to export technology, it is generally required to clearly demonstrate to the potential buyer that by the use of technology, it is possible to manufacture good quality products at a globally competitive price in conditions existing in his country.

Modes of Technology Export

Technologies are generally exported through any one or a combination of the following modes:

i) Export of know how;

ii) Export of Designs and Drawings;

iii) Setting up of joint ventures in the host country;

iv) Export of Turnkey projects including export of plant and machinery;

v) Consultancy Export including export of technical services and training;

vi) Export of capital goods, components and raw materials on long term basis.

Export of know-how is accompanied with transfer of detailed technology know-how documentation, supervision in plant commissioning and training of know how recipients personnel. Export of Designs and Drawings involves handing over of the designs and drawings of a project in exchange for a lump sum fee. Setting up a joint venture involves participation in equity of a newly formed company by way of cash remittance, capitalization of lump sum fee for know how, technical and consultancy services. Turnkey projects and constancy exports involve lump sum payment for plant and equipment and services offered.

Technology Exports – Indian Scenario

India is known for its intellectual prowess, rich bio-diversity and vast natural resources. India is on the threshold of major growth in its trade, commerce and industry, in consonance with the policies of liberalization and globalization being followed by the Government of India since 1991. India, the second largest populated country in the world, the fifth largest economy in the world on a purchasing power parity basis, is strategically situated in the South Asian Region and has made substantial and steady economic, industry and technological progress. India has over the years developed strong S&T infrastructure for human resource development as well as for R&D, primarily aimed at achieving technical self reliance and enhancing domestic technological capabilities in various areas of national importance. Today, India has one of the world's largest technical workforce, estimated to be in excess of 4 million engineers, scientists and technicians. The technological infrastructure includes 325 national laboratories and R&D institutions under CSIR, ICMR, DRDO, ICAR and others, over 1250 in-house R&D centres of industry and around 450 non commercial scientific and industrial research organisations recognized by DSIR. In addition, strong industrial production capabilities have been built up in several areas, based on indigenous as well as exported technologies.

The industrial experience and technological capabilities acquired by India in select areas over the years is relevant to other developing countries and there exists a vast potential for export of technologies, projects and services. Sporadic efforts have been made by several organisations in the country to export technologies. In strategic areas like defence, space, atomic energy, etc. Indian scientists developed the technology to meet her requirements. It is only recently the Department of Electronics and the Department of Defense Production are identifying defense related technologies which will be suitable for exports. In the area of computer software India's strength in developing technology and also provide technical services is being widely recognized.

Today as several developing countries are moving close to achieving the status of industrialized nations, economic and industrial globalization is foremost on the agenda of many nations including India which wish to become global players. Specific data on technology exports by various countries is not readily available but a study of two types of technology indicators make international or inter-regional comparison of technological activity possible. One such indicator is the R&D expenditure by various countries as it is a measure of resources made available for science and technology activities in any country. Nations that spend relatively large amounts on R&D in the industry tend to be relatively quick in reaping the benefits of new technology, even though they may not be the original innovators. The Gross Domestic Expenditure on Research and Development (GERD), as a percentage of Gross Domestic Product (GDP) for different areas in the world in 1996 are given in Table 1.

Table 1: GERD/GDP Ratios for Different Areas in the World		
Regions	GERD/GDP (%)	Rank
European Union[1]	1.9	4.5
European Free Trade Association	2.3	3
Central & Eastern European Countries (CEEC)[2]	1.5	6.5
Israel	1.9	4.5
Commonwealth of Independent States	0.9	10
USA	2.8	1.5
Canada	1.5	6.5
Latin America	0.4	15
Middle and Near East[3]	0.5	13
Sub-Saharan Africa	0.4	15
North Africa	0.4	15
Japan	2.8	1.5
NICs[4]	1.3	8
China	0.7	12
India	0.8	11
Other Countries in Far East	0.1	17
Australia and New Zealand	1.2	9
World Average	**1.8**	-

Note:

1. European Union: 15 member countries viz. Austria, Belgium, Denmark, Finland, France, Germany, Greece, Ireland, Italy, Luxembourg, Netherlands, Portugal, Spain, Sweden & UK
2. CEEC: Estonia, Latvia and Lithuania
3. NICs: Newly industrialized countries of Republic of Korea, Malaysia, Hong Kong, Singapore

Source: Constructed on the basis of data obtained from World Science Report, 1998.

It can be clearly seen that the USA and Japan are leading at 2.8% each so far as the percentage of expenditure on R&D is concerned. The India's expenditure at 0.8% enjoys 11th position of GDP is far lower than the United States, EU, Japan, CIS and NICs and it is also less than half of the world average. It is significant to note that Japan which imported technology, improved on the imported technologies and were able to export products based on those technologies to the very countries from where they imported the technology in the first instance.

"Patent" is another technology indicator since it is the basic product of technological activity. The patent recognizes an invention, such as an industrial process or a new product or material. Technological activity can be measured by Patent Production which indicates the level of inventiveness and creativity in technology for industrial purposes. An indication of the technological production can be had by looking at the Patents granted to various countries in Europe and USA as given in table 2.

Table 2: Technological Production, Measured by Patents granted in Europe and the USA 1996

Regions	European Patents World share(%)	US Patents World share(%)
European Union	45.4	18.6
European Free Trade Association	3.2	1.5
Central and Eastern European countries	0.2	0.1
Israel	0.4	0.4
Commonwealth of Independent States	0.2	0.1
USA	27.3	48.7
Canada	0.8	2.3
Latin America	0.1	0.2
North Africa	0.0	0.0
Middle and Near East	0.0	0.0
Sub Saharan Africa	0.1	0.1
Japan	20.9	25.0
NICs	0.5	1.3
China	0.0	0.1
India	0.0	0.0
Other countries in Far East	0.0	0.0
Australia and New Zealand	0.6	0.5
World Total	**100.00**	**100.00**

Source: Constructed on the basis of data obtained from World Science Report, 1998

It can be seen from the European Patenting Figures that the major technological capabilities are shared by Europe (nearly 50% of the world total), the USA (27%) and Japan (21%). No other country is above 1%. A look through the United States patenting data, USA accounts for 48.7% while EU and Japan account for 18.6% and 25% respectively. India's share in the European and United States patents is insignificant and therefore, India does not contribute in this table.

In India's case, the contribution of technology to exports can be judged by looking at technology intensive exports. Technology intensive exports include export of capital goods, computer software, management and technical services, construction and turnkey projects, etc. and earnings from joint ventures set up abroad. Exports under these categories during 1995-96 is given in Table 3.

Table 3: Technology Intensive Exports from India during 1995-96

	Exports	
	(Rs in crores)	**(%)**
Export Sector		
Capital Goods	2780	40.54
Computer Software	2350	34.26
Management and Technical Services	500	7.29
Joint ventures	403	5.88
Wholly owned subsidiaries	75	1.09
Exim Bank Export contracts		
a) Construction	38	0.56
b) Turnkey projects	712	10.38
Total	**6858**	**100.00**

Source: Constructed on the basis of data obtained from "Promotion of Technology Exports from India" by Ashwani Gupta, 1997

Conclusions and Policy Implications

It is apparent that technology export is a difficult exercise and India has to go a long way before establishing itself as a technology exporter. It calls for extensive market surveys, negotiations, demonstrations, trainings, documentations etc. She has strong technological and industrial capabilities in several areas which can be shared with other developing countries for mutual advantage. Serious efforts need to be undertaken to promote exports of technologies and services to select countries, including the SAARC region. While technology generation is important, equally significant is protecting the technologies legally through patents.

In the context of technology exports, India has to begin with generation of technology. In this age of information technology, at least India must do is to see that we have access to all the technologies. This will mean that we must strengthen our national informatics infrastructure so that every exporter or R&D lab gets up-to-date information, both relating to technology as well as business opportunities for technology related exports. Our advantage is that our scientific manpower has excellent potential and it is cost effective.

Efforts must be made to establish a relationship between our research and educational establishments, industry and the government. This will, provide the basic framework for generation, testing and marketing of technologies first within the country and then exporting them abroad.

Since we are in an increasingly competitive era of global trade, we must examine seriously whether we can also follow the strategy of Japan i.e. buy technology and add value to it or develop the same further into commercially exploitable products or services. This has to be taken up in a systematic manner and as a conscious strategy so that we also develop the type of capability which Japan has developed.

The services of NRI technocrats should be utilized by India in developing technologies and try to use their knowledge to set up technology related labs or export facilities.

Strategic policy interventions and policy measures including attractive incentives need to be evolved to boost technology exports.

Appropriate National Mechanisms should be evolved to develop and maintain a data base on technologies exported and other related information of commercial and technical nature. A regular publication on technologies exported and their analysis should be brought out, as has been already initiated by DSIR.

Keeping in view the capabilities and potential for technology exports, and the pressing need to enhance our high value added exports on sustainable basis, a Technology Export Promotion Centre may be set up with the involvement of concerned agencies and the government.

References

A compendium on Technology Exports from India (1996). Department of Scientific and Industrial Research, Ministry of Science & Technology, New Delhi.

The Financing of Exports (1997), International Trade Centre UNCTAD/WTO.

Promotion of Technology Exports form India (1997), Department of Scientific and Industrial Research, Ministry of Science & Technology, New Delhi.

Technology Promotion – Experiences of Selected Asia Countries – Asian and Pacific Centre for Transfer of Technology, 1995.

World investment Report (1996), Investment, Trade and International Policy Arrangements – UNCTAD.

-oOo-

15

SERVICE QUALITY IN PUBLIC SECTOR BANKS: AN EMPIRICAL INVESTIGATION

Mushtaq Ahmad Bhat

Abstract

In a liberalised and competitive environment, as the race to compete and survive intensifies, business firms discover that their offerings becoming dangerously similar to one another. The service products of airlines, banks, fast foods, and the like equally measure up to one another's specifications. Under such circumstances quality service offers a way of achieving success among competing services. Firms will prosper or decline, depending upon the quality of service they provide to their customers. In view of its (service quality) gaining importance, an attempt has been made, in the present paper, to study service quality of public sector banks with a view to offer suggestions to make overall service quality of banks more effective and efficient.

Introduction

Interest in service quality is obvious when one thinks about it. Poor quality places a firm at a competitive disadvantage. If customers perceive quality as unsatisfactory; they may be quick to take their business elsewhere. Recent years have witnessed a veritable explosion of discontent with service quality at a time when the quality of many manufactured goods seems to have improved significantly.

From a marketing standpoint, a key issue is whether customers notice differences in quality between competing suppliers or not! Improving quality in the eyes of customers pays off for the companies that provide it. Data from the Profit Impact of Market Strategy (PIMS) research show that a perceived quality advantage leads to higher profits (Buzzell and Gale, 1987). Berry and Parasuraman (1991) also hold the view that high quality service gives credibility to the field sales force and advertising, stimulates favorable word-of-mouth communications, enhances customers' perception of value, and boosts the morale and loyalty of employees and customers alike. Thus, it is clear that service quality offers a way of achieving success among competing services. Particularly, where a number of firms that offer nearly identical services are competing within a small area, such as banks, establishing service quality may be the only way of differentiating itself. Such differentiation can yield a higher proportion of consumers' choices and, hence, mean the difference between financial success and failure. In a liberalized and competitive environment, therefore, only those banks would be effective in delivering goods, which provide excellent service quality. Almost, all the banks perform same functions. Therefore, the customer takes into account the relative efficiency while choosing a particular bank. Moreover, banks carry on business with public money and, therefore, customers expect better service from them.

The most recent trend in many service organisations is to consider quality service as a critical factor in enabling them to achieve a differential advantage over their competitors (Albrecht and Zemke, 1985; Berry, Bennett and Brown, 1989; Leonard and

Sasser, 1982; Ross and Shetty, 1985). Increasingly, quality is becoming a key variable in strategic planning. Further, the organisations which are becoming leaders in quality service are characterized by the commitment of top management and a corporate culture that encourages a consumer and quality focus throughout the company (Albrecht and Zemke, 1985; Marshall, 1985). In India, may academicians and practitioners (Brahmanandam and Narayana, 1990; Elias, 1982; Nageswar and Pramod, 1990; Nageswar, 1987; Nandakumar, 1995; Sesha Sai, 1999; and Sundaram, 1984) have highlighted the need for better service quality in banks, mostly public sector banks, and offered guidelines for improvement in bank services. These studies have also warned public sector banks that if the present trend of customer dissatisfaction continues unabated, time is not far away when these banks will loose their valuable customers to competitors (especially private and foreign).

In light of above research findings, quality service is critical to banks' success particularly in today's increasingly competitive environment. In view of the tremendous importance of service quality in banks, an attempt has been made, in the present paper, to study service quality and its dimensions in banks and suggest, on the basis of study results, ways and means for improving service quality with a view to make overall banking service more effective and efficient.

Service Quality

Despite the appreciation of the importance of service quality in strategic planning and for corporate success, there are no clear cut definitions of quality or dimensions for setting quality standards and measuring subsequent quality delivered and received. Most of the suggested definitions focus on meeting customer needs and requirements. For example, service quality is "a measure of how well the service delivered matches customer's expectations" (Lewis and Booms, 1983), or "providing the customer with what he wants, when he wants it, and at acceptable cost, within the operating constraints of the business and "providing a better service than the customer expects" (Lewis, 1988). Too often the term 'quality' is used as if it were a variable itself such as conformance to specifications, the degree to which customer specifications are satisfied, a fair exchange of price and value, fitness for use, freedom from variation and doing it right the first time (Garvin, 1988; Kotlar, 1999; Woodruffe, 1998).

Additionally, a number of definitions refer to the importance of the client's/ customer's perceptions of quality (Takeuchi and Quelch, 1983) which are consumer's attitudes or judgements resulting from comparisons by consumers of expectations of service with their perceptions of actual service performance (Berry, et.al., 1985,1988; Gronroos, 1982; Lewis and Boom, 1983). Berry (1980), along with Booms and Bitner (1981), argue that, due to intangible nature of services, customer uses elements associated with the physical environment when evaluating service quality. Managing the evidence and using the environmental psychology are often seen as important marketing tools. Levitt (1981) proposes that customers use appearances to make judgements about realities, and less tangible a product the more powerful is the effect of packaging in judging that product. Hostage (1975) for his part, believes that a service firm's contact personnel comprise the major determinant of service quality, while Lewis and Booms (1983) propose that service quality resides in the ability of the service firm to satisfy its customer needs, i.e. customer satisfaction, Purasuraman, et.al., (1985) found that consumer's perceptions of quality are influenced by various gaps which lead to service quality shortfalls and, in particular, that the "quality perceived in a service is a function of the gap between customer's desires/expectations and their perceptions of the service that is actually received," i.e., service quality is a measure of how well the service delivered meets the expectations of service. Quality has, thus, become one of the main concerns of company officials (Leonard and Sasser, 1982) and is becoming a strategic variable which greatly affects marketing and production policies in many service firms.

Dimensions of Service Quality

As the understanding of service quality has emerged, researchers have developed conceptualizations of the dimensions of service quality. Lehtinan and Lehtinan (1982) refer to process quality, as judged by consumers during a service, and output quality judged after a service is performed. They also make a distinction between physical quality (products or support), interactive quality (where the dimensions of quality originate in the interaction between the customer and the service organization), and corporate quality (Lehtinan and Lehtinan, 1991). Gronroos (1984) discusses the technical quality of service encounters – i.e., what is received by the consumer –and the functional quality of the process – i.e., the way in which the service is delivered, to include the attitudes and behavior, appearance and personality, service mindedness, accessibility and approachability of customer contact personnel-together with corporate image dimension of service quality. Barry (1980), along with Booms and Bitner (1981), argue that due to intangible nature of services, customers use elements associated with physical environment when evaluating service quality. Levitt (1981) proposes that customers use appearances to make judgements about realities, and the less tangible a product the more powerful is the effect of packaging in judging the product. Gummesson and Gronroos (1987) synthesized the Gronroos's Model with one from manufacturing and incorporate design, production, delivery and relational dimensions of quality. Hostage (1975) believes that a service firm's contact personnel comprise the major determinant of service quality.

The most widely reported set of determinants of service quality is that of Berry and his colleagues, Parasuraman, Zeithaml (1985,1988). They suggested that the criteria used by consumers that are important in moulding their expectations and perceptions of delivered service fit ten dimensions: tangibility; reliability; responsiveness; communication; credibility; security; competence; courtesy; understanding/knowing the customer and access. Subsequent research, analysis and testing has led to five dimensions of service quality – SERVQUAL (Parasuraman, Zeithaml and Berry, 1988)

1. Tangibility: physical facilities, equipment, appearance of personnel
2. Reliability: ability to perform the promised service dependably and accurately
3. Responsiveness: willingness to help customers and provide prompt service
4. Assurance: knowledge and courtesy of employees and their ability to convey trust and confidence

5. Empathy: caring, individualized attention the company provides to its customers.

Selection of the Instrument

In developing a survey questionnaire, knowledge from previous research, group discussions among customers and review of the service quality literature was taken into account. In particular, SERVQUAL was tested among a number of customers and all its dimensions were felt important. The numerous examples of industry-specific empirical studies using SERVQUAL (see for example, Lewis (1987), hotel services; Brown and Swartz (1989), medical services; Lewis (1991), service quality in banks; Saleh and Ryan (1991), was, therefore, chosen as an ideal instrument for studying service quality in banks.

The Samples

The present study is limited to Northern India, which includes J&K State, Punjab, Haryana and Delhi. However, the survey was confined to urban areas only keeping in view the concentration of banks in these areas as well as the paucity of time and financial resources of the researcher. The study is further limited to two public sector banks only in Northern India, namely State Bank of India (SBI)*and Punjab National Bank (PNB).* These banks were purposely selected for the present study keeping in view their role and involvement in shaping the economic destiny and in instrumentalising the process of social and economic transformation in Northern India. Specifically, in terms of advancing credit and deposits, employee strength and branch network, they stand at the top (for details, see IBA Bulletin (Special Issue) March, 2002, xxiv, (3), pp, 264-299). Further, present study is limited to retail banking only as it constitutes nearly eighty per cent of the total banking business of public sector banks (Srivastava, 1994).

The study is based upon the experiences and opinions expressed by bank customers regarding their expectations and perceptions about the quality of service they are receiving from their respective banks. For this purpose, a sample of four hundred bank customers was taken from sample organizations. While choosing a bank customer, for present study, the method of simple random sampling was used. All important demographic characteristics like age, level of education, level of income, profession and geographic location of the bank were taken into consideration while choosing bank customers. All these characteristics have an important bearing upon bank customers' evaluation (regarding expectations and perceptions) of service quality. The effort was made to give a balanced representation to above demographic characteristics to make the sample representative.

Results and Discussion

In line with the objective of the study the main area of questioning and analysis concerned customer expectations and perceptions in relation to service quality dimensions: tangibility, reliability, responsiveness, assurance and empathy. Expectations and perceptions were measured on a seven point scale starting from strongly disagree to strongly agree. Mean differences between customer expectations and customer perceptions were calculated separately for the two banks. This was followed by a t-test to determine the level of significant difference. The main parameters are discussed as under:-

Tangibility

It is evident from Table 1.1 that service quality of PNB is better as compared to SBI on all elements of tangibility. The SERVQUAL score of PNB on physical facilities and neatness of employees is comparatively better as compared to SBI. The negative SERVQUAL scores on all elements of tangibility particularly physical facilities and up-to-date equipments demands substantial investment on said elements of tangibility, which will improve service quality to a great extent. Tangibility particularly computerisation of banking operations, internet and intranet based services, ATMs etc., will take care of most of retail banking which constitutes eighty percent of the total banking business. This will reduce workload of front line staff and will provide a way to quick response. This observation is in line with the Rangarajan Committee (1989) report, which stressed mechanization of Indian banking industry. The Committee had rightly commented that when banks are in tough competition with other financial intermediaries that are fully equipped and automated, there is a need for a greater measure of computerization. It pointed out that for the Indian banking system to be more competitive internally and to remain in step with wide ranging innovations taking place in industry abroad, a radical change in work technology is imperative (Bide, 1997). Many authors and practitioners have suggested to adopt banking technology as a means to improve customer services (Ammyya, 1996; Godse, 1997; Middleton, 1994; Saraf, 1997). The technological advancement, the world over, is so rapid and widespread that isolating banking and technology from each other is relatively an impossible preposition in today's fast changing competitive environment. Lakshmi (1991) in an empirical study reported that 73% of the respondents felt that the banks are being maintained in a good fashion is quite contrary as far as the findings of present study are concerned. In the said study, Lakshmi reported that forty-eight per cent respondents opined that the bank furnishing was just adequate and sixty three per cent of respondents felt that dressing was ordinary. Such a sad state of affairs has again come to the light as far as neatness of employees and physical facilities are concerned.

Reliability

Table 1.1 brings to light minor variation in SERVQUAL scores of the banks, under reference, on all elements of reliability. The low negative SERVQUAL scores reveal that these banks are doing well on reliability in comparison to other dimensions of service quality. Srivastava (1994) along with Brahmanandam and Narayana (1990) reported in their studies that banks do not start their operation at specified time, which results delays in transactions. Staff members usually report late by 15 to 30 minutes, while customers keep on waiting. Even while dealing with customers, they do not hesitate to leave their seats on some pretext or the other. The result is delay. The same sad state of affairs exists in banks, under study, because the public sector banks lack positive work culture. Muniraj (1994) along with Ramachandra (1992) have similar observations about the work culture in banks and have recommended discipline as one of the marketing strategy to improve customer service. Srivastava (1994) in his study also confirms that only twenty per cent of the customers view the working conditions as appealing for business like transactions, the rest eighty per cent are highly critical about it.

Table 1: Comparative SERVQUAL Scores of Banks		
Service Quality Elements	**Mean**	
	SBI	**PNB**
Tangibility		
Upto date equipment**		
Physical facilities*	-331	-283
Employees are well dressed and neat appearing*	-1.79	-1.52
Communication material	-1.84	-17.74
Reliability		
Promise to do something by a certain time, doing it	-1.22	-1.13
Being sincere in solving the problem	-1.19	-1.10
Performing the service right the first time	-1.19	-1.09
Providing the service at the promised time	-1.14	-1.07
Keeps records correctly	-0.48	-0.40
Responsiveness		
Telling customers exactly when service/s will be performed	-1.47	-1.19
Employees providing prompt service to customers	-2.23	-2.03
Employees who are always willing to help	-1.73	-1.60
Employees who are never too busy to respond to customers requests	-1.27	-2.25
Assurance		
Employees who are trustworthy	-1.62	-1.59
Feeling safe in transacting with the bank	-0.31	-0.39
Employees who are courteous	-1.83	-1.79
Employees who have the knowledge of answer customers questions	-1.55	-1.60
Empathy		
Bank that gives individual attention	-1.55	-1.51
Convenient operating hours	-2.09	-2.27
Employees who give personal attention	-1.68	-1.58
Bank which has your best interests at heart	-1.80	-1.88
Employees who understand specific needs of the customer	-1.94	-1.98

No of respondents for each bank=200; df,396; level of significance. p>0.01;**p>0.05

Responsiveness

The SERVQUAL scores of PNB on all elements of responsiveness are better in comparison to the SERVQUAL scores of SBI .However, there is significant difference ($p>0.01$) as far as telling customers exactly when service/s will be performed wherein PNB relatively scores high. The difference on the remaining elements of responsiveness is negligible. The low negative SERVQUAL scores of both the banks reveals poor service quality standards on responsiveness, particularly, employees providing prompt service to customers' and employees who are too busy to respond customers requests , wherein respondents of related banks have reported low perceptions regarding service quality. In the absence of banking technology, the large volume of work results in delays (poor response). However, Nageswar (1987) and Nageswar and Pramod (1990), in their studies, brought to light the fact that large corporate clients are able to get efficient and speedy service from their banks mainly because of the knowledge and efficiency of their own staff and the liaison with the banks, the small investors/ entrepreneurs are required to run to the banks for their work themselves. Since retail banking/personal banking constitutes eighty percent of the total banking business, which means that majority of bank customers face the problem of lack of concern from their respective banks. Banking technology, which was absent during 90's, has increased customer aspirations today and as a result they expect quick response from their banks. Bhattacharyay and Ghose (1989), while highlighting urban bank saver's opinion, reported that only nine per cent clerks' are slow while as thirty nine per cent are very prompt and fifty two per cent usually prompt in providing services to customers. This state of affairs existed prior to 90's when we had controlled economy. Today customers will have a different perception on responsiveness of banks as they are in close competition with foreign banks, which are backed by sophisticated banking technology. The present study's findings are not in agreement with the views as reported by above mentioned scholars keeping in view the changed and competitive banking environments.

Assurance

The low negative SERVQUAL scores of both the banks on feeling safe in transacting with the bank brings to light that respondants of related banks are by and large satisfied with this element of assurance. The high negative SERVQUAL scores of both the banks on employees who are consistently courteous and employees who have the knowledge to answer customers' questions reveals poor service quality standards as far as said elements of assurance are concerned. This research finding is in line with the findings of Srivastava (1994). He reported that approximately 50% of the customers feel that bank employees are formal and casual in their approach while dealing with customers. However, the findings of Bhattacharya and Ghose (1989) are not in agreement with the above findings. They reported that about eighty four per cent respondents feel that banks have courteous employees. Lewis (1991) reported that honesty and trust-worthiness are highly rated personal qualities among the US bank employees. This follows that courteous, trustworthiness, and knowledge of employees to answer customers questions play a significant role in determining the quality of service of banks, wherein these banks are deficient. This fact has also been brought to light by Sundaram (1984) and Gurdeep (1994) who hold the view that present customer service systems lack motivation and initiative, adversely affect the services offered, the process delaying the service and the poor motivation is de-sensitizing the service. Banks have almost become bureaucratic organisations. Such statements lead us to conclude that banks do not have good working conditions as has also been revealed by Srivastava (1994).

Empathy

Table 1 brings to light that respondents of both the banks are dissatisfied as far as convenient banking operations and employees who understand specific needs of the customer are concerned. This is quite evident from the respective high negative SERVQUAL scores of the banks. The weak position of these banks on empathy suggests that heavy investment in banking technology is needed, which will definitely take care of said elements of empathy. Lakshmi (1991) highlighted this fact, in an empirical study, where 70% of the respondents opined that the present business timing of most banks was not at all convenient. As already mentioned, public sector banks, in India are operating in all segments, in particular, government transactions, which increase their work-load and in absence of large number of ATMs', banks continuously have to face complaints from their customers regarding operational hours and individual attention.

Conclusions and Suggestions

The findings of this paper lead us to the conclusion that service quality of public sector banks, under study, is very poor as is clear from high negative mean scores. The results of the study also makes it clear that service quality between two public sector banks does not differ significantly except on tangibility where PNB has taken a lead. The main reason for this empirical evidence is uniform work culture in public sector banks. Apart from uniform culture, public sector banks also have uniform control/direction, uniform services, uniform HRD policies etc. Srinavasa (1996) also reported this fact in SWOT analysis of public sector banks. Sesha Sai (1999) has rightly observed that service quality has two main elements, viz., creation and delivery of service. The creation of service includes range of services, designing of services in terms of customer conveniences; beneficial features and others are quite common in public sector banks. In the same way, delivery of service covers features such as speed, accuracy, promptness, reliability, attitude of front line staff are again common in public sector banks. Since these banks have little control over the creation of services because of uniform direction/control, the employees play a pivotal role in the delivery of these services. Bank management, however, can make these services more effective through proper HRD policies/practices but these again are common among public sector banks. Of course PNB has taken a lead as far as tangibles are concerned which has given them slightly a differential edge in delivery of quality services

The findings of the study draw attention to the fact that service quality of public sector banks, under study, is very poor on tangibles and responsiveness dimensions of service quality. These findings suggest heavy investment on tangibles particular computer based banking, tele banking, anywhere and anytime banking, etc. This will help in delivering quick and accurate services to customers besides reducing the workload of front line staff and thereby providing ways to employees to respond to customer requests.

Banks should also conduct frequent training programmes in areas like prompt cash payments and receipts at the counter, efficient pass book and statement service, prompt collection and remittance services, early decisions on credit applications and quick attention to complaints as these areas have direct bearing on customers service quality.

Banks must conduct studies on customers' perception of banking services and customers' awareness regarding banking schemes to know where bank stands as far as delivering quality services and services available in the bank are concerned so that corrective measures are accordingly taken.

Banks must pay attention to potential failure points and service recovery procedures, which become integral to employees training. In other words, it amounts to empowering employees to exercise responsibility, judgement and creativity in responding to customers' problems.

In order to overcome growing consumer dissatisfaction it is suggested that banks should make commitment to service quality and the creation of an appropriate culture. The organizational culture may require change, towards employee orientation to the company, and everyone's orientation to the external customer. This change starts at the top; the customer care process must begin with senior management's commitment to employees and customers, ideally with strong and visible leaders. The top management must adopt and drill it down the line concept of customer as given by Mahatma Gandhi, Father of the Nation: "A customer is the most important visitor to our premises. He is not dependent on us. We are dependent on him. He is not an interruption to our work. He is the purpose of it. He is not an outsider to our premises. He is part of it. We are not doing a favour by serving him. He is doing us a favour by giving an opportunity to do so."

The suggestions as highlighted above, if rightly perceived and properly implemented, will certainly go a long way in improving service quality in banks. Since consumer behaviour is dynamic in nature and consumer expectations change continuously, as the level of income, education or socio-economic environment changes, there is always need for research and in-depth study to bring out, from time to time, the factors responsible for consumer satisfaction/dissatisfaction in banks. The present paper has brought out some research gaps, which have a strong bearing on service quality vis-à-vis performance in banks. It is, therefore, suggested that more detailed investigations into such vital issues need to be taken up by separate comparative and contextual studies.

References:

Ammayya, T. (1996) "Developing Competitive Advantage Through Absorption of Technology in Knowledge, Skills and Attitudes of People", IBA Bulletin, Vol.XVIII, No.12, October-December, pp.38-42.

Berry, L. L., Zeithaml, V.A. and Parasuraman, A. (1985) "Quality Counts in Services Too", Business Horizons,May-June,pp.44-52

Berry, L. L., Zeithaml, V.A. and Parasuraman, A. (1988) "The Service Quality Puzzle", Business Horizons, July-August.

Berry, L.L. (1980) "Services Marketing is Different" Business" Vol.30, (May-June), pp. 8-30

Berry, L.L. and Parasuraman, A. (1991) "Marketing Services: Competing Through Quality", Maxwell Macmillan International, New York, pp.175-203

Bhattacharaya, B.N. and Ghose, B.K. (1989) "Marketing of Banking Services in the 90s,: Problems and Perspectives", Economic and Political Weekly, February 25, Vo.24, No.8.

Bhide, M. G. (1997), "Information Technology in Banks" IBA Bulletin, Vol.68, No.4, October-December, pp.149-152.

Booms, B.H. and Bitner M.J. (1981) "Marketing Strategies and Organisation Structures for Services Firms", in Zeithaml V.A. Panasuraman A, and Berry L.L (1985) "Problems and Strategies in Service Marketing", Journal of Marketing Vol., 49, No.2 pp.33-46.

Brahmanandan, G.N. and Narayana, M.S. (1990) "A Study on Customer Service in Commercial Banks", Indian Journal of Marketing, Vol.20, No.5, January, pp.7-8 & 16.

Brown, S.W. and Swartz, T.A. (1989), "A Gap Analysis of Professional Service Quality", Journal of Marketing, Vol.53, April, pp.92-100.

Buzzell, R.D. and Gale, B.T. (1987) "The PIMS Principles – Linking Strategy to Performance" in Christopher H Lovelock (1996) "Service Marketing"3rd Ed., Prentice Hall, New Jersey, p.462.

Elias, A. H.(1982) "Indian Banking Service." Journal of Indian Institute of Bankers, Vol. 35, NO.3, pp.119-124

Garvin, D.A. (1988) "Managing Quality" Free Press, New York, pp.40-41.

Godse, V.T. (1997) "Banking Technology: Challenges Ahead for Banks", IBA Bulletin, Vol.68, No.4, October-December, pp.180-182.

Gronroos, C. (1982), "Strategic Management and Marketing in the Services Sector" in Parasuraman A., Zeithaml V.A and Berry L.L (1985) "A Conceptual Model of Service Quality and its Implications for Future Research", Journal of Marketing, Fall Vol., 49, pp.41-50.

Gronroos, C. (1984) "A Service Quality Model and its Marketing Implications", European Journal of Marketing, Vol., 18, No.4, pp.36-50

Gummensson, E. and Gronroos, C. (1987) "Quality of Products and Services: A Tentative Synthesis Between Two Models", Research Report, Services Research Centre, University of Karlstad, Sweden.

Gurdeep, S. (1994) "Marketing of Services in Banking Sector: Challenges Ahead", in Bidhi, C. (1994) "Marketing of Services" (Ed.), Rawat Publications, New Delhi, pp.82-90.

Hostage, G.M. (1975) "Quality Control in a Service Business", Harvard Business Review, July – August, pp.98-106.

Kotlar, P. (1999) "Marketing Management: The Millennium Edition", Prentice Hall of India, New Delhi, pp.50-58.

Lakshmi,V.M. (1991) "Bank Marketing : A Long Way to Go",Quarterly Economic Report of the Institute of Public Opinion,Vol.34.No.3,July-Sept.,pp.43-50

Lehtinen, U. and Lehtinan, J.R. (1982) "Service Quality: A Study of Quality Dimensions", Working Paper, Service Management Institute, Helsinki, Finland.

Lehtinen, U. and Lehtinen, J.R. (1991) "Two Approaches to Service Quality Dimensions", The Service Industries Journal, Vol. 11, No.3, pp.287-303.

Leonard, F.S. and Sasser, E.W. (1982), "The Incline of Quality", Harvard Business Review, September-October; Vol.60; No.5; pp.163-171..

Levitt, T. (1981) "Marketing Intangible Products and Product Intangibles", Harvard Business Review, May – June, pp.94-102.

Lewis, B. (1991), "Service Quality: An International Comparison of Bank Customers Expectations and Perceptions", Journal of Marketing Management, Vol.7, pp.47-62.

Lewis, B.R. (1988) "Customer Service Survey: A Major UK Bank" August, Financial Service Research Canter, Manchester School of Management, MIST; in Lewis, B. (1991), "Service Quality: An International Comparison of Bank Customers Expectations and Perceptions", Journal of Marketing Management, Vol.7, pp.47-62.

Lewis, R.C. (1987), "The Measurement of Gaps in the Quality of Hotel Service", International Journal of Hospitality Management, Vol.6, No.2, pp.83-91.

Lewis, R.C. and Booms, B.H. (1983) "The Marketing Aspect of Service Quality" in Lewis, B.R. (1981) "Service Quality: An International Comparison of Bank Customers Expectations and Perceptions", Journal of Marketing Management, Vo.,7, pp.47-62.

Lewis, R.C. and Booms, B.H. (1983) "The Marketing Aspect of Service Quality" in Emerging Perspectives on Services Marketing; L. Berry, G. Shostack, and G. Upah (Eds)., American Marketing Association, Chicago, pp.99-102.

Marshall, C.E. (1985) "Can we Be Consumer-Oriented in a Changing Financial Service World", The Journal of Consumer Marketing, Vol.,2 No.4., Fall pp.37-43.

Middleton, P. (1994) "Towards Globalisation and International Competitiveness", IBA Bulletin, Vol.XVI, No.11, November, pp.8-11.

Muniraj, R. (1994) "Strategies to Improve Customer Service in Banks", The Banker, June, pp.31-34

Nageswar, R. (1987) "Customer Service in Banks Must Improve", Yojana, Vol.31, No.13, July 16-31, pp.20-31.

Nageswar, R. and Pramod, P. (1990) "customer Services and Banks", Yojna, Vol.34, No.13, July 16-13, pp.15-22.

Panasuraman, A., Zeithaml V.A. and Berry. L.L. (1988), "SERVQUAL: A Multiple Scale for Measuring Consumer Perceptions of service Quality", Journal of Retailing, Vol.64, No.1, Spring, pp.12-40.

Panasuraman, A.., Zeithaml V.A. and Berry. L.L. (1985), "A Conceptual Model of Service Quality and Its Implications for Future Research", Journal of Marketing, Vol.49, Fall, pp.41-50.

Ramachandra, R.B. (1992) "Where the Bankers are not Market-Friendly", The Banker, Vol. 39 No.9. pp.26-28.

Ross, J.E. and Shetty, Y.K. (1985), "Making Quality a Fundamental Part of Strategy", in Lewis B. (1991) "Service Quality: An International Comparison of Bank Customers Expectations and Perceptions", Journal of Marketing Management, Vol. 7, pp.47-62.

Saleh, F. and Ryan, C. (1991), "Analysing Service Quality in the Hospitality Industry Using the SERVQUAL Model", Service Industries Journal, Vol.11, No.3, pp.324-343.

Saraf, W. S., (1997) "Banking Technology: Agenda Ahead", IBA Bulletin, Vol.68, No.4, October-December, pp.153-155.

Sesha Sai, P.V. (1999) "Customer Service – Some HRD Interventions", IBA Bulletin, Vol.XXI, No.2, February, pp.11-16.

Srivastava, A.K. (1994) "Customer Service in Banks: Need for a Marketing Approach" in Bidhi, C. (1994) "Marketing of services" (Ed.), Rawat Publications, New Delhi, pp.25-38.

Sundaram, S. (1984) "Customer Service in Banks at Crossroads", The journal of the Indian Institute of Bankers, Vol.55, No.4, pp.217-223.

Takeuchi, H. and Quelch, J.A. (1983), "Quality is more than Making a Good Product", Harvard Business Review; July-Aug; pp.139-145.

Woodruffe, H. (1998) "Services Marketing" Macmillan India Ltd., New Delhi, pp. 95-105.

Section V: Finance & Accounting

16

GAP IN THE INDIAN AND INTERNATIONAL GAAP

Mohi-ud-Din Sangmi
Syed Javed Iqbal Kamili

Abstract

With the liberalisation and globalization of economy, the scenario of the business in India has undergone a paradigm shift. The investors perceive the opening of boarders for the MNCs to operate the business in the Indian soil critically. Inquisitive investors in these companies are interested in the performance of these companies, which is reflected in their financial statements. Preparation of financial statements is based upon Generally Accepted Accounting Principles (GAAP). These principles have now taken the shape of Accounting Standards. If different companies within a country prepare their financial statements on the basis of different accounting standards, it may reflect ambiguous pictures about the performance of these companies. To do away with this ambiguity, a common accounting language is inevitable. A common accounting language has a direct impact on the resources allocation dynamics of the capital markets. The International Accounting Standards seem to be much awaited answer to the bewilderment of diversity in accounting standards world-wide. It is in this backdrop, International Accounting Standards Committee (IASC) and various international agencies came forward to harmonize accounting practices internationally. India is a member of both the World Trade Organisation (WTO) and International Accounting Standard Committee (IASC). Due to the fact that Indian economy is now being integrated with the global economy, the accounting standards followed in her companies must be in tandem with the International Accounting Standards. In this paper, an attempt has been made to identify the gaps between Indian and International accounting Standards with the objective of suggesting measures towards harmonization of Indian and Global Accounting Practices.

Introduction

The equity markets are not today what they were a decade before. The efficiency of the capital markets has increased due to the liberalisation and globalization of the economy. The opening up of the markets has brought many issues on the forefront, which includes the consolidation of the financial statements and equity accounting. The business stakeholders like shareholders, customers, creditors, employees and governmental bodies are monitoring the companies, which are operating both at national and international levels. Accounting reports provide the information by which millions of investors judge corporate performance and by reference to which they make investment decisions. Everyday, decisions concerning the allocation of resources of vast magnitude are made on the basis of accounting information. The companies are now conscious that they need to go beyond the boarder to grow and compete. The investors for the

MNCs to operate the business in the Indian soil are observing the opening of the boarders minutely. A close competition has emerged among the national and international companies. Interested investors in these companies are keen to know the progress and performance of these companies, which is reflected through the presentation of financial statements. In view of the trans-national operations of the MNCs and the changes in the economic policy of the country, financial statements need to be prepared on the basis of unambiguous and commonly accepted accounting language which is based on Generally Accepted Accounting Principles (GAAP), popularly known as Accounting Standards. As adoption of different accounting principles causes difficulties in making relative evaluation of performance of the companies. This phenomenon hinders the valuation and consequently the decision making process. On the other hand, compressibility of accounting principles facilitates better decision making and enhances the efficiency of resources allocation. A common accounting language would in all probability eliminate the need for a laborious reconciliation process (that of preparing sets of financial statements to comply with different accounting standards). Imagine two MNCs merger candidates sharing a common accounting language, the benefits in such situations are immense, for it directly impacts the merger deal (Rajeshwer 2000).

This necessitates the country's accounting practices should not work in isolation but have to be a part of the world's integrated economy. This is possible when the gap between the Accounting Standards of India is bridged with the accounting standards issued by the IASC. This will lead to harmonisation of Indian accounting standards with the international accounting standards.

International Accounting Standards

The concept of establishing international accounting standards germinated around the turn of the 20th century at the first International Congress of Accountants held at St. Louis in 1904, reached maturity with the formation of the international accounting standards committee (IASC) at the tenth International Congress of Accountants by the leading accounting bodies of nine nations in 1973. Its membership at present is composed of accounting bodies from more than 90 countries. The objectives of the IASC are as follows:-

i) to formulate and publish in the public interest accounting standards to be observed in the presentation of financial statements and to promote their world wide acceptance and observance; and

ii) to work generally for the improvement and harmonization of regulations, accounting standards and procedures relating to the presentation of financial statements (Martin and Roberta 1999).

The IASC has moved forward with great speed and has issued 41 accounting standards (see Appendix 1). The standards are intended to take care of conventional problems such as disclosures of accounting policies, valuation of inventories, depreciation, information to be discussed in the accounting policies, valuation inventories, information to be discussed in financial statements and their consolidation. Accounting treatments of various issues such as taxes, leases, construction contracts, intangible assets, property, plant and equipment, revenue, employee benefits, financial instruments, investments property, segments reporting, government grants, business combinations and so on. Since its inception the IAS has been followed by a number of countries in the World, a survey on the use and the application of IAS (See Appendix II) reveals that in majority of cases, national standards, law and/or practices confirmed with the IAS (Rathore, 1996).

In another survey conducted by Street, Gray and Bryant (1999), it was revealed that 50 percent of companies surveyed were fully complying with all the IASs while 58 percent noted companies with some limited exceptions and only 2 percent of the companies surveyed did not follow the IASs. Over the years, more and more adherents are joining fray of the common accounting code. The German Government proclaimed that it would allow the use of IAS for domestic purpose. France is also considering the issue. More significant is the European Commission's announcement of IAS. The EU announced its support for the IAS in November, 1995. Similarly, the Australian Stock Exchange is pressing for accepting the IAS and Korea has recently informed the IASC that it will move moving closer to using IAS. In Japan, the Tokyo Stock Exchange has decided to accept Singapora and Hong Kong Accounting Standard for cross boarder listing. Which represents an important attitudinal change since both are based on IAS (Rajeshwer 1997).

The Indian Accounting Standards

Being one of the signatories of the IASC, India also realised to formulate its own set of accounting standards on the pattern of IASs. These standards are set, taking into consideration her economic, legal and cultural environment. Thus, the Accounting Standards Board (ASB) was established in April 1977 under the auspices of the Institute of Chartered Accountants of India. The Board has issued twenty three accounting standards, which are listed in the Appendix III. The accounting standards issued are related to, disclosure of accounting policies, valuation, changes in financial positions, contingencies and events accruing after the balance sheet date, net profit or loss for the period, prior period items and changes in accounting policies, depreciation accounting, accounting for construction contracts, accounting for research and development, revenue recognition, accounting for fixed assets, accounting for the effects of changes in foreign exchange rates, accounting for government grants, accounting for amalgamations, accounting for retirement benefits in the financial statements of employees, borrowing costs, segments reporting, related party disclosures, leases, earning per share, consolidated financial statement, accounting for investments in associated companies, consolidated financial statements, etc. Although the standard setting process has been there since 1977 but legally the standards became mandatory only after 1998 when Companies Amendment Ordinance inserted sub-sections (3A) & 3B) to section 211 of the Indian Companies Act, making is obligatory for all the companies to comply with the accounting standards issued by the ASB in India.

The land mark change in the Indian Accounting Standards history has happened on 15th June 2001 when the Government of India for the first time constituted an independent known as National Advisory Committee on Accounting Standards, under sec 2 (210A) of the Indian Company's Act, 1956. This has given a new credence to the accounting standard setting process in India. But despite of the fact that Indian Accounting Standards in India were to be developed in consonance with the international GAAP, however there is a lot of gap between Indian and international GAAP. In the lines that follow, an attempt has been made to highlight the gaps between Indian and International GAAP (accounting standards) with a view to help to bridge such gaps.

Gap in the Indian and International GAAP

There are two types of gaps in the Indian and International Accounting Standards.

1) Difference in the standards
2) Absence of the standards

1) Difference in the standards

Cash Flow Statements: *Accounting Standard No. 3 (IAS 7)*

Cash flow statement is a basic financial statement. It explains changes in cash and cash equivalents during a period. Cash equivalents are short-term, highly liquid investments subject to insignificant risk of changes in value.

Information about the cash flows of an enterprise is useful in providing users of financial statements with a basis to assess the ability of the enterprise to generate cash and cash equivalents and the need of the enterprise to utilize those cash flows. The economic decisions that are taken by users require an evaluation of the ability of an enterprise to generate cash and cash equivalents and the timing and certainty of their generation.

Cash flow statements should classify changes in cash and cash equivalents into operating, investing and financial activities.

Operating may be presented using either the direct or indirect methods. Direct method shows receipts from customers and payments to suppliers, employees and government (taxes), etc. Indirect method begins with accrual basis net profit or loss and adjusts for major non-cash items.

Investment disclosure separates cash receipts and payments arising from acquisition or sale of property, plant and equipment; acquisition or sale of equity or debt instruments of other enterprises (including acquisition or sale of subsidiaries); and advances and loans made to, or repayment from, third parties.

Financing Discloses separately cash receipts and payments arising from an issue of share or other equity securities; payments made to redeem such securities; proceeds arising from issuing debentures, loans, notes and repayments of such securities.

Cash flows from taxes should be disclosed separately within operating activities, unless they can be specifically identified with one of the two headings.

Under the International Accounting standard both direct and indirect methods are used for operating of cash flow statements. But under the Indian Accounting Standard only indirect method is allowed to be used. Moreover, the cash flow statement to be prepared under AS-3 of India differ in approach to the cash flow statement required to be prepared under section 10 of the Companies Act.

Accounting for Retirement Benefits in the Financial Statements of Employers: *Accounting standard 15 (IAS 26)*

The IASC has issued IAS 26 on Employee Benefits, which replaces the existing IAS 19 on Retirement Benefits. While the earlier standard dealth only with employee benefits at retirement, the new standard identifies five categories of benefits and Short-term *Employee Benefits*.

The short-term employee benefits such as wages, salaries and social security contributions, paid annual leave, and paid sick leave, profit sharing and bonuses and non-monetary benefits for current employees. The standard requires an enterprise to recognise these benefits when an employee has rendered service in exchange for those benefits. An obligation under profit sharing and bonus plans results from employee service and not from a transaction with the owner. Therefore, an enterprise recognize the cost of profit sharing and bonus plans not as a distribution of net profit but an expenses.

Post – Employment Benefits

Post – employment benefit plans are formal or informal arrangements under which an enterprise provides post-employment benefits for employees. The standard classifies post-employment benefit plans as defined contribution plans and defined Benefit plans.

Defined Contribution Plans:

Under defined contribution plans, an enterprise pays fixed contribution into a separate entity or fund and has no legal or constructive obligation to pay further contribution if the fund does not hold sufficient assets to pay all employee benefits relating to employee service in the current and prior periods. The standard requires that the contribution to a defined contribution plan should be recognized as an expense when an employee has rendered service in exchange for those contributions. Where such contribution do not fall wholly within 12 months after the end of the period in which the employees render the related service, they should be discounted. The standard requires that disclosure of the amount be recognised as an expense for such plans.

Defined Benefit Plans

Under the defined benefit plans, the enterprise's obligation is to provide the agreed benefits to current and former employees. These plans may be unfunded or they may be wholly or partly funded by contribution by an enterprise and sometimes its employees.

Termination Benefits

Termination benefits are employees benefits payable as a result of either an enterprise's decision to terminate an employee's employment before the normal retirement date, or an employee's decision to accept voluntary superannuation in exchange for those benefits. The standard states that the event which gives rise to an obligation is the termination rather than employee service. Therefore, an enterprise should recognise termination benefits only when it is demonstrably committed to either terminate or provide termination benefits. Where termination benefits fall due more than twelve months after the balance sheet date, they should be discounted.

Equity Compensation Benefits

These are the employees' benefits under which the employees are entitled to receive equity finacnial instruments issued by the enterprise, or the amount of the enterprise's obligation to employees depends on the future price or equity financial instruments issued by the enterprise. The standard requires disclosure regarding nature and terms of equity compensation plans, accounting policy, and amount recognised in financial statements, but does not specify recognition and measurement requirements.

Other long term employee benefits

These are the employee's benefits, which do not fall due wholly within 12 months after the end of the period in which the employees render the related service. These benefits include long-term compensated absences, jubilee or other long service benefits, profit sharing and bonuses payable 12 months or more after the end of the period in which the employees render the related service, etc. the standard requires a simpler method of accounting for these benefits than for post-employment benefits.

Indian Accounting Standard on Retirement Benefits As-15 deals with only retirement benefits in the financial statements of employers. It distinguishes between defined contribution schemes and defined benefit schemes. In respct of the defined contribution schemes, AS 15 requires charging off of the contribution payable by the employer to the statement of profit and loss. However, in respect of the defined benefit schemes, it requires actuarian valuation of the accruing liability.

Accounting for Investment:

Accounting Standard 13 (IAS 40)

This statement deals with accounting for investment in the financial statements of enterprises and related disclosrues requirements. Investments are assets held by an enterprise for earning income by way of dividends, interest, and rentals, for capital appreciation or for other benefits to the investing enterprises. Assets held as stock in-trade are not "investment". A current investment is an investment that is by its nature readily realisable and is intended to be held for not more than one year from the date on which such investment is made.

A long term investment is an investment other than a current investment.

Under the AS 13 disclosure of long term investments should be made at market values. However, there is no requirement to disclose fair values under Indian GAAP for other instruments such as loan and financial hedges. International GAAP requires fair value disclosure of all financial instruments and also provides guidelines on the methods that can be used to compute the fair values.

Moreover, AS 13 requires current investments to be carried at the lower of cost and market value, and long term investment at cost, except for other than temporary declines in values. The aggregate market values of quoted long term investments are required only to be disclosed, not adjusted, whereas international GAAP allows and in some cases requires, long term investment to be marked in market values.

Accounting for the Effects of Changes in Foreign Exchange Rates

Accounting Standard 11 (IAS 21)

An enterprise may have transactions in foreign currencies or it may have foreign branches. Foreign currency transactions should be expressed in the enterprise's reporting currency and the financial statement of foreign branches should be translated into the enterprises reporting currency in order to include them in the financial statements of the enterprises.

Exchange differences arising on foreign currency transactions should be recognised as income or as expense in the period in which they arise in exchange differences arising on repayment of liabilities incurred for the purpose of acquiring fixed assets, which are carried in terms of historical cost, should be adjusted in the carrying amount of the respective fixed assets. The carrying amount of such fixed assets should, be to the extent not already so adjusted or otherwise accounted for, also be adjusted to account for any increase or decrease in the liability of the enterprise for making payment towards the whole or a part of the cost of the assets or for repayment of the whole or a part of the monies borrowed by the enterprise from any person, directly or indirectly, in foreign currency specifically for the purpose of acquiring those assets.

The carrying amount of fixed assets, which are carried in terms of revalue amounts, should also be adjusted in the manner described as above. However, such adjustment should not result in the book value of a class of revalued fixed assets exceeding the recoverable amount of assets of that class, the remaining amount of the increase in liability, if any being debited to the revaluation reserve, or to the profit and loss statement in the event of inadequacy or absence of the revaluation reserve.

Under AS-11, Accounting for the effects of changes in foreign rates, require the capitalisation of exchange differences arising on repayment of liabilities for the purpose of acquiring fixed assets even after the asset is put to use. International GAAP does not allow such foreign currency transactions differences to be capitalised. As a result, significant foreign exchange differences that are expressed under International GAAP are capitalized under Indian GAAP

Accounting for Research and Development

Accounting Standard (AS 8) (IAS 38 intangible assets)

This statement deals wit the treatment of costs of research and development in financial statements.

This statement does not deal with the accounting implications of the following specialized activities:

1. Research and development activities conducted for others under a contract
2. Exploration for oil, gas and mineral deposits
3. Research and development and activities of enterprises at the construction stage.

Research is original and planned investigation undertaken with the hope of gaining new scientific or technical knowledge and understanding. Development is the translation of research findings or other knowledge into a plan or design for the production of new or substantially improved materials, devices, products, processes, systems or services prior to the commencement of commercial production.

Intangible assets, applies to all the intangible assets that are not specifically dealt with in other International Accounting Standards. It applies, among other things to expenditure on: advertising, training, start up and research and development (R&D) activities. AS 8 if modified on IAS basis will enable users to understand among other things, the types of intangible assets that are recognized in the financial statements and the movements in their carrying amount (book value) during the year. IAS 38 also requires disclosure of the amount of research and development expenditure recognized as an expense during the year.

2) Absence of the standards

Income taxes (IAS 12)

IAS 12 among other things provides the following:

accrued deferred tax liability for nearly all taxable temporary differences;

accrued deferred tax assets for nearly all deductible temporary differences if it is probable a tax benefit will be realised;

accrued unused tax losses and tax credits if it is probable that they will be realised ;

use tax rates expected at settlements; and

current and deferred tax assets and liabilities are measured using the tax rate applicable to undistributed profits.

As there is no accounting standard in India on the subject, the deferred tax accounting is absent in India except in the accounts of new multinationals. Companies only account for the tax provisions based on the current tax law. Consequently, there is also no requirement for companies to reconcile their effective and statutory tax rates in the financial statements.

Financial Reporting in Hyperinflationary Economics *(IAS 29)*

Hyperinflation is indicated cumulative inflation over three years to the extent of 100 percent or more. In such circumstances, financial statements should be presented in a measuring unit that is current at the balance sheet date. Comparative amounts for prior periods are also related into the measurement unit at the current balance sheet date. The absence of such standard may affect the Indian companies in super inflationary conditions.

Disclosure in the financial statements of books and Similar financial Institutions *(IAS 30)*

This standard prescribes special disclosures for banks and similar financial institutions. A bank's income statement should group income and expense by nature and should report the principal types of income and expense. Income and expenditure items may not be offset except (a) those relating to hedges (b) assets and liabilities for which the legal rights of offset exists.

The significant role of the banks in the Indian changing economic scenario cannot be underestimated. The separate accounting standard for the banking financial statements and disclosure procedure is a requirement in modern days.

Reporting of interest in Joint venture *(IAS 31)*

A joint venture is a contractual arrangement subject to joint control. These are of three types:

Jointly controlled operations

Jointly controlled assets; and

Jointly controlled entities

There is a need to have a policy document (standard) to be followed in this direction.

Financial Instruments: Disclosure and Presentation *(IAS 32)*

This standard is a must for India now, as the Indian businesses cannot turn a deaf ear to the disclosure and presentation of financial instruments in their annual reports because of the developments in the money i.e. capital market instruments and their significant role in the financial system of the country especially when derivatives are allowed to be traded in India.

Interim Financial Reporting *(IAS 34)*

Although quarterly interm financial reporting is prescribed under SEBI, however, in the absence of a standard which has legal obligation, does not fulfil the objective for which SEBI has enacted this provision.

Similarly, a separate standard for discontinuing operations is the need of the hour.

Impairment of assets (IAS 36)

Impairment of Assets deals mainly with accounting for impairment of goodwill, intangible assets and property, plant and equipment. The standard includes reqirements for identifying an impaired asset, measuring its recoverable amount, recognizing for reversing any resulting impairment loss, and disclosing information on impairment losses or reversals of impairment losses. IAS 36 presdribes how an enterprise should test its assets for impairment which is absent in India at present.

Intangible Assets *(IAS 38)*

Intangible assets, applies to all intangible assets that are not specifically dealt with in other international accounting standards. It applies, among other things, to expenditure on advertising, training, start up and research and development (R&D) activities. Since Indian companies are undertaking huge R&D activities now, such a kind of standard in India is a must in the days to come.

Investment property *(IAS 40)*

An enterprise should recognize normal purchases and sales of financial assets in the market place at trade or settlement date. Certain value changes between trade and settlement dates are recognized for purchase if settlement date accounting is used. Such standard also would help in Indian companies to correctly specify their investment property.

Conclusions

From the above description, it may be concluded that if India has to be a successful player of world economy in the years to come, she has to reform its Generally Accepted Accounting

Principles (GAAP) in tandem with the demands of the International GAAP. Then only the economic reforms undertaken recently can bear fruits for her business organisations and citizens. The gap in the Indian and International GAAP as identified in the above lines needs to be pondered over by the policy planners, accounting and financial regulators and business houses in order to usher in a better, transparent and viable corporate culture.

References

Anuradha Jain (1998). "Employee Benefits", The Chartered Accountant, April, ICAI, New Delhi.

George Gerelik (1999). "The Setting of accounting Standards: Canada, the United Kingdom, and the US". The International Journal of Accounting, Vol 2, 1999.

International Accounting Standards Committee, "Survey of the Use and Application of International Accounting Standards", IASC, Londoh, July 1998.

Jain, C.M. (2000). "Accounting Requirements under Tax Laws and Indian Accounting standards", Indian Journal of Accounting, Vol. XXXI

Martin E. Taylor and Roberta Ann Jones (1999). "The Use of International Accounting Standards Terminology: A Survey of IAS Compliance Disclosure", The International Journal of Accounting, Vol 34, No. 4.

Rajeshwer, Ch. (1997). "Harmonization of Accounting Standards", The Chartered Financial Analyst, October, ICFAI, Hyderabad.

Rathore, Shirin (1996), International Accounting, Prentice Hall of India, 207.

Street, Donna, L, Gray, Sidney, J. and Pryant Stephaine M. (1999). "Acceptance and Observance of International Accounting Standards". An Empirical study of Companies claiming to comply with IASs", The International Journal of Accounting, Vol. 34(1) 11-18

"Treading towards Transparency". The Accounting World, Vol. I(3), March, 2001.

Appendix I

List of International Accounting Standards

IAS 1	Presentation of Financial Statements
IAS 2	Inventories
IAS 3	Replaced by IAS 27 and IAS 28
IAS 4	Replaced by IAS 16 and IAS 38
IAS 5	Replaced by IAS 1
IAS 6	Replaced by IAS 15
IAS 7	Cash Flow Statements
IAS 8	Profit and Loss for the period, Fundamental Errors and Changes in Accounting Policies
IAS 9	Replaced by IAS 38
IAS 10	Events after the Balance Sheet date
IAS 11	Construction Contracts
IAS 12	Income Taxes
IAS 13	Replaced by IAS 1
IAS 14	Segment Reporting
IAS 15	Information reflecting the effects of changing prices
IAS 16	Property, Plant and Equipment
IAS 17	Leases
IAS 18	Revenue
IAS 19	Employee Benefit
IAS 20	Accounting for Government grants and disclosure of Government Assistance
IAS 21	The effects of changing in foreign exchange rates
IAS 22	Business Combinations
IAS 23	Borrowing Costs
IAS 24	Related Party Disclosure
IAS 25	Replaced by IAS 39 and 40
IAS 26	Accounting and Reporting by Retirement benefits plans
IAS 27	Consolidated Financial Statements and Accounting for Investments in Subsidiaries
IAS 28	Accounting for Investments is associates

IAS 29	Financial Reporting in hyper-inflationary economies
IAS 30	Disclosure by Banks etc.
IAS 31	Financial Reporting of interests in joint venture
IAS 32	Financial instruments: Disclosures and presentations
IAS 33	Earning per share
IAS 34	Interim financial reporting
IAS 35	Discontinuing operations
IAS 36	Impairment of Assets
IAS 37	Provision for contingent liabilities and contingent assets
IAS 38	Intangible assets
IAS 39	Financial Instruments: Recognition and Measurement
IAS 40	Investment Property

Source: International Accounting Standards Committee, London, 2002.

Appendix II

Survey on Use and Application of IAS

Standard	IAS adopted as National law of standard	IAS used as basis for National law or standard	National law or standard developed separately & conforming with IAS	No National requirements for National practice conforms with IAS	National law of standard developed separately but does not conform with IAS	No National requirement and National practice does not conform with IAS
IAS 1	6	6	23	5	3	2
IAS 2	5	4	26	2	7	1
IAS 3	6	4	18	10	4	3
IAS 4	6	6	28	5	1	-
IAS 5	6	5	25	7	3	-
IAS 7	6	4	23	9	1	3
IAS 8	6	3	26	3	6	2
IAS 9	6	4	16	9	7	3
IAS 10	6	6	26	6	1	1
IAS 11	6	5	19	9	3	2
IAS 12	6	3	14	8	7	6
IAS 13	6	4	23	10	2	1
IAS 14	6	2	6	7	5	17
IAS 15	4	-	6	12	4	18
IAS 16	6	3	25	9	2	-
IAS 17	6	3	15	4	6	10
IAS 18	6	4	16	12	2	2
IAS 19	5	4	4	9	4	9
IAS 20	5	1	16	12	4	4
IAS 21	6	5	16	8	6	4
IAS 22	5	2	13	9	6	7
IAS 23	6	4	15	12	2	14
IAS 24	3	1	13	7	3	14
IAS 25	3	2	14	10	6	4
IAS 26	3	3	4	9	3	13

Source: IASC Survey on Use and Application of IAS, London.

Appendix - III

List of Indian Accounting Standards

IAS 1	Disclosure of Accounting Policies
IAS2	Valuation of Inventories
IAS 3	Cash flow statements
IAS 4	Contingencies and events occurring after the Balance Sheet Date
IAS 5	Net Profit or Loss for the prior period items and changes in accounting policies.
IAS 6	Depreciation Accounting
IAS 7	Accounting for Construction Contracts
IAS 8	Accounting for Research and Development
IAS 9	Revenue Recognition
IAS 10	Accounting for Fixed Assets
IAS 11	Accounting for the effects of changes in Foreing Exchanges
IAS 12	Accounting for Government grants
IAS 13	Accounting for Investments
IAS 14	Accounting for Amalgamations
IAS 15	Accounting for Retirement Benefits in the Financial Statements of Employees
IAS 16	Borrowing Costs
IAS 17	Segment Reporting
IAS 18	Related Party Disclosure
IAS 19	Accounting for Leases
IAS 20	Earnings per share
IAS 21	Consolidated Financial Statements
IAS 22	Accounting for Taxes on Income

Source: Compendium of Accounting Standards, Institute of Chartered Accountants of India, 2001.

17

CONVERSION OF FINANCIAL STATEMENTS TO US GAAP

L. K. Jha

Abstract

For the last three decades, each country has been following certain accounting practices which were mainly drawn on the pattern of International Accounting Standards. But due to liberalisation, the corporates in India felt the need to mobilise finances from the US markets through ADRS, GDRs etc. which necessitated the Indian companies to prepare their financial statements not on Indian Accounting Principles but on the basis of standards issued by the Financial Accounting Standards Board (USA), popularly known as US GAAP. In this paper an attempt has been made to provide a framework for converting the financial statements prepared on Indian GAAP to US GAAP.

Introduction

In India, the statements on Accounting Standards are issued by the Accounting Standards Board to establish canons that have to be complied with to ensure that financial statements are prepared in accordance with generally accepted accounting principles in the country (hereafter referred to as GAAP). These standards are largely drawn from the International Accounting Standards, as India is a member of the International Accounting Standards Committee (IASC). However, these have been suitably modified to cater to the requirements of the local business.

The challenges that are tackled in the harmonization of the IASC and US GAAP are, therefore, relevant in the Indian context. A significant criticism of International Accounting Standard (IAS) that the standards are too broad and general to ensure that similar accounting methods are applied in similar circumstances or that similar results are consistently achieved may be applied to the Indian GAAP as well. An example is the accounting for expenses incurred under a voluntary retirement scheme, in which the methods used range from pay as you go to amortization of the present value of future pension payments over the period of benefit. In order to improve comparability, the number of alternatives that are allowed in the implementation of the standards would need to be reduced.

In certain peculiar areas, such as banks, insurance companies and public utilities, disclosures in the financial statements are guided by statute, and the accounting policies would require review for restatement under US GAAP. The main difference between Indian and US GAAP is given as follows:-

Area	US GAAP	Indian GAAP
Fixed Assets valuation	Carried at historical cost only downward revaluation is permitted for impairment. Exchange fluctuations on loans taken for, purchase of assets are expensed when incurred	Usually at historical cost. Revaluation of fixed assets is permitted. Exchange fluctuations on loans are capitalised.

Capitalised interest costs	Capitalisation is required	Actual interest costs incurred on the installation or construction of fixed assets are capitalised
Long-lived assets	Assets, including intangibles, are reviewed for impairment, which is measured as the carrying amount of the assets minus the undiscounted future cash flows. Restoration of recognised impairment losses is prohibited	Assets retired from active use of held for disposal are stated at book value or net realisable value.
Research and develop-ment costs	Expensed when incurred (with the exception of development costs in, specialised industries). Purchased R&D may be capitalised if it has alternative future use	Research and development costs may be capitalised if the criteria of technical feasibility of the product, resource availability and existence of market, are met.
Leases	Capital leases reflected in the fixed assets of lessee, operating leases disclosed in footnotes	The asset is reflected in the books of the lessor. The lessee expenses the lease rentals payable during the year.
Inventory valuation (year end)	Carried at the lower of cost or replacement cost	Carried at the lower of cost and net realizable value
Loans (asset)	Impairment of loans is measured as the present value of the expected future cash flows discounted at the loans effective interest rate minus recorded investment in the loan.	Impairment of loans is provided for in accordance with the Reserve Bank of India prudential norms (for the financial sector), or on the basis of recoverability (for others).

	Impairments is considered for each loan individually	
Deferred revenue expenditure	Deferral is not generally permitted	Expenses such as pre-operative expenditure, restricting costs and the costs of voluntary retirement schemes are generally amortised over a period of 3-5 years.
Investments in marketable securities	Securities are individually marked to market with unreaslised gains or losses taken to current income	Current investments are carried at the lower of cost or market value
0-20 percent ownership	Securities are individually marked to market with unrealized gains or losses taken to share holders equity.	Long term investments are carried at cost less provision for diminution in value.
20-50 percent	Equity method of accounting, inter company profit effect is eliminated	Treatment as current or long term based on intention. Dividend income is recognised when received
51-100 percent	Consolidated, using pooling of interest (up to 2001) or purchase accounting. Minority interest is dis-closed as a line item. Inter company transactions are eliminated	Consolidation is not required. Carried at cost, as long term investments, profits of subsidiary are recognised to the extent dividend is received. Losses of subsidiary are nor reflected.
Deferred taxes	Computed under the liability method. Tax expenses for the period is, determined through the changes in the deferred tax assets and liabilities.	Accounted for under the tax payable (flow through method), though the liability method is recommended.

Debt	Long term debt is valued at present value; all other debt at face value	Principally valued at face value
Good will	Taken to balance sheet and amortised, over a period not exceeding 40 years 20 years under consideration	Purchased goodwill is capitalised and amortised over the expected period of benefit or charged against available capital reserves.
Dis-continued operations	Discontinued operations are separately identified segments. Income from operations and gain/loss, on loss, on disposal are disclosed separately	Gain/loss on disposal of segments are shown gross, as extraordinary items

Effect of the differences on the Financial Statements

The differences in the accounting and disclosure requirements under US GAAP and Indian GAAP would impact upon:

Item	Financial Statement Impact
Revaluation of fixed assets	Total assets and shareholders equity is overstated
Capitalisation of exchange fluctuations	Total assets and shareholders equity is overstated
Excess depreciation	Fixed assets, total assets and shareholders equity are overstated. Net income is understated
Deferral of R&D and other expenditure	Total assets, current earnings, overstated with future earnings understated due to the amortisation of expenditures
Impairment of loans and long lived assets	Assets and shareholders equity are overstated
Lease accounting	Fixed assets and total liabilities are under-stated in the books of the lessee

Long term investments	In the absence of consolidation, the revenues, expenses, assets and liabilities of the holding company are understated. Losses of subsidiaries are not reflected. Inter company transactions are not eliminated in the books of the parent company
Deferred income taxes	Net earnings and shareholders equity overstated and liabilities understated.
Completed contract accounting	Total assets, shareholder equity and net income are understated.
Goodwill write off	Total assets, shareholders equity and net income are understated, if amortised over a shorter period

The analysis by investors and others, of the information contained in the financial statements, specific areas of differences and their impact on the financial statements from the viewpoint of an analyst using the Indian Financial statements are given as follows:-

Conversion of Financial Statement to US GAAP

Conversion of financial statements prepared under Indian GAAP to US GAAP requires careful planning in the following areas:-

i) Identification of significant accounting policies that would need to be disclosed under US GAAP and the differences that exist between the Indian GAAP accounting standards and these standards;

ii) The extent of training required within the organisation to create an awareness of the requirements under US GAAP that is required in order to restate the accounts;

iii) Subsidiaries and associate companies and restatement of their accounts is conformity with US GAAP;

iv) Reconciliation of differences arising on restatement to US GAAP in respect of income for the periods under review and for the statement of shareholders equity;

v) Preparing the proforma financial statements, complete with accounting policies and disclosures.

Conclusion

The conversion of financial statement in accordance with the US GAAP may appear to be formidable. However, as the Indian accounting standards are built on the foundation of International accounting Standards, on which a truly global GAAP might be built, there is no cause for concern, as it is easier to restate accounts that are prepared on the basis of IAS (and Indian GAAP) to US GAAP, rather than the other way around.

-0o0-

18

PROFESSIONAL ETHICS FOR ACCOUNTANTS: A FRESH LOOK

Kalim Wahidi

Abstract

In the environment which is ruled by greed and lust for wealth, there is widespread corruption, law breaking, even the unethical practices and immoral acts are being resorted to by certain individuals to attain their spurious motives. In this paper, a cursory look at the ethical practices in business is taken and the author with the help of the codes of conduct issued by the professional bodies at the International and at the national level stresses that there is a tremendous need for the accountants to follow the ethical codes, act honestly with integrity and responsibility, because they are the custodians of trust of those stakeholders of business who have little time, skill and expertise to know whether their funds are used judiciously or not. In this direction, the author reminds the accountants to be accountable to their conscience and answerable to God.

Introduction

Ethics is a branch of philosophy. It seeks to identify and clarify the presuppositions of human conduct having to do with good and evil. It attempts to elucidate the concepts of morality and Justice. According to the American Heritage Dictionary, ethics is the study of the general nature of morals and of the specific moral choices to be made by the individual in his relationship with others.

Ethics and ethical are often used synonymously with morals and moral. The ethics or morality of persons or groups, consists not merely in what they habitually or customarily do, but in what they think it is fitting right or obligatory to do. The word right here is used in the sense of proper or just. Right conduct is incompatible with excess or deficiency in feelings and actions.

Ethical concerns permit all human activities. Business activity is one of the many human activities. It comes within the ambit of ethical concerns, Ethical issues arise in connection with core ethical values of honesty or justice. Ethical concerns are also an issue when actions and decisions affect other people either by helping them or by harming them. Ethical issues also arise when other people's rights and interest are not at stake. Whenever there is a choice to be made between values, or a better and a worse way of doing things ethical judgement is involved.

Ethics concerns itself with good life. It lends direction in the matter of what constitutes good life and how good life should be lived. Some of the components of the good life which each individual will aim for, may well conflict with the dictates or moral law and it is through the application of the moral law, as a regulative instrument of human behaviour, that the good life, though possibly different for each individual and capable of yielding individual happiness. yet conforms to ethics and deserves the title of good life. For the achievement of the good life, as just described, the moral laws are as necessary as the criminal laws. Though the individual is moral by nature. and he is able, through reason, to recognise the variety of moral acts, yet he is constantly driven by animal instincts residual from his evolutionary process -

that may well conflict with the imperatives of morality and reason, and the question is to what extent the observance of the moral laws should be left to individuals or to the applications of a moral code in some universally acceptable form. Good for a man is an activity of soul in accordance with the best and most perfect kind of virtue.

Ethical Trends in Society

Ethical conduct by members of all professions is highly valued in society. Codes of conduct, codes of ethics, and canons of law provide ample evidence of these values. Even without such codes and concerns, professionals should feel a strong obligation to act ethnically because it is in the best interests of both themselves and society.

However, many observers of the contemporary scene are disturbed by what is seen as an increasing blend towards ethical behaviour in society, or at the least a pronounced increase in the impact that unethical behaviour has on daily living. Only a cursory examination of news events is needed to confirm this trend.

Many in the accounting profession are particularly disturbed by recent revelations of wrongdoing in the field of business and finance. Improprieties by those who own, manage or finance business operations can directly damage in the eyes of the public, the accounting profession's reputation for the integrity of its services.

Finance and ethics

In the 21st century the ethical challenges for the professionals working in finance and accounts have multiplied, especially due to the introduction of computer technology in business. Governments all over the world are struggling to formulate laws for identification of place of income accrual in international transactions conducted through internet. Financial matters seem to present many ethical problems. One key reason to this is the sheer pervasiveness of finance. Finance is the language of business; expressed and recorded in accounts. Finance underlines all that a business does. If the language of' finance is corrupted, if it is systematically used in ways that are incorrect or not meaningful or inconsistent, it will be impossible for those managing the business to understand what the business is doing or what it should be doing.

Accounting professionals such as Chartered Accountants are entrusted with the task of looking into fairness of financial recording and reporting. A trade mark of true professionals is their willingness to accept a rigorous set of ethical principles and to follow these principles in the conduct of their daily affairs. The acceptance of these ethical principles requires that professionals maintain a higher standard of conduct than is called by law. Professionals are required to consider carefully the implications of alternative actions and to conduct themselves in a manner that is not only lawful but proper.

Model for Making Ethical Decisions by Accounting Professionals

Donal H. Taylor and G. William Glezen have given the following model that could be used by accounting professionals who face critical ethical questions in their work;

1. Gather or identify all the relevant facts about the situation that rises the ethical issue and creates the need for an ethical decision (determine the nature of the proposed tax deduction).
2. Consider the individuals or groups that will be affected (like stakeholders). In the like case of the questionable tax deduction this may include the client, the CPA, the internal Revenue Service, and society as a whole.
3. Consider the alternative courses of action (include the deduction in the tax return, try to convince the client of the inadvisability of including the deduction in the tax return, resign from the engagement, etc.).
4. Consider the possible results or consequences of each course of action (collect your usual fee but risk an audit by the internal Revenue Service and the possible loss of reputation, lose the tax client but enhance your reputation for integrity and "feel better" about your sense of ethics, etc.).
5. Compare the courses of action with the standards for the ethical questions raised (the code of conduct of your

profession, your own moral principles that evolve front binding life's experience).

6. Select a course of action from among the alternatives.

The model outlined above lays stress on the need to deliberate in a way that the society reposes confidence in the professional accountants.

The Accounting Profession's code of Professional Conduct

Most professional bodies/associations have written codes of professional conduct. Although each profession adopts codes of conduct that are useful in its unique operating environment, there is a general commonality among them.

1. Members of each profession are usually expected to maintain a higher standard of conduct than required by the law. To paraphrase, "it's not necessarily ethical even if it's lawful."
2. The principles, codes, canons, and such of each profession usually contain positive admonishments designed to encourage ethical conduct and project a positive image to the public.
3. Professions also expressly prohibit certain acts on the part of their members. These acts are .simply not compatible with the high ethical standards that ensure quality work, clients' trust, and a positive public image.

The professional codes of conduct stress on the following values :-

1. Responsibility
2. Public Interest
3. Independence
4. Objectivity and Integrity

These values of professional code of conduct have been defined by the International Federation of Accountants (Santas, 1997), in its guide-line on Professional Ethics for the Accountancy Profession. It states:

"*Persons who pursue a vocation in which they offer their knowledge and skills in the service of others have responsibilities and obligations to those who rely on their work. An essential prerequisite for any group of such persons is the acceptance and observance of professional ethical standards regulating their relationship with clients, employers, employees, fellow members of the group and the public generally."*

The ethical requirements of any accountancy body should be based upon the following fundamental principles by which an accountant should be governed in the conduct of his professional relations with others:-

a) **Integrity:** An accountant should be straightforward, honest and sincere in his approach to his professional work.

b) **Objectivity:** An accountant must be fair and must not allow prejudice or bias to override his objectivity. When reporting on financial statements which come under his review he should maintain an impartial attitude.

c) **Independence:** When in public practice an accountant should both be, and appear to be, free of any interest which might be regarded, whatever its actual effect, as being incompatible with integrity and objectivity.

d) **Confidentiality:** An accountant should respect the confidentiality of information required in the course of his work and should not disclose any such information to a third party without specific authority or unless there is a legal or professional duty to disclose.

e) **Technical Standards:** An accountant should carry out his professional work in accordance with the technical and professional standards relevant to that work.

f) **Professional Competence:** An accountant has a duty to maintain his level of competence throughout his professional career. He should undertake work which he or his firm can expect to complete with professional competence.

g) **Ethical Behaviour:** An accountant should conduct himself in a manner consistent with the good reputation of the profession and refrain from any conduct which might bring discredit to the profession.

The Institute of Chartered Accountants of India has formed a code of conduct for its members (ICAI, 1988). The code of conduct given by The Institute of Chartered Accountants of India is formulated in two schedules. There are three parts of the first schedule. The first and second parts deal with professional misconduct in relation to chartered accountants in practice and those in employment respectively. The third part applies to all chartered accountants. Where a chartered accountant is found to be guilty of misconduct listed in any of the three parts of the First Schedule, the Council of ICAI has the power to reprimand the guilty chartered accountant. The Second Schedule lists circumstances in which a chartered accountant in practice would be deemed to be guilty of professional misconduct. It also specifies two such situations in which any member of ICAI would be so guilty.

Conclusion

Ethical concerns for professional accountants are manifold. These problems remain as long as every society practices its own ethical standards. Globalization of economies of individual states with the help of information technology provides a ray of hope in this matter. When the whole world starts functioning as a single Unit or a single society then the political science will be able to pronotmce a dictum on what is universal good and what should be the code of conduct for accounting professionals. The doctrines of religion will provide valuable guidance in this regard.

References

Code of Conduct by Institute of Chartered Accountants of India, Eighth Edition 1988.

De Costa Santas, (1997). Telesophy: An integral system of Philosophy, Minera Press, London.

Taylor, K. H. and Glezen, G. W. Auditing, Integrated Concepts and Procedures, Fifth Edition, John Wiley & Sons, Inc.

Teleosphy, An Integral System of Philosophy by Arnirico da Costa Santos 1997, Minera Press, London.

--oo--

19

EMERGING PATTERN OF TAXING GLOBAL BUSINESSES

Baddar Alam Iqbal

Abstract

Public expenditure has been on the rise continuously with an increase in the functions of the governments of developed and developing countries. Therefore, it has now become the most vital constraint of every government to generate adequate volume of revenues to finance their development needs, sine-quo-non for speedy and gradual rise in the volume and value of business world over. Hence, these days governments are heavily dependent upon taxation as the chief source of revenue for providing effective and efficient infrastructural facilities for accelerating the pace of growth and development. Therefore, it is correct to say that tax is not an evil. it is the price to be paid by the business to the governments to have efficient and effective infrastructural facilities. The present paper is an attempt to highlight the emerging pattern of taxing global business .It also deals with the European Union (EU) scenario and Indian scene with regard to corporate tax rate. Comparison is also made in respect of corporate tax rates among developing economies. Some guide posts have been made for rationalization of taxing global businesses.

Introduction

It has now become the most vital constraint of every government to generate adequate volume of revenue to finance their developmental needs, sine-quo-non for accelerating the volume and value of business world over. Temporary revenues may be obtained by borrowings, but these borrowings eventually have to be repaid. Some revenues are generated from government corporations, administrative and judicial operations, and from other sources, but the major chunk of revenue comes from taxation. Therefore, today governments are heavily depended upon taxation as the chief source of revenue for providing effective and efficient infrastructural facilities for developing the business. Hence, tax is not an evil, it is price to be paid to governments by the business to have and use efficient and effective infrastructural facilities.

In this backdrop, the need of the day is to mobilise public revenue for meeting the rising spendings which is a vital economic function of Sovereign states. Reduction in tax rates often tops the list of electoral promises. World over, among various segments of tax structure, by the governments, one of the most vital facets has been corporate tax as most powerful means of getting or collecting revenue. The worldwide trend has been to slash tax rate in respect of some of the corporate firms so that increased benefits should accrue as a result of a widened tax base, ensuring a rising number of corporates coming forward to pay taxes.

Developed World Scenario

The most significant trend has been that corporates the worldover, pay lesser taxes than individuals and normally these taxes are ranging between 30 to 38 per cent. The maximum tax rate has been in case of Canada with a tax rate figure of 38 per cent during the year 2000 and the lowest tax rate is in case of Germany with a tax rate figure of 30 per cent (table 1).

Table 1: Trends in Corporate Tax Rates in Developed World during the year 20000

Country	Tax Rate in %
USA	35
UK	31
Italy	37
Australia	36
Japan	35
Austria	34
Germany	30
Belgium	33
Denmark	32
Netherlands	35
Canada	38

Source: World Development Report,

Data set out in Table 1 reveals that developed countries have much rationalized tax rates in regard to corporate firms and disparities are not of much alarming nature. So far as the developing countries are concerned the situation is different.

Developing Economies' Scene

There are disparities of alarming nature in regard to corporate tax rate structure. The tax rates are ranging between 15 per cent and 35 per cent. The largest corporate tax rate has been in case of India, Sri Lanka, Argentina and Russian Federation i.e. 35 per cent and the lowest possible corporate tax rate has been in regard to Brazil i.e. 15 percent (table 2). In case of Latin American continent the disparities are of alarming nature. In case of Argentina the tax rate stood at 35 per cent, while in case of Brazil the tax rate has been just 15 per cent. In Southeast Asian economies, whereas, Indonesia and Thailand have tax rate of 30 per cent, South Korea and Malaysia levy 28 per cent tax on corporates. In East Asia, China has the highest corporate tax rate as compared to Hong Kong with a tax rate figure of 16 per cent.

China, South Africa and Thailand have similar tax rates i.e. 30 per cent.

A Comparison

If data on corporate tax rates are compared, the disparities have become of more alarming nature i.e. corporate tax rates are ranging between 15 per cent and 39 per cent. The Canadian corporate firms pay 38 per cent as corporate tax. Those in the United States of America pay 35 per cent. The same in India (without the surcharge).The corporate tax rate in the United Kingdom is 31 per cent. Brazil and the Hong Kong have come up as tax heavens for investors.

Table 2: Developing Economies: How they are Taxed during the year 2000

Country	Tax Rate in %
Argentina	35
Russian Federations	35
Sri Lanka	35
India	35
China	35
China	30
South Africa	30
Thailand	30
Indonesia	30
Malaysia	28
South Korea	28
Hong Kong	17
Brazil	15

Source: World Development Report, 2000-2001

Tax Scenario in EU

During the last more than 3 years, the European Commission(EU) has been doing concerted efforts through the "debate" on the ifs and buts in regard to strategy to harmonise EU tax rates especially at the corporate level. In January 2001, the European Commission did "retreat" its controversial drive to harmonize tax structure for EU (of 15 member countries). There are wider disparities in corporate and other tax rates (30 per cent to 37 per cent) depend on prosperity mentality and expectations of corporate firms in each nation from their respective tax system. This all has resulted into wider political ramifications for ruling parties. But the most pertinent aspect is that now European Politicians are looking for a face saving exit out of the controversial tax policy. Similarly, apart from psychological and social issues. There are wider disparities in regard to individual incomes, firms income ad national wealth of member countries of the EU. According to Bolkestein, EU's Internal Market and Tax Commissioner" the Commission will hence focus on problems encountered by businessmen and individuals in single market".

Tax structure scenario has further become more complicated by EU's proposed expansion as within a decade or two. It could have nearly 25 to 30 members .from the former communist ruled regions of Europe who have languished in poverty. Since the collapse of the USSR during the last year of decade 80s i.e. 1989. they are committed and engaged in the needed process of rebuilding their respective economies as a free market economies and must base on multi-party democracy and must govern on the basis of rule of law.

The Nice summit of EU Government leaders in December 20OQ have failed to identify pragmatic policy options to streamline taxation rates and system especially business tax rates. The Nice summit has also failed to convince members to agree upon on a more qualified majority voting on tax issues. since the present system is handicapped by individual members' veto system.

These days, the EU is offering a single market with 370 million consumers and this particular market is being considered as one the world's highest purchasing power which is also backed by Euro (single currency of EU) which was introduced in January 1999. Since December 1998, the EU is busy in the process of initiating and adopting common rate of corporate taxation to wipe out harmful tax competition among 15 member countries. The coming days looked inviting with prospects of a single currency and a standard Pan-European tax regime. Very recently, in an unprecedented step, the Finance Ministers of 15 member countries have also initiated an idea of a "code of conduct on corporate taxation" which is being considered a one of the most significant stone towards having a common tax regime in regard to business in EU.

Apart from the 15 member nations of the EU aiming at standardising taxation regime, individual nations have also rightly agreed to refrain from competition with fellow members by offering an attractive tax breaks to investors in specific sectors, industries and regions. In this regard, Germany, France and Italy have already started work on a major tax reform exercise in January, 1998. The very purpose of this exercise to bring reforms in respect of their existing cumbersome and heavy tax regime. In the EU the Italy has the highest corporate tax rate as high as 37 per cent. While Germany has the lowest corporate tax rate as low as 30 per cent (table I). On an average German tax payer at corporate level has to bear additional burden of social security costs. This has prompted many corporate firms to shift their manufacturing base outside Germany. Added to this, in recent months of 2001 many cases of tax evasion have been reported in Germany and it is forecasted that tax evasion would become a growing problems EU policies are trying hard to neutralize the negative affect of high degree of taxation by creating and initiating a needed environment of .wealth creation through reducing and rationalizing tax burden on European people and firms.

Indian Scenario

The National council of Applied Economic Research (NCAER) very recently has suggested to Finance Ministry to take into consideration a case of reducing corporate tax rate which is highest in developing world and also even higher than some other developed nations namely the UK(31 per cent), Australia (34 per cent). Belgium (33 per cent). Denmark (32 per cent), and has been affecting India's business community and, therefore, there is an immediate need to take such steps to give fillip to investment and thus to economic growth.

The Council in its review of the economy too concludes that the gross domestic product (GDP) would be growing by nearly 6.15 per cent during the current fiscal inline with official estimates. The NCAER has made out a case for reduction in tax rates. Taking an illustrative case of the surcharge on corporate tax, the Council has said that the surcharge imposed two years was meant to be temporary. If the rate had been decreased and the corporate tax rebate was reinvested. there would have been a rise in real GDP growth which is still the need of the day. While *prima facie* there would be loss of revenue. The additional growth would also improve tax collection which would also reduce fiscal deficit.

In India the investment scenario and climate have been of depressing nature resulted into reduced profit margins. Hence, in the wake of higher energy related costs, the tax rebate would provide the needed stimulus to new investment which is the need of the hour for Indian economy. In this regard the NCAER suggestion is worth considering. According to NCAER a 10 per cent reduction in the existing corporate tax rate would result into an increase of 0.36 per cent in India's gross domestic product (GDP). On the other hand, inflation will go up by a marginal margin of 0.19 per cent, or percentage points. But on the other side, fiscal deficit as percentage of the India's GDP would go down by a margin of 1.5 per cent. Added to this, the Council has also pointed out that the positive impact of additional investment on growth would be obvious as higher demand in a situation of excess capacity would certainly result into additional output further resulted into price stability. The existing trends reflect excess capacity and a fiscal stimulus will result into an additional source of demand and hence output and growth

It is an undisputed fact that there are more beneficial spin-offs or benefits when investment is financed by domestic savings instead of foreign investment entering into a country like that of India. The difference is always because of the impact of the foreign inflow on the exchange reserves and money supply, if they are not properly sterilized. Higher volume of money supply, always implies higher prices (inflation), resulted into lower growth in consumption expenditure. In both the instances of investment and growth, fiscal deficit as a ratio of GDP of India declines as growth materializes without revenue loss.

Conclusion

From the foregoing analysis, it is clear that there has been wider disparities in terms of corporate tax rates both in developed world as well as developing world. But the disparities are of a learning nature in case of developing world ranging between 15 per cent and 35 per cent. In case of India, tax rate is quite high or highest. Hence, there is an immediate need of making existing tax rates more rationalized and competitive so that foreign investment could inflow in developing world in general and India in particular which is the need of the day. Hence, to facilitate a rise in investment expenditure, the Government of India must, give up on immediate tax revenues and must induce the investors confidence through tax cut in regard to corporate firms which is the need of the hour.

-oOo-

20

DIRECT AND INDIRECT TAXES

G. Q. Mir

Abstract

An efficient and effective system of taxation whether direct or indirect creates an atmosphere condusive for economic growth. A new era in the development of tax policy, structure and administration is needed. A transformation not only of tax structure but also of attitudes, habits of thoughts and action is required. The tax paying public should change its attitude towards its tax obligation in the direction of compliance. The government and tax department must begin to look at the tax system as an important determinant of economic efficiency and welfare. The attitude and outlook of the tax administration should undergo a thorough reorientation. After making these observations the author states that a tax system cannot be satisfactorily implemented unless it is generally acceptable to tax payers. Much also depends upon the reasonableness and fairness of the system and upon the tax rates and the manner in which the tax proceeds are used by the government. The author concludes that the scope of direct taxes can be widened by incorporating agricultural income into its ambit. It is also desired to have an indirect tax system which could and should be used to influence the choices of consumers and producers e.g. discouragment of consumption of harmful commodities, conserving scarce resources and protecting environment. This paper addresses all these issues in the Indian context.

Introduction

The Constitution of India does not define the word "tax". Cooley (1994) in his Constitutional Law defines this word as under:-

> *The word "taxes" in its most enlarged sense embraces all the regular impositions made by the government upon the person, property, privileges. occupation and enjoyments of the people for the purpose of raising public revenue.*

Taxes are compulsory payments which citizens in a country are required by law to make to the government for defraying the cost of providing public services and financing transfer payments. Taxation is an important instrument of fiscal policy used for influencing the magnitude and direction of investment in the economy. An appropriate design of tax policy is necessary for stabilizing the price level .promoting economic growth and improving social welfare. In the days of classical economics, taxation served as a revenue collecting device for meeting government expenses for protection of society and the maintenance of administration. Its allocative role was neglected. (Subramaniyam, et al., 1993)

After the emergence of Keynesian economics the functional role of taxation received increasing attention. It was realized that it not merely raises revenue for the government but also affects economic activities via changes in effective demand. It can be used tor achieving a balance between private and public expenditure in order to improve welfare without impairing incentives to private entrepreneurs. Distributive justice along with promotion of economic development through public intervention should be the aim of taxation policy, but with least injury to efficiency in the private sector. Thus taxation policy is intended for the attainment of the following objectives:

i) to meet the developmental programmes and thus strengthen the country's potential;
ii) to control and arrest inflation;
iii) to do away with disparities in income and wealth;
iv) to eliminate and reduce regional disparities.

Taxes in any country are of two types: Direct taxes and Indirect taxes. A direct tax is paid by the person on whom it is legally imposed, while an indirect tax is imposed on one person but paid partly or wholly by another. Income tax and wealth tax are a few examples of direct taxes, whileas sales tax and excise duty are the examples of indirect taxes.

Direct Taxes

In direct taxes the assessee and the taxing authorities are in direct contact and the assessee has to pay tax out of his own pocket. A 'tax consciousness' is developed inasmuch as the payer of such a tax is definitely conscious of making a contribution to the welfare resources of the state and can be expected, also, to take interest in removing governmental waste and inefficiency. In actual practice, however, the taxpayers tax-consciousness might turn to be of the reverse type, whereby they direct their attention to tax avoidance and tax-reduction and develop apathy towards governmental lapses.

One of the chief features of direct taxes is progressive tax incidence. It means that the rate of tax varies with progressive increasing amount of income. That is more rich is subjected to a higher rate of tax as compared to less rich. So no uniform rate of tax to variable incomes. This is based not only on reasonable classification but also on a scientific base. In other words, there is the science of direct taxation, the base of which is a delicately formulated concept of equitable measure of a person's taxable capacity. The word, equity is the very soul or life of direct taxes. Therefore, direct tax is not a haphazard levy to be manipulated by the Finance Minister as a financial talisman for raising revenue.

The principle of progressive tax incidence has thus given birth to the direct taxes as useful but delicate instrument for bringing about a bloodless or non-violent reduction in the disparities of income and wealth among the individual members of human societies.

Direct taxes did not dominate the tax structure of developed countries in the initial stages of their economic development. But today, all the developed countries of the world give much importance to direct taxes as a means of generating savings and promoting further investment. On the other hand underdeveloped countries like India are compelled by low levels of income, inefficient and corrupt administration and greater taxpayer resistance which ultimately inhibit the growth of direct taxes.

Since the inauguration of the Five Year Plans, significant changes have taken place in the structure of direct taxes keeping in view the changing needs and conditions of the nation. Several incentive devices have also been provided in the direct tax structure in order to encourage savings and investments by the individuals and corporations. However, all these measures have failed to achieve the desired result (Subramiyan et al, 1993). The contribution of direct taxes in India is relatively low because they cover only a small segment of the population. The Direct Tax System has become a most unjust and unfair system under which more income / wealth escape tax than that which is taxed in the hands of a few assesses. There is much more untaxed income / wealth in India than taxed income / wealth. This untaxed income / wealth which is called black money income or wealth escapes tax due to concealment / evasion / non-disclosure. Generation of such black income per annum is estimated to be anywhere between Rs. 40,000 crores to Rs. 60,000 crores of which on an average rate of tax at 40 percent, the tax altogether escaping assessment and collection ranges between Rs. 12,000 crores to Rs. 20,000 crores per annum; which is higher than the actual official tax collection under Direct Tax System (Suba Rao, 1992). The socialistic objective of levelling down inequalities of wealth has miserably failed. There is more inequality of wealth than ever before. More than roping of black money into tax net, correct and effective steps of minimizing if not altogether stopping generation of black money are urgently required. Repeated attempts to please the habitual tax evaders by offering amnesty have miserably failed in unearthing even a meagre quantity of total untaxed money / wealth. The connivance between tax evaders and tax enforcement staff cannot be ruled out in this regard. It has been alleged in the several quarters that India is the "highest taxed country" in the world. The high rate of direct taxes have not only inhibited further investment but also encourage tax evasion on large scale which created a parallel economy in the country.

Indirect Taxes

Indirect taxes account for 85.4 percent of the combined tax revenue of the centre and the states. (Tax Reforms Committee, 1991). The incidence of indirect taxes falls on final users of the commodities but the government is collecting it from producers / traders. The plus point in this tax is that it is not paid consciously. So the chances of its evasion and avoidance are less. Indirect taxes are also more condusive to curbing inflation which is inherent in the development programmes of developing economies and promoting productive investment. The indirect taxes are regressive as they fall equally on the rich and the poor alike. Yet the regressive nature of these taxes may be lessened by imposing heavier taxes on luxury and semi luxury goods.

In the interest of revenue and welfare, some objectives should be kept in mind while fixing the indirect taxes. It is best to adopt a tax structure which will leave the relative prices of inputs and consumer goods unchanged and which would least disturb the choices of consumers and producers. This could be done when most of the goods and many services are levied to tax at a single rate or at a few rates. Tax theory and international experience also indicate that this constitutes the best "neutral" way of raising the bulk. of the indirect tax revenue. A single rate tax or a tax with two or three rates is manageable. This was also supported by Indirect Taxation Enquiry Committee (1978) Report. Departure from neutrality can be made but it must be justified. From looking at the tax structure in several countries, one could make the inference that those who advised governments to levy multiple rates on different commodities either had assumed that the state had the right to interfere with the pattern of consumption and it liked and could ignore any loss of welfare involved, or were unaware that unnecessary and unintended interference in the form of tax induced changes resulted in loss of welfare that could and should be avoided.

Secondly, it is generally desired that indirect taxes must fall more heavily on the better off consumers. This re-distributive objective would justify some differentiation in rates. That would mean a departure from neutrality. Therefore, one needs to work out here a compromise between the objectives of efficiency and equity. Thirdly the state, acting on behalf of society must desire to discourage the consumption of harmful commodities such as alcohol and levy higher rates on those commodities. And fourthly higher rates of taxes on some raw materials could be levied to induce economy in the use of those materials in production of consumption for reasons of conservation and protection of the environment.

The criterion of neutrality would suggest that different imported commodities should be subjected to the same rates of taxes as the corresponding domestic products. Here again departure from neurality could be justified on the basis of non-revenue objectives namely living some degree of protection to domestic industry especially in a developing country. For example, in the state of Jammu & Kashmir to give boost to local industry the woollen and silken garments manufactured outside the state can be subjected to high rate of tax.

However, the protective import duties should be just sufficient to give a reasonable degree of protection. They should not be fixed at higher levels merely to raise revenue. While raising import duties may be a convenient way of increasing revenues, the adverse impact of high duties on the efficiency of , resource use in the economy would be disastrous in the long run. It is also to be noted that widely varying rates of protective import duties would lead to inefficient allocation of resources in the economy. The spread of protective import duties must be moderate and the differentiation in rates must be deliberately made for achieving specific economic and social goals (Indirect Taxation Enquiry Committee, 1978).

An efficient and effective system of taxation, whether direct or indirect, creates an atmosphere conducive for economic growth. On the other hand an ineffective and inefficient system tends to generate the phenomenon of black money by encouraging tax evasion, the evil effects of which are disastrous. Direct taxes, in fact, should collect more revenue from those sectors which generate most of the national income. In India, agricultural income was kept outside the purview of direct taxes for a long time in spite of the fact that a large portion of the national income comes from agricultural sector. The high rate of economic growth experienced in Japan has been made possible to a great extent by the active role which agricultural taxation has played in that country. So, in order to provide inter-sectoral equity the agricultural income should also be treated at par with income from other sources. The revenue recovered from agriculture can be spent on institutional improvement and the development of infrastructure in the rural areas.

A tax system cannot be satisfactorily implemented unless it is generally acceptable to the taxpayers. The degree of willingness to comply with the tax law depends firstly on non-economic factors, such as, the social millieu and the degree of civic consciousness on the part of the population as well as threat of prosecution in the breach of law. Given the extent of willingness to comply, the accountability of a tax structure or system will crucially depend on the perception of the population of its fairness in its inherent structure as well as in the system as it operates, the reasonableness of its burden and its simplicity. The manner in which the tax proceeds are used by the government also determines the willingness to bear the burden of taxation. If the tax proceeds are used productively and in the public interest, there would be greater general willingness to pay due taxes. Reasonable rates of taxes are also an important factor in determining the acceptability of the tax system (Tax Reforms Committee, 1991).

In India, the major and minor levies imposed by the centre and the states together add up a substantial total burden which most people are unwilling to bear. In fixing the rates of anyone particular tax, say, the stamp duty or property tax, the existence of and the rates of other related taxes are rarely taken into account. For example, the burdens of stamp duty and property tax are not taken into account in fixing the rates of income tax on rental income from house property, net wealth and capital gains tax. Besides, the impact of inflation on real tax liability is generally ignored with the result that the total tax burden often tends to rise inequitably.

It is also stated that a sound tax system should strive to satisfy the criteria of administrative ease and simplicity, fairness, economic efficiency, certainty and stability. A complicated tax system is difficult to administer (Tax Reforms Committee, 1991). It also spawns disputes and litigation because of differing interpretations of complicated provisions in the tax law. Tax structure and laws in several developing countries had become complicated for two major reasons: The first was the desire on the part of policy makers and their advisers to use the tax system for achieving many objectives besides raising revenue. This has led to the introduction of a plethora of incentive provisions into the tax laws. Since then, there has been a general disillusionment with the effectiveness of the provisions and a growing conviction that the provisions have made the tax laws too complicated to understand and to enforce, leading to much disputation. Also, with many deductions and exemptions the rates of tax had to be higher in order to raise the given amount of revenue.

The second reason why the tax system had become complicated and difficult to enforce was the desire strongly felt in the post war years to make the direct tax systems the main instrument for the reduction of economic inequalities. This had led to the introduction of highly progressive rates of income tax supplemented by a gift tax, a long-term capital gains tax and a net wealth tax. Apart from the impact on incentives which those taxes exerted, the taxpayers began to look for loopholes to minimize the tax burden which they considered to be too high. Attempts at avoidance and evasion were countered by the enactment of additional provisions in law. With this process continuing the law got more and more complicated.

However, the various objectives alluded above still require to be kept in view when simplifying taxes. The issue here is not the desirability of the pursuit of objectives such as economic growth, health and education for all and removal of poverty. Taxes, particularly direct taxes, are only of the possible instruments available to the government to further these objectives. Expenditure policy, interest rate policy, restructuring of the legal framework, public distribution and public works programmes are among the other instruments at the disposal of the government. Any modification of tax provisions which reduces its simplicity, certainty or stability in order to pursue objectives other than the objective of raising revenue required by the public sector in an equitable manner should be undertaken only after carefully weighing the relative merits of alternative instruments (Subba Rao, 1992).

A new era in the development of tax policy, structure and administration is needed. A transformation not only of tax structure but also of attitudes, habits of thoughts and action is needed. The tax paying public should change its attitude towards its tax obligation in the direction of compliance. The government and the tax department must begin to look at the tax system as an important determinant of economic efficiency and welfare. The attitude and outlook of the tax administrators should undergo a thorough reorientation. The tax administration must strive to build a collaborative and not adversarial relationship with the tax paying public. While the tax evaders must be dealt with strictly in accordance with the law, the ordinary taxpayer should receive ample help in fulfilling his tax obligations.

A change in attitude regarding the compliance cannot come about merely through exhortation. A credible structure of sanctions against non-compliance is crucial to the establishment of an equitable system of taxation. Dissatisfaction with the existing system has as much to do with the failure of the system to bring tax offender to book as with the wasteful use of the funds raised by the government through taxes. The success of reform would depend much on government's will in strengthening tax enforcement and bringing the tax department under effective control. Alongwith the need for changes in attitudes, there is also a need for a change in perception. The irrational and unnecessary complicated tax structure and the deficiencies in procedures and laws leading to an excess of expenditure of time and effort on disputes are as much an impediment to growth of the economy as any other component of the earlier policy regime. Thus, it has to be understood that radically transforming the tax structure and improving tax administration is an integral part of structural reform of the economy as a whole which is being attempted by the government.

Conclusion

Thus, it is clear from the above that the importance of direct taxes in India has been declining. Moreover, it has been observed that direct taxes have so far remained ineffective in performing their re-distributive role of rendering inequality in the distribution of income and wealth. Inadequate taxation of the agricultural sector, frequent raising the exemption limit, political bias, inefficient tax administration, existence of non-monetary sector, tax evasion etc., are some of the important characteristic features of Indian direct taxes structure. Unless, these loopholes are rectified, it is hardly possible to have an effective and efficient direct tax structure in the fiscal economy of the government.

It is also desired to have an indirect tax system which is basically neutral. But for achieving some important social objectives, the tax system could and should be used to influence the choices of consumers and producers e.g., discouragement of the consumption of harmful commodities, conserving scarce resources and protecting environment. It is strongly felt that taxation would have to play an important role in checking pollution and ensuring that those who cause it or benefit from activities causing it should be made to pay for the costs of nullifying the effects of pollution and of taking compensatory action. Therefore, in the case of corporations and business in general there might have to be a shift from income taxation to taxation of pollution.

References

Cooley, Thomas, M. (1994). General Principles of Constitutional Law in the United States of America, 4th edn., Boston, Little Brown & Co, p. 61

Government of India, Ministry of Finance, Indirect Taxation Enquiry Committee, Final Report, 1978: 119.

Government of India, Ministry of Finance, Tax Reforms Committee, Interim Report, December, 1978: 15-16.

Subbarao, T. (1992). The Direct Tax System: Suggestions for Structural Changes Leading to Taxes without Tears. Journal of the Indian Law Institute, October-December, Vol. 34, Number 1, 9.

Subrahmanya, K. N. and Sreekantaradhya, B. S. (1983). Taxation and Centre-State Financial Relations, New Delhi, Deep and Deep Publications, p. 53.

21

HARMONIZATION OF COMMODITY TAXATION: A CASE OF VALUE ADDED TAX SYSTEM

Bashir Ahmad

Abstract

The issue of commodity taxation reforms is a matter of considerable significance in a developing country like India because unfair and cascading type of tax system can prove deterimental for overall economic growth in the present era of globalisation. India has not been able to attract heavy Foreign Direct Investment (FDI) because of high inflationary costs, which are mainly tax induced. In this context, the concept of Value Added Tax (VAT) system is becoming increasingly popular worldover as a ready recipe for correcting the various evils of commodity taxation. Against this background, in this paper an attempt has been made to examine the indirect tax reforms undertaken so far in India and also analyse the lessons of such reforms. An attempt has also been made to analyse the possibility of adoption of a comprehensive value added tax system as a means to achieve harmonization in commodity taxation.

Introduction

The international financial and fiscal scenario has undergone a transformational change during the last decade. Even today the winds of change on the economic landscape continue to blow fast as a result of the dynamic interaction of technological advancements, governmental policies and market forces. While the processes of deregulation and liberalization are contributing to improved allocation of financial resources and market efficiency, these changes have simultaneously brought forth issues of judicious fiscal management and its consequences for the overall tax system. These continuing developments have significant implications especially in the fields of taxation; as such tax reforms have assumed a prominent place in the government fiscal agenda during the recent years. The main reasons for the tax reforms can be attributed to the perception that tax system practised sofar was unfair, complex, cumbersome and detrimental to economic efficiency. Tax reforms were also inevitable in the present competitive economic environment for the purpose of widening of personal and corporation tax base and for restructuring commodity taxation through the use of Value Added Tax System, a greatest innovation of century in the field of fiscal policy.

Indian Tax System: Rationale

Though taxation is the main source of revenue to the exchequer and its importance for welfare state like India can never be under estimated. But leaving aside the sense of duty and patriotism on the part of tax payers, taxes are impalatable as they inflict burdens. The progress in income tax structure coupled with a plethora of exemptions, preferences and numerous incentive/ provisions led to the widespread feeling of unfairness. In addition to this, political hurdles and constitutional difficulties experienced by the union government, introducing income tax on the agricultural sector which is basically confined to the states, has made the total tax system of the country unfair, un-equitable, uneconomical and uncertain.

Despite the fact that indirect taxes constitute the main part of the Indian tax system, there happens to be no well defined rationale and fiscal norms for raising revenues on this score. With the existence of multiplicity of excise and sales tax rates, the industrial costs have escalated due to "cascading effect", as such have hampered the industrial growth badly. Consequently, India has turned out to be a high cost economy. However, when the Indian market, which remained dormant and isolated from international markets until the mid 1980's is coming out of cozy cocoons cannot motivate foreign investors if it continues to be a high cost economy on account of defective commodity taxation system. Thus, it becomes imperative for fiscal policy planners and economists, to look into the individual items of indirect tax levies, so as to examine the tax incidence and relative progressivity and regressivety as well as inflationary potential of each tax and then to suggest suitable alternatives in duties which will make the whole structure of commodity taxes less regressive and inflationary. In this context, it is *sine quo-non* for planners to ensure that overall structure of taxation is optimal, simple, transparent, less distorting, broad-based and fair as well as efficient, in terms of certain well defined canons like neutrality, certainty, economy, productivity, equity and diversity.

For attempting any kind of tax reforms, the fiscal planners have to take care of the attitude of the government for having more reliance on indirect taxes of various kinds. This kind of attitude can be perceived from the table 1, which depicts the Central Government tax revenue as percentage of Gross Domestic Product (GDP).

As is evident from the table 1, the ratio of corporation tax and income tax to GDP is either showing fluctuating trend or marginal decline over the period 1990-91 to 1999-2000, while as ratio of indirect taxes (i.e. customs and excise duty) to GDP is showing healthy growth over the same period. Further, the ratio of indirect taxes to GDP ranges between 70% to 75%. Thus heavy reliance an indirect taxes coupled with heterogeneity and all the drawbacks of cascading type of tax system is harmful to the healthy growth of the economy. Under this situation it is difficult for the fiscal decision makers to take in hand the indirect tax reforms because temporarily it may bring down the revenue, which may not be liked by the government on account of political pressures. Thus, present ratio of indirect taxes to GDP should first be brought down and compensating it by increasing direct tax ratio and service tax revenue. After this attempt, the decision regarding overall overhauling/reforms of indirect tax system can be taken in hand.

Table 1: Gross Tax Revenue as %age of GDP

Years	Corporation Tax	Income Tax	Customs Duty	Exercise Duty	Others	Total
1990-91	0.94	0.95	3.64	4.33	0.31	10.16
1991-92	1.20	1.30	3.41	4.31	0.37	10.33
1992-93	1.19	1.06	3.18	4.13	0.43	10.10
1993-94	1.17	1.06	2.58	3.69	0.31	8.82
1994-95	1.37	1.19	2.65	3.70	0.23	9.14
1995-96	1.39	1.32	3.03	3.40	0.27	9.41
1996-97	1.36	1.34	3.15	3.30	0.30	9.45
1997-98	1.32	1.13	2.65	3.16	0.92	9.19
1998-99	1.35	1.15	2.31	3.03	0.29	8.16
1999-00	1.95	1.38	2.47	3.16	0.24	8.80

Source: The Economic Times, New Delhi, August 24, 2001.

Tax Harmonisation: Need and Objectives

With the onset of the continuous process of deregulation, liberalisation and globalisation, the study of commodity taxation has assumed greater significance. In view of this, policy makers and economists are seriously thinking in terms of harmonization and rationalisation of indirect tax structure. Government of India have/had setup indirect Taxation Reform Committee (ITRC) in this direction under the chairmanship of Raja J. Chelliah in 1992. The committee observed that like other countries, the Indian indirect tax system is also suffering from serious ailments and chronic among them is "cascading effect". Since tax competition and tax exporting with resultant distortions and inter jurisdictional conflicts are commonly associated more with indirect taxes, as such harmonization of commodity taxation is now assuming more significance and becoming main focussed area in India.

The need for the harmonization of indirect tax system arises due to number of weaknesses with which existing commodity taxation system suffers from viz. in-elasticity (revenues not corresponding to economic growth and structural changes), complexity (difficulties in administering and compliance), inefficiency (economic distortions), inequity (unequal treatment of individual and businessmen in similar circumstances) and lack of failures (benefits to those who can defeat the system). The rationalization of commodity taxation is also required because multiplicity of rates, exemptions, allowances and deduction under the existing indirect tax system have given birth to chaotic situation wherein not only revenue and equity difficulties arise but also distortions in the capital markets are witnessed.

In this context, the broad aims of indirect tax reforms should revolve around harmonization of tax rates, exemptions, deductions, administrative procedures, centre-state financial relations and distribution of revenue between centre and state governments. Further, it should be aimed at mitigating tax induced inflation, minimizing tax pyramiding and overlapping or snow-balling effect of indirect taxes (i.e. cascading effect). Thus, its study in welfare state like India assumes more significance because it being one of the principal fiscal instruments in raising revenue and securing redistribution.

Value Added Tax : A Recipe for Tax Harmonization

In the wake of rediscovery of the virtue of commodity taxation reforms, economists, viz. Agarwalla (2000), Poddar (1990), Purohit (1993) and Singh (2000) suggested the replacement of commodity taxes like excise and sales tax by a comprehensive VAT, with a view to reducing their "cascading effect". Generally any tax in commodity taxation is related to selling price of a product. In present technological era when raw material passes through various stages and processes till it reaches to ultimate stage, output of the first manufacturer becomes input for second manufacturer, who carries out further processing and supply it to third manufacturer. This process continues till a final product emerges. This product then goes to distributor/wholesaler who sells it to retailer and then it reaches to the ultimate consumer. In case tax is to be paid on selling price of a product the tax burden goes on increasing after every stage or production. As stage of production and/or sales continues, each subsequent purchaser has to pay tax again and again on the material which has already suffered tax. This is called "cascading effect". The adoption of VAT is a ready medicine for eliminating this effect and its purpose is to reduce production costs and prices and thereby to check the induced inflation in the economy.

Under VAT system, tax is imposed on the commodity at each stage in the chain of transactions/processes on the value addition, till the product or service reaches to the final consumer. Thus, it is a tax levied on the value addition of a commodity at each stage of production or distribution carried out by a business firm. Due to various merits of VAT, the system has been adopted in over 60 countries including countries in Africa, Asia, Europe, Middle East, South America and even China. However, it is not simple to operate the VAT in a country like India unless it is levied at national level. The basic problem arises from the question as to how to treat inter state trade. There are three possible alternatives for operating a system of destination based VAT viz. (i) National VAT (ii) State VAT or (iii) Concurrent or Dual VAT.

National VAT is a system of commodity taxation under which both central excise and sales tax is replaced on all goods and services with arrangement for revenue starting. The levy implemented through parliamentary legislation and administered by the union government. State VAT is a system wherein centre leaves it to the states to lay the tax on domestic trade in the form of VAT, replacing both central excise and sales tax. However, a few special excises on sumptuary and luxury items would be levied by the centre. Concurrent VAT is a system in which both centre and states replace their excise and sales tax by VAT and levies VAT independently.

Despite of its drawbacks, VAT is the greatest fiscal innovation of the century achieved in the field of commodity taxation. This can be used as a ready recipe for harmonization of commodity taxation because it has power to cure the chronic disease i.e. "Cascading effect" of traditional commodity taxation on the one hand and can reduce distortions in the incentive structure for investments, exports and production on the other hand. In view of these facts, India introduced VAT in 1985 in a modified form (MODVAT). It was termed as MODVAT as it was restricted only to the manufacturing stage. This is virtually an extension of the provisions of set offs for excise and countervailing duties paid on inputs with the objective of relieving inputs from taxation, without adopting a full fledged VAT. Over the years it has been experienced that though MODVAT has been gradually extended to many items which primarily had been left out, but for a number of reasons, much headway in indirect tax reforms has not been made. Main reasons contributed to this is existence of multiplicity of tax rates which have impeded the adaptation of one comprehensive VAT. In this context endeavours are now being made through negotiations for implementing a uniform VAT across all states in the country. The implementation of recommendations of the committee of State Finance Ministers (1995 and 1998) and of the chief Ministers (1999) provides basis for replacement of sales tax by VAT.

In order to eliminate their problems of multiple rates on outputs and inputs, allowing credit for tax paid on inputs on case to case basis, the union budget 2000-2001 introduced a new scheme of CENVAT in place of MODVAT. Principally there is no difference between two systems, however, procedures have been simplified indeed in CENVAT scheme. It has been restricted to VAT on central excise duty and CVD only. CENVAT credit is available only on inputs used in or in relation to manufacture of a final product and is available in respect of duty paid on capital goods only.

The union budget 2001-2002 took a further step towards rationalisation of exercise duty by retaining CENVAT @ 16% and reducing the three rates of special excise duty to a single rate of 16%. But complete replacement of traditional commodity taxation in near future looks like a dream, as major hurdles of centre-state financial relations is difficult to sort out, because states ae not willing to handover their share to the centre.

Conclusion

To sum up, the gradual opening up of the economy has set in the testing time for efficient fiscal system in general and judicious commodity taxation in particular. The changing economic environment, therefore, calls for more elastic, equitable, transparent, simple, less distorting, broad based and practicable commodity tax system. Since the crucial factor for better economic growth and development is strong financial base, which in turn is to a greater extent dependent on productive and competitive fiscal management. Therefore, before to construct high-tech broad based information super high-ways, the first priority should be given to streamline the lanes and by-lanes of fiscal system in the country, so that the economic growth and development journey which so far was saddled with accidents, may prove smooth in future after complete delegation, liberalization and globalization process takes place. In this context, concerned agencies should place more emphasis on harmonization and rationalization of indirect tax system, with a view to remove all the aspects of a cascading effect, distortions in internal trade and eliminate distortions in resources allocation and administration. Better medicine for tax harmonization in the field of the central excise and the state sales tax system is adoption of the Value Added Tax system. VAT, though is useful prescription for harmonization of commodity taxation but it is not prudent to extend VAT blindly to the retail or even wholesale stage in manufacture process. In this context, it is suggested that for curing the present ills of commodity taxation it is proper to have CENVAT for all commodities at national level and state VAT for chaotic state sales tax.

Reference

Agrawalla, R. K. (2000). "Optimal Commodity Taxation: A Survey of Theoretical Literature". Business Analyst, Vol. 21, No. 1.

Final Report of the Tax Reforms Committee (Chairman Raja J. Chelliah), Government of India, New Delhi, 1992.

Government of India, "Ministry of finance, Interim Report of the Indirect Taxation Enquity Committee (Jha Committee), April, 1977.

Poddar, S. N. (1990). "Value Added Tax at the State level" in M. Gillis, C. S. Shoup and G. P. Sicat (eds.), Value added Taxation in Developing Countries (World Bank).

Purohit, Mahesh C. (1993). Adoption of Value Added Tax in India - Problems and Prospects", Economic and Political Weekly, March 6.

Singh, A. P. (2000), "Indirect Tax Reforms - Moving Towards a single Uniform VAT", PNB Monthly Review, Vol. 22, No. 8.

The Economic Times, New Delhi, August 24, 2001, Delhi Edition.

Union Budget 2000-01and 2001-2002, Ministry of Finance, Govt. of India, New Delhi.

22

FDI - BOON OR BANE?

Mohammad Shafi

Abstract

The farce perception of host countries that foreign investment is shrouded with "foreign domination" is fast disappearing. Now there is wider appreciation both in political and economic circles, for foreign Investment within the framework of a host country's Developmental programme. Today, both capital exporting countries and capital recipient countries have introduced a range of incentives to attract and entice foreign Investment. Tax benefits, Investment guarantees, financial assistance offered by capital exporting countries and the policies adopted by capital recipient countries which include decontrolling the conditions of entry of foreign capital; lifting of restrictions on the remittance of profits and repatriation of capital; and framing of convenient regulations for operation of foreign capital. The benefits of foreign investment to a host country far outweigh the costs tagged with it, particularly in the realm of external economies.

Of late, many countries including India have become cherished destinations for foreign Investment but the actual inflow of FDI to India is far less than the projected approvals. The present paper seeks to analyse and interpret the benefits and costs attached with foreign investment and also puts forth broad spectrum of arrangements available with a host country vis-à-vis its selection of foreign Investment.

Introduction

A large number of countries have been making use of foreign Investment in the form of capital and technology to accelerate the pace of their economic development. Several capital exporting countries, in this regard, have introduced a range of incentives that include Tax benefits, Investment guarantees and the financial assistance to private investors. However, of far greater importance than the measures adopted by capital recipient countries themselves, which have waived off controls over the conditions of entry of foreign capital; lifted restrictions on the remittance of Profits and the repatriation of capital; and framed convenient regulations for operations of foreign capital. Of late, there has been paradigm shift in the attitude of capital recipient countries from the hard lines one to the compromising one. Today, there are hardly any complaints from any private investor claming "the favourable climate" does not exist and the host country no longer sticks to that so caused fear of "foreign domination" (Yadapadithaya: 2000). Presently the host countries are now framing policies in the light of development Planning in which Participation of Private Foreign Capital has a due place in such policies. The execution of development requires reinforced governmental activity and huge investment on the part of international Private enterprise. However, the private investor must correctly visualize the requirements of the host country and must try to fit into the host country's developmental plan. At the same time the concerned government should give a meditative thought to the proposed foreign investment if the risks attached to the business are too high and the returns too low. Thus the Development planning should be devised in such a way so as to fulfill the mutual interests of both the international private investor and the host country.

However, the present malice in the developing economies vis-à-vis private capital participation is marked by a mixture of restrictions and incentives. On the one hand, varieties of governmental regulations restricting foreign investment from entering certain key sectors of the economy; imposing of limitations on the extent of foreign participation in ownership or management specifying conditions on the employment of domestic and foreign labour; limiting the amount of profits and impose exchange controls on the remission of profits and repatriation of capital. The other impediments or deterrents (FDI) may include (a) huge foreign indebtedness of the host country, (b) unstable governments, (c) foreign exchange problems, (d) entry requirements and bureaucracy, corruption and technological pirating. However, on the other hand, a progressive liberalization policy by governments towards private foreign capital has taken place during the last few years. Governments of many countries have realized that the benefits of foreign investment are far reaching and as such have, therefore, devised a package of incentives to foreign investors which include, *inter alia*, assistance in securing information on investment opportunities, establishment of facilities such as industrial estates, Protection tariffs of commodities that compete with those produced by foreign investors, tax concessions and special legislation for the protection of foreign investments.

Types of foreign Investment

Foreign Investment may be categorized into two broad areas, viz, Foreign Direct Investment (FDI) and Portfolio Investment. The Foreign Direct Investment covers the wholly owned subsidiaries, Joint ventures and Acquisitions. While as, the portfolio Investment covers the investments by foreign Institutional Investors (FIIs) and Investments in GDRs and FCCBs.

However, the Present paper is restricted to the study of Foreign Direct Investment(FDI).

Advantages of Foreign Investment

The benefits of foreign investment are manifold. From the stand point of national economic benefit, the essence of the case for encouraging an inflow of capital is that the increase in real income resulting from the act of investment is greater than the resultant increase in the income of the investor. If the value added to output by the foreign capital is greater than the amount appropriated by the investor social returns exceed private retains. (Gerald M. Meier: 2000). With the rise in productivity of foreign Investment there is sure to be some direct benefits to some other income group as mentioned below:

1. **Domestic Labour:** Domestic labour may get higher real wages because of the increase in productivity. This phenomena will increase employment opportunities.
2. **Consumers:** If the investment is cost-reducing in a particular industry consumers of the product may gain through low prices. If the investment is product-innovating consumers benefit from better quality products or new products.
3. **Government:** With the whopping increase in foreign trade resulting from foreign capital Investment, the fiscal revenues of the government are sure to increase.
4. **External Economies:** One of the greatest advantages of foreign investment is likely to come from external economies. Undoubtedly, the direct foreign Investment brings to the host country not only foreign capital but also managerial expertise, technological knowledge, technical personnel administrative organization and product innovations. The stimulus and fervour provided by foreign investment to the domestic industry encourages the domestic capitalists to put in additional investments. Similarly, the other greatest advantage to the recipient country is the access to foreign knowledge and technology. This knowledge is quite helpful in overcoming managerial and technological gap. This knowledge is interpreted in common parlance as *private technical assistance*. The private technical assistance and *Demonstration effect* that are integral features of a private foreign investment have a far proliferating effect on other sectors of the economy (Francis Cherunilam: 2000) towards building the basic infrastructure, it will facilitate more investment. Even if the foreign investment is in a particular industry, it will boost domestic investment by reducing costs and creating demand in other industries. Foreign investment

many lead to training of workers in new other labour force working in other industries or these trained workers may be later employed by local firms.

Dangers of foreign Investment

Foreign investment is bereft with many dangers Foreign capital is inherent with a strong drawback of unabsorptive capacity of the recipient country i,e, the capacity of the country to utilize the foreign capital efficiently. Lack of feasibility projects, infrastructural facilities, technical knowledge inputs, personnel inefficiency or inadequacy of administrative machinery etc. are important factors rendering the recipient country un-absorptive of foreign investment. Moreover, the following criticisms are leveled against foreign capital.

(1) Private foreign capital tends to flow to high profit area rather than to the priority sectors.

(2) The technologies brought in by the foreign investor may not be adapted to the consumption needs, size of the domestic market, resource availabilities, stage of development of the economy, etc.

(3) Through their power and flexibility the multi-national corporations can evade or undermine economic autonomy and control and their activities many be inimical to the national interest of particular countries. (Francis Cherunilam: 2000)

(4) To encourage foreign enterprise, the govt. of the host country may have to provide special facilities to undertake additional public services, extend financial assistance or subsidize inputs. These have a cost in absorbing government resources that could be used elsewhere.

(5) Tax concessions may have to be offered to domestic investor as well so as to save one from scathing political criticism.

(6) One of the serious issues is that which is associated with balance of payments. Pressure of the balance-of-payments position may become unbearable when the foreign debt has to be serviced. If the amount of the foreign exchange required to service the debt becomes larger than the amount

of foreign exchange being supplied by new foreign investments, the transfer mechanism will then have to create a surplus on current account equal to the debit items on account of payment of interest, dividends, profits, and amortization on the foreign borrowings (Domar, 1990).

The indirect dangers pose a greater threat in so far as the likely pressure on international reserves are concerned. The host country will be unwilling to exercise measures on balance-of-payments adjustments in order to find sufficient foreign exchange for the remittance of external suggest import quotas, tariffs and exchange restrictions may suppress the demand for imports but they do so at the expense of productivity and efficiency. The alternative of currency devaluation may cause the country to have the heavy cost of deterioration in terms of trade changes in income distribution (Yadapadithaya: 2000).

Past Trends and Future of FDI in India

Historical retrieval reveals that the earlier governments of independent India were quite receptive of FDI. However, as the socialist vision of India was taking shape under the prime ministership of Jawahar Lal Nehru, the thrust shifted to indigenous industrial development and curbs on foreign investment became more and more rampant with the passage of time. Ironically, the infrastructural base for massive industrialization was quite limited. Now the subsequent governments relied back on FDI. The foreign investors upto the late 1960s had no restrictions on the remittance of profits and dividends. It may be surprising to note that the first comprehensive restrictions on FDI came in late 1960s and early 1970s. This was the period marked with socialist populism of Indira Ghandhi and the swadeshi thinking of the erstwhile Jana sang acquired a tangible form. Morever, MNC enterprises established in the earlier phase had begun to become profitable, profits and remittances had become very sizeable. These seemed even larger after the devaluation of the rupee in 1967. Such a political and economic environment necessitated the restrictions on FDI from 1970s onwards.

The assumption of power by Indira Ghandhi in 1969 brought a spate of restrictions. By the beginning of 1980s the Indian manufacturers came to be identified with technological obsolescence and high costs. However, there was a paradigm shift in India's policy with the assumption of power by prime Minister, Rajiv Ghandhi. Investment cases began to be expedited quickly and by now there was consensus in all political ideologies that foreign investment was a must for India's sustained economic and industrial development.

FDI Infow

Despite the signing of numerous MOUs by Indian firms with foreign collaborators the actual inflow of FDI has lagged far behind the proposals sanctioned. In 1997, the govt. cleared proposals worth $1572 million. The actual inflow was only one fifth of this amount.

India : The cherished destination for FDI

India is a country identified prominently by its abundant natural resources, the rapidly expanding huge market, the availability of talented and skilled man power. In addition to these the change in attitude and the mind set of people willing to strive for the best and get recognized as a major economic power house is an added advantage vis-à-vis foreign investment (Gosh, 1994).

Presently the pace of reforms has accelerated the confidence of foreign investor -- has jumped hıgh as is evidenced by surging in flow of foreign investment both direct and indirect.

According to "FDI Confidence Index' prepared by 'AT Dearney' (an international Management consultancy firm) India occupies a pivotal position as the most favoured destinatıon for the International FDI and its position is 7th after the LIS, Brazil, China, the UK, Poland and Germany, Not-Withstanding its seventh position, the actual FDI received by India is nowhere near the amounts that actually flowed to the top ten FDI receiving countries (Table 1). In 1997 India received FDI worth $ 3.3 billion. The top ten recipients of FDI that year were US $ 91 billion, china $ 45 billion, the U.K. $ 37 billion, France $ 18 billion, Brazil $ 16 billion and Singapore, Sweden and Australia $10 billion each. More-ever, even countries ranked far below India received far more FDI.

As we are quite conversant with the fact that before July 1991 only selective foreign investments and collaboration were permitted by the Indian Government. However, since August 1991 with a massive liberalization programme, the investments from LIS and other countries increased sharply (Tables 1 & 2).

Table 1 : The Top 10 Recipient countries of FDI (1997)		
Rank	**Country (Recipient**	**FDI Received (in US $ billion)**
1.	USA	91
2.	CHINA	45
3.	UK	37
4.	France	18
5.	Brazie	16
6.	Belgium	13
7.	Mexico	12
8.	Singapore	10
9.	Sweden	10
10.	Australia	10

Source: Business India, December, 14-27, 1998, P.48

Table 2: Indo-US Collaborations and Investments in India				
Year	**Number of approvals Indo-US collaborations**		**Approvals US share in (%)**	
	Number	**Total (%)**	**US $ million**	**% to total**
1981	85	21.85	2.51	20.70
1982	110	18.54	5.20	8.00
1983	135	20.05	13.43	22.45
1984	147	19.54	7.52	7.91
1985	197	19.24	32.61	31.66
1986	189	19.75	22.98	27.46
1987	196	22.98	22.76	27.41
1988	191	20.63	67.09	40.52
1989	127	20.99	37.33	19.63
1990	133	19.96	19.22	26.87
1991	177	18.61	75.95	34.80
1992	329	21.84	429.84	31.68
1993	296	20.18	1103.56	39.11
1994	348	18.77	1111.92	38.09
1995	470	20.80	2246.50	21.90
1996	437	18.97	2840.64	27.82
1997	130	21.49	1270.66	22.7782

Source : The Economic Times, January 20, 1999, P.20.

The trend in approvals and actual inflows of FDI reveal that there has been a sharp decline over the years (Table 1.3). The actual in flow of FDI accounted for 47.7% (in US $) of approvals in 1991. The corresponding percentage is just 21.1% in 1997.

Table 3: Foreign Direct Investment : Approvals and Actual Flows

Year	Approvals Rs. Crore	Approvals US $ million	Actual flows Rs. Crore	Actual flows US $ million	Actual inflow
1991	739	325	351	155	47.7
1992	5256	1781	675	233	13.1
1993	11189	3559	1786	574	16.1
1994	13590	4332	3009	958	22.1
1995	37489	11245	6720	2100	18.7
1996	39453	11142	8431	2383	21.4
1997	57149	15752	12085	3330	21.1
1998	*25103	6132	8433	2073	33.8
Total	189968	54,268	41,490	11806	21.7

* Upto Sept 1998, figures are provisional.

Source : Economic Survey, 1998-99, Ministry of finance Economic Division Government of India, 1999, P. 87

The FDI has shown a distinct preference for core sector (1.4). The core sector has attracted FDI worth Rs 101002 crores making a contribution of 57.9% and consumer goods have attracted 13.2% followed by services and capital goods.

Conclusion

There has been a general perception among poorer countries that the costs tied up with foreign investments far outweigh the benefits. Now realities have emerged and there is wider appreciation, both in political and economic foras, of Foreign Investment within the framework of a host country's developmental programme. Today the host country issues investment guarantees as an attraction to foreign investor. The positive inducements leading to better opportunities for profit-making have to be put forth before the foreign investors.

However, while considering measures to seek foreign investment, a developing country would never like to go for indiscriminate foreign investment. The objective is always to derive maximum national economic gain, as assessed by the host country through benefits and costs.

Presently the latest approach to attract foreign investment has been to focus attention on alternative arrangements for procuring foreign capital, management technology and marketing capabilities without the foreign ownership and control. Now the problem for this host country is to evaluate the benefits and lots of alternative arrangements for unputing the investing firms capabilities and then to secure by inducements the best feasible alternative. The alternative arrangements span an entire spectrum. The one extreme end of the spectrum is the traditional form of foreign capital investment involving 100% foreign equity on a life long stay in the host country. This arrangement the host country is feasible only in areas where joint mix of capital, technology and management can not be allocated in any other way. Within this arrangement sometimes would visit on national participation in case of further expansion of the enterprise. Moving still further in the same arrangement, the host county may in order to dilute the foreign equity, ask for a joint venture at a very outset and also establish a limited time span for any foreign equity participation.

However, within the other alternative arrangements the host country may altogether exclude foreign capital and acquire the managerial and technological knowledge through other contractual arrangements. Licensing arrangements, technical services arrangements, engineering and construction contracts and co-production agreements can prove to be of considerable benefit to a developing country.

To sum up, foreign investment is like a double–edged sword; if it is properly allocated and efficiently utilized by the recipient country, it will surely prove to be a boon. And, the indiscriminate use of foreign investment may otherwise, render breed inefficiencies in every other sector resulting in undercutting of growth of the economy and the welfare of the nation hence shall prove a bane.

-oOo-

23

MUTUAL FUND PRODUCT INNOVATION

N. A. Gilkar

Abstract

Mutual Fund (MF), an investment product, mobilizes savings and provides stability to capital market. MF organisations in public and private sector have launched a variety of MF products in the country catering to the specific financial needs of investors. A humble attempt, in this paper has been made to have a glimpse of the present macro scenario and strategies to be evolved to make MF product innovations by a particular organisation. The analysis reveals that because of volatility in the market, assets under management (AUM) of MF industry slashed by 19.83 percent during fiscal ending March, 2001 against a prior period hike posted to the tune of 65.03 percent. The private sector played a convincing role and debt products dominated MF industry. In the first instance, the organisation under study should launch ethical funds coupled with income products, growth products and tax plan products etc. in open-ended as well as close-ended options.

Introduction

Investment is a sacrifice of the certain present value for the uncertain future reward. Mutual Fund (MF) organisations market a variety of investment products in financial sector and have been playing a significant role in mobilising savings and providing stability to capital market. In India MF industry commenced operations in the year 1964 with the setting up of Unit Trust of India (UTI) and public sector Banks and financial institutions began to enter. MF business since 1987. Indian capital market experienced a remarkable change after liberalisation in early 90's and has further promoted development of MFs by widening canvas for private sector operations. The opening of MFs to private sector in the year 1993 has been a harbinger to tougher competition and launching of a variety of MF products more suited to specific financial needs of investors. Of the total 37 players in MF industry, 11 are in public sector including UTI, whereas, the remaining 26 are in private sector, operating more than 350 schemes ending March, 2001. In the formation and working of MFs various key players involved are Sponsor, Trustee, Asset Management Company(AMC) and Custodian. MF industry is regulated by Securities & Exchange Board of India (SEBI). Association of Mutual Funds in India (AMFI) is a self regulatory organisation set up by Mutual Funds.

Innovation, a new way or method of doing things, provides an attractive source of competitive advantage. Innovation has two dimensions as how good a firm is at (i) innovating internally, and (ii) finding external opportunities for innovation (Shah, 1998). Many MF organisations abroad have floated property funds, art funds; energy funds, ethical funds, ecological and environmental or green funds. In USA a MF organisation has launched a religious oriented scheme viz. 'Christian Investment Vehicle' which promises typically avoiding investment in socially undesirable activities (Bansal, 1997). Of late, in India sponsors have been giving a serious thought in designing better MF investment products. MF products are the schemes launched from time to time. MFs both in public and private sector have started adding innovative features in their schemes. In today's environment when investors hesitate to subscribe to MFs, a variety of innovative features can be conceived and products accordingly designed, by effectively involving R&D and Marketing sections of MF organisations, as detailed below. An inbuilt safety and quick liquidity will make MFs a challenge for bank deposits (Bansal, 1997).

- GIC MF, for the first time offered insurance warrants. For prompt liquidity, investors have been offered payment for units being repurchased within 48 hours.
- JM MFs offered investors a choice shifting laterally or jumping from one scheme to another of their schemes at the NAV-based value without any associated cost.
- Alliance MF has promised quarterly declaration of its portfolio as against yearly which was promised for first time by Morgan Stanly
- IDBI MF in its maiden scheme IDBI-I-NIT'95 has ensured investor against capital erosion by offering a safety net. It offers to repurchase NIT'95 at par from original allotees upto 5000 units per investor for one year from the date of allotment.

Again, MFs have been looking at children for innovative business avenues. After UTI, HDFC Mutual Fund in private sector followed the suit. The SBI MF targeted at this segment and accordingly, filed with SEBI for "Children's Fund". As a part of its innovative marketing strategy the fund explored the possibility of staffers 'adopting' schools in various parts of the country to conduct painting and music competitions targeted at students. Parents would be subscribing to the "Children's Fund" given the fact that they want to provide for long term needs of their children (Arun, 2001).

Objectives of the Study

The J&K Bank Ltd., one of the well-performing banks in the country, has been striving for diversification to explore new business opportunities in the context of new millennium challenges. Accordingly, the bank has an agenda for launching of Mutual Fund business. It is in this backdrop that the present paper makes a humble attempt to study the opportunity in the context of present macro scenario and suggest strategies to be evolved by the bank in this regard. The main objectives of the present paper are:

i) To study the sector-wise and product-wise behaviour of Assets Under Management (AUM) of Mutual Funds to have a glimpse of the present macro scenario.

ii) To study the strategies with regard to MF product development, product promotion, accessibility of MF products, etc to be evolved by the J&K Bank.

iii) To study the contributions of academic institutions imparting commerce education in up-bringing manpower for financial services sector.

The Present macro Scenario

The Annexture I analyses sector-wise AUM and reveals that UTI registered a year-on-year (yoy) decline of 24.20 percent at Rs 58017 crores as on March 31, 2001 against an increase of 43.56 percent at the end of previous year. Similarly, AUM of Bank sponsored funds too fell by 57.50 percent at Rs 3333 crores ending March, 2001 against a hike of 43.07 percent recorded for the fiscal 1999 – 2000. However, institutional sponsored funds managed to hold on the AUM position at Rs 3507 crores as on March 31, 2001 as compared to 3570 crores during previous year, registering a nominal decrease of 1.76 percent as against 27 percent upward movement ending March 2000. The public sector (aggregate) AUM, thus, posted a decline of 26.26 percent from Rs 87959 crores to Rs 64857 crores and showed an increase of 42.76 percent during the year 1999 – 2000, from Rs 61612 crores to Rs 87959 crores. Whereas, AUM of private sector funds (aggregate) increased marginally by 2.73 percent from Rs 25046 crores to Rs 25730 crores against a substantial flip of 265.10 percent from Rs 6860 crores ending March, 1999 to Rs 25046 crores ending March, 2000. An introspection of the following analysis clearly indicates that private sector played a convincing role in the MF industry, consequently the share of public sector MFs has declined from 8.98 times (1999) to 3.51 times (2000) which further reduced to 2.52 times ending March, 2001.

Table 1: Sector-wise AUM (%)				
Year	**Public**	**Private**	**Mix**	**Total**
1999	89.98	10.02	8.98 : 1	100
2000	77.83	22.17	3.51 : 1	100
2001	71.60	28.40	2.52 : 1	100

Table 2 similarly, analyses product-wise AUM which reflect that equity funds decreased by 39.74 percent as against debt. funds which increased by 1.56 percent ending March, 2001. However, during the fiscal 1999 – 2000, the equity funds went up by 254.18 percent against a marginal increase of 3.07 percent registered by debt. funds. Liquid funds, on the other hand, exhibited an increase in AUM to Rs 6445 crores from Rs 4597 crores, thus posted a hike of 40.20 percent ending March 2001 against an increase of 28.80 percent ending March 2000. The debt. funds dominated MF industry. The analysis revealed that because of volatility in the market, AUM slashed down by 19.83 percent during the fiscal ending March 2001 against prior period hike to the tune of 65.03 percent. The following analysis further reveales that upward / downward changes have not moved in the same direction in respect of equity, debt or liquid funds during the period under study.

Table 2: Product-wise AUM (%)						
Year	**Equity Funds**		**Debt. Funds**		**Liquid Funds**	
	Content	**Index**	**Content**	**Index**	**Content**	**Index**
1999	24.14	100	70.64	100	5.22	100
2000	51.81	215	44.12	62	4.07	78
2001	38.94	161	53.94	76	7.12	136
Mean	38.30	159	56.23	79	5.47	105

Competitive Analysis and Strategies

Competition is inherent in the market where two or more suppliers of a product operate and it affects every business whether small or big. As such, JK Bank MF, as and when launched, has to identify competitors and study dimensions governing competition. Accordingly, strategies are to be evolved to counter competition and enter the market. JK Bank MF would be entrapped in competition both from within as well as from outside. The financial products offered by the J & K Bank Ltd. in the shape of term and demand deposits would pose a stiff competition from within. The out side competition would be posed by MF products marketed by MF organisations operating in the industry. The status of deposits mobilization by Jammu & Kashmir Bank Ltd for last seven years is analysed in table 3.

Table 3: Deposits Mobilisation in Jammu & Kashmir Bank Ltd.

(Rs. in crores)

Years	Cash Inflows		Cumulative	
March 31	Amount (Rs.)	Joy ± Growth %)	Amount (Rs.)	Index
1997	762.96	-	3658.14	100
1998	1224.31	+60.47	4882.45	133
1999	1561.58	+27.55	6444.03	176
2000	2978.06	+90.71	9422.09	257
2001	1745.99	-41.37	11168.08	305

Source: Annual Reports of the Jammu & Kashmir Bank Ltd.

The above analysis in Table 3 reveals that for the year ending March, 2001 the deposits inflow recorded a negative growth of 41.37% over previous year. Otherwise, the cash inflow from deposits mobilisation by the bank during the earlier years reflected a positive growth of 60.47% (1998), 27.55% (1999) and 90.71% (2000). Similarly, the cumulative deposit mobilisation has also been effected by ± joy growth. The launching of a MF product would definitely have an effect on the Deposit Mobilisation by the bank.

It has also been evidenced by the fact that AUM of Bank sponsored MFs have exhibited a decreasing trend per rupee of public sector MFs as well as the MF industry. AUM of Bank sponsored MFs per rupee of AUM in public sector and MF industry on the whole have slashed sharply from 8.90 to 5.14 and from 8.00 to 3.68 paise respectively during the period under study. The indices in respect of both variables have not moved down in the same speed. The bank sponsored MFs in the whole industry has comparatively shown a faster downward trend.

Table 4: Assets under Management, Bank sponsored MFS per rupee of MF Industry

Years	Public Sector MFs		MF Industry	
	Paisa	Index	Paisa	Index
1999	8.90	100	8.00	100
2000	8.92	100	6.94	87
2001	5.14	58	3.68	46
Mean	7.65	86	6.21	78

Marketing Strategy

"Marketing–mix is the set of marketing tools", says Philp Kotler (1994), "that the firm uses to pursue its marketing objectives in the target market". The concept is equally relevant to MF products like other physical goods or services to be developed and designed, prices determined, product promoted and made accessible in the target market. Each of these tools entail planning by JK Bank MF to match the expectations of potential investors in MF products. "Any competitive strategy is to achieve a sustainable advantage," suggests Michael Porter (1985), "and the customers must continue to view the advantage as of value to them." In doing so it is important to consider goals and strategic options. Initially, the goal of JK Bank MF would be to enter the market, so a proactive approach is required, which could be effected first with newer MF products with differentiation, innovations and attractions. Product innovation would enable JK Bank MF to outperform its competitors by attracting and retaining investors for longer period. Accordingly, the Bank needs to develop an effective in-house R&D cell manned with competent specialists having varied experiences in the field to focus on designing and developing new and unique MF products. Also, the Bank has to be strong enough to find outside the state of Jammu

& Kashmir opportunities for these innovative products. Thus, a close co-ordination established in activities is a pre-requisite to achieve the objective. As for example: Ethical funds, innovative MF product, integrate personal values, societal concerns and investment performance. Socially responsible investing ethical MF products consider investors' financial needs and impact of investment on society and environment. "The primary criteria of ethical funds," says Rajgopalan (2000), "mainly addresses social, environmental and ethical concerns of investors. The underlying idea is to promote economic equity and foster a clean environment." Ethical fund investors include individuals, and institutions such as trusts, universities, hospitals, foundations, non- profit organisations, NGOs, temples, churches, and religious establishments. Ethical MF products thus have great future in J&K in particular and in the country in general with the huge potential investors possessing a deep value - based culture.

At this stage JK Bank MF, needs to attract those investors who like to gain from the fund performance and stay with the Bank MF as such, the Bank should reach out to such investors and convince them of this fact. The need of the hour, thus, is to educate the potential investors about the principles of prudent investing to take a reasonable long-term view of equity investments and not getting swayed by short-term volatility. A wide range of potential investors in J&K state and particularly in Kashmir are not aware of investing their money in MFs. A massive education programme, as a promotional strategy, spread across the state needs, therefore, to be launched and concerted efforts in this regard would effect flow of investment in MFs being launched by JK Bank MF. Equally, the prospective investors have to be made fully aware of their rights and obligations. Thus, the Bank can promote investor education through writings, seminars, conferences, talks, meetings, cultural programmes, painting and music concerts, etc.

JK Bank MF would virtually enjoy an advantage in a small geographical market segment due to its unique geographical position. At macro level, the leading MF organisations are strong to protect their market share. The Bank would need to analyse strengths and weaknesses of other MF organisations already in the market. This analysis would help it to make SWOT (strengths, weaknesses, opportunities, threats) analysis of the bank MF. A SWOT Analysis of the bank has been attempted and given in Fig.(b). JK Bank MF would move into the local market segment on the premise that the potential investors in the geographical area have by then developed a desire through promotion for the MF product and that the competitors have not been in a better position to serve this geographical area as is evident from the fact that UTI has been operating in the market segment for a long period but has not made any remarkable impact. A variety of MF products cater to the needs of various investors according to their financial position, risk tolerance and return expectations. The aim is to provide (i) capital appreciations and (ii) income by periodical distribution of dividend. JK Bank MF may commence MF business by offering equity funds (Growth funds) in order to avoid competition from within and by investing majority of funds in equities the shocks of volatility of capital market would be averted as the MF investors would think of long-term as against short term investment. It would provide capital appreciation over medium to long term period.

Close-ended MF products are listed in the stock exchanges and are traded like equity shares. The unit holders can enjoy liquidity by trading their units in the stock exchange. The JK Bank MF at its infancy stage by launching close-ended Growth product would not directly be involved in repurchase and resale of its units.

Organisational

S	W
♦ A large branch network would give the bank much needed reach	♦ A great deal has to be done with regard to improving customer service
O	**T**
♦ Looking at expanding retail reach in urban and rural areas	♦ Competition from MF organisations will increase with the investors becoming educated in MF operations.

Environmental

Fig A: SWOT Analysis

People (employees) have to perform a very important role in MF product marketing and build and maintain a favourable image of the Bank, provide solutions when problems arise, render special help to investors in need and maintain harmonious relationship. They should be well trained, motivated, enthusiastic and friendly to serve the investors in a pleasant and responsive way and advise them without under or over playing the importance of MF products being launched by the bank. The employees engaged in designing, developing and implementing different marketing programmes, depending on the needs of investors, have to conduct research, collect information, prepare prospectus and offer documents and other material for promotion and their main responsibility is to bring the front office employees upto date on the latest trends in the MF business. Finally, people involved in planning and developmental activities are responsible to design attractive MF schemes and plan strategies for the MF product development. Continuous feedback for different MF products is to be obtained from front office employees so as to incorporate innovative changes in the products to be launched as desired by the investing public from time to time. Process denotes the way a particular action is carried out and, as such, MF product marketing of the Bank should have to take care of all the procedures, mechanisms and activities which are practised when a MF product is being launched. Some of these processes are statutory in nature like SEBI (MF), Regulations '93 which require compliance. SEBI, as the regulatory body, enjoys the freedom of inspecting a mutual fund and take action against it for any violations of any provisions of the regulations (Paingrahi, 1996). While some others are practised to facilitate easy control of different activities. Physical evidence in MF business deserves a special attention as the investors would like to see, evaluate and compare the products before making a purchase decision. In MF products, an investor estimates the amount of satisfaction in terms of return/capital appreciation against a risk especially when he chooses from a variety of MF products flooded in the market by different MF organisations.

This diversification of its operations would provide an opportunity to the J&K Bank to unlock the value of large branch network especially with unparalled access in the state of Jammu &

Kashmir, where each branch is serving an average populations of 29000. It will provide a ready forum for the bank to sell its MF products to the clients belonging to different economic strata of the society at varied geographic locations.

Academic Contributions

The present economic management placed a responsibility upon the commerce education institutions to develop human capital for manning different organisational structure and authority layers in economic institutions. The factors of competition are getting strengthened. The syllabus, accordingly, have to be updated and training programmes meaningfully evolved and adopted to the changing pattern of the economic management. The restructuring by replacing outmoded and outdated courses by professionally acceptable and job-oriented ones to prepare students fruitfully respond to the usage of the time. Thus, without this, it is believed that it would be difficult to tackle the changing currents of market forces.

To assess the role played by academic institutions imparting commerce education in upbringing the trained manpower, it has been noticed that both at college and University levels, the following courses of study enjoy core level position in the instruction structure:

Curriculum		
S.No	***Courses of Study***	***Stage***
1.	Investment Management	B.Com.
2.	Securities Analysis and Portfolio Management	M.Com

Commerce Education in Kashmir has been striving to impart necessary financial services inputs in changing business environment to the students. The commerce students are equipped with tools and techniques which they can use to work effectively, successfully and with high dedication in the field of MF industry.

Conclusion

Private sector has augmented its market share in MF business in the country. At 'launching stage' in MF business the paper concludes, the strategies evolved by JK Bank MF to counter competition and build investor confidence would be: (i) Product promotion with mass education of investors, (ii) Innovative ethical product development; (iii) Pursuing investment objectives through launching 'close-ended' growth product by majority investment of funds in equity preferring capital appreciation. However, the JK Bank MF at 'growth stage' would launch 'open-ended' income products by investing substantial funds in debt. instruments as a majority of investors by then would have been aware of the mutual fund business in the state.

Good corporate governance is equally important for the Jammu & Kashmir Bank MF. Focus on enhancing unit holders value, protecting and improving the value of investments, efficient services to unit holders, disclosure practices as per SEBI regulations and regulatory compliance are the corner stone aspects of the corporate governance. Towards this, the bank would continuously strengthen and upgrade its fund management set-up and capabilities. The monitoring of fund performance in relation to targets, benchmark indices and peer performance are the key issues. The changes in the operating environment have necessitated to promote good corporate in the companies in which the bank would invest and have relationship. Thus, the bank has to continuously monitor the performance of these companies and take post investment actions for safeguarding its investments.

References

Agarwal, G. D. (1992). "Mutual Funds and Investor Interests", Chartered Secretary, Vol. 22(1) 23-24.

Ansari, M.N.A. (1993), "Mutual Funds in India: Emerging Trends", The Chartered Accountant, Vol. 42(2): 88-93.

Arun Iyer (2001). "Mutual Funds Look at Kinds for New Business Avenues". The Economic Times, 11 July; 16.

Bansal, L. K. (1995), "Signals from Annual Reports of Mutual Funds", Chartered Secretary, Vol. 25(4): 822-826.

Bansal, L. K. (1996), "Mutual Fund Investors Taken for granted by AMCs", Chartered Secretary, Vol. 26(4): 365-366.

Bansal, Lalit, K. (1997). Mutual Fund Management and Working, Deep. and Deep Publications, New Delhi.

Barna, S. K. et al. (1991), "A Regulatory Framework for Mutual Funds", Economic and Political Weekly, Vol. 21(5): 55-59.

Barua, S. M. et al. (1991), "Master shares: A Bonanza for large investors", Vikalpa, Vol. 16, (1): 29-34.

Batra, G. D. (1991), "Growth and Performance of Mutual Funds in India", Indian Management Studies (Punjab University), Vol. III, (1&2): 97-102.

Bhatt, N. M. (1990), "Mutual Funds: Some Regulatory issues", The Economic Times, Banglore (ed.), January 7.

Dewan, Sonica (1998), "Mutual Funds in India: A review", Business Analyst, Vol. 19, (1): 105-115.

Fortune (1991), "Mutual Funds and Offshore Funds in India", Fortune India, March 1, 34-40.

Gandhar, V. (1992), "The Changing Pattern of Mutual Funds in India", The Management Accountant, Vol. 27(11): 924-928.

Gopal, Madan (1990), "Mutual Funds in India: The Future is Bright", The Banker, Vol. 60(12): 15.

Gupta, A. P. (1991), "Mutual Funds in India", The Indian Journal of Commerce, Vol. XLIV, (167): 132-134.

Gupta, R. (1989), "Mutual Funds", The Management Accountant, Vol. 24(5): 320-322.

Jain, Deepak, (2001). "Issues in the Area of Marketing" Dossier, The Economic Times, New Delhi, 8-14, June, 23.

Jaiswal, R. (1994), "Money Market Mutual Funds", The Chartered Accountant, Vol. 43(2): 125-128..

Jammu & Kashmir Bank (2001). Trust Newsletter, 40-5.

Jayadev, M. (1995), "Valuation of Mutual Fund Units", The Chartered Secretary, Vol. XXV, (10): 957-961.

Jhamb, M. (1991), "Mutual Funds Dominate Market Capital, Yojana: Vol. 35(23): 8-10.

Kably, Lubna (1995), "New Accounting Values: The Money Managers", Business Standard, 11 May.

Kaura, M. N. et al. (1995), "Performance of Growth Oriented Mutual Funds: An Evaluation". The Applied Finance, Vol. 1, (1-14).

Kumar, S. (1994), "Computing NAVs – When Arithmetic Confounds", The Economic Times, Banglore (ed.) January 6.

Lalwani, S. J. et al (1998), "Mutual Funds: A New Dimension in Emerging Scenario of Financial Institutions", Indian Journal of Banking and Finance. Vol. 21(1): 63-69.

Nagalia, A. K. (1995), "Investment Schemes for the Middle Class and Retired People", in Gupta and Srivastava (Edit), Development of Stock Market in India, Anmol Publications, New Delhi: 105-116.

Paingrahi, M. S. (1996), "Mutual Funds: Growth, Performance and Prospects", Economic and Political Weekly, Vol. 31(12): 765-775.

Panigralin, M.S. (1996). "Mutual Funds: Growth, Performance and Prospects", Economic and Political Weekly, Vol. 31(12): 765-775.

Philip Kotler (1984), Marketing Management, Analysis, Planning and Control, London.

Porter. Michael (1985), "Competitive Advantage: Creating and Sustaining Superior Performance", the Free press, new York.

Raghu, M. R. (1997), "Receipe for Mutual Fund Performance", The Chartered Financial Analyst, Nov. 62-64.

Rajgopalan, T. (2000), "On Ethical Funds, "The Chartered Secretary P.1524.

Rajkumar, U. et al. (1998), "Emerging Trends of Mutual Funds in India" Indian Journal of Banking and Finance, Vol. 21(1): 79-89.

Ramola, K. s. (1992), "Mutual Fund and the Indian Capital Market", Yojana, Vol. 36(24): 11-12.

Sadhak, H. (1991), "The Alternative saving Media", The Economic Times, 30 April 9.

Sahu, R. K., et al (1993), "The Role and Future of Mutual Funds in India", The Management Accountant, Vol. 28(2): 91-93.

Sanghvi, A. R. (1994), "Mutual Funds", The Chartered Accountant, Vol. 43(8): 816-819.

Sarkar, A. K. (1991), "Mutual Funds in India: Emerging Trends", The Management Accountant, Vol. 26, (3): 171-194.

Semi-ud-Din (1992). Presidential address, 45th All India Commerce Conference, Bangalore.

Sengupta, A. K. (1991), "Mutual Fund – Scenario and Strategic Issues", Banking Finance, Vol. IV, (5): 3-8.

Shah, A. et al. (1994), "Performance Evaluation of Professional Portfolio Management in India", CMIE, April 10.

Shah, A. M. (1998). "The Differential Advantage: Sources of development and Their Management", The Business Review, Vol. 14(1&2), 69-79.

Shukla, S. (1991), "Master share and Canshare Performance Evaluation", The Economic Times, December 9.

Vengopalan, S. (1992), "Mutual Funds and company Law", Chartered Secretary, Vol. 22(10): 1003-1004.

Vidyashanker, S. (1990), "Mutual Funds – Emerging Trends in India", Chartered Secretary, Vol. 20(8): 639-640.

-oOo-

Annexture I: Sector wise Assets under Management (Rs in Crores)

	March 31, 1999		± Flow		March 31, 2000		± Flow		March 31, 2001	
		(%)	(Rs.)	(%)	(Rs.)	(%)	(Rs.)	(%)	(Rs.)	(5)
UTI	52,320	77.86	(+)23227	43.56	76,547	67.73	(-)18,530	24.20	58017	64.05
Bank sponsored	5481	8.00	(+)2361	43.07	7842	6.95	(-)4509	57.50	3333	3.68
Instt. Sponsored	2811	4.12	(+)759	27.00	5370	3.15	(-)63	1.76	3507	3.87
Public Sector	61,612	89.98	(+)26,347	42.76	87,959	77.83	(-)23102	26.26	64,857	71.60
Indian Pvt. Sector	1016	1.48	(+)1315	129.43	2331	2.07	(+)1039	44.57	3370	3.72
Predominantly Indian owned JV funds	3040	4.45	(+)6684	219.86	9724	8.60	(-)1104	11.35	8620	9.51
Predominantly Foreign owned JV funds	2804	4.09	(+)10187	363.30	12991	11.50	(+)749	5.76	13740	15.17
Private Sector	6860	10.02	(+)18186	265.10	25046	22.17	(+)684	2.73	25730	2840
MF Industry	68472	100	(+)44533	65.03	113005	100	(-)22418	19.83	90,587	100

Source : Computed and constructed from the AMFI news letters for relevant years.

24

NEW DIMENSIONS OF INSURANCE SECTOR: AN INDIAN PERSPECTIVE

Surjeet Singh Risam

Abstract

In order to reduce the risks, remarkable development in the area of commerce and business took place with the emergence of insurance sector. By being insured, the risk is being multiplied with others. With the passage of time, insurance became a full sector of commerce and got promoted and managed on the lines of other business sector. This paper is an attempt to highlight the recent policy paradigm under taken in the Indian economy so far as the insurance sector is concerned. An humble attempt has been made to highlight the new challenges and opportunities which the Indian insurance companies face in view of the new financial milieu.

Introduction

The insurance sector had its beginnings in the early part of last century, when the concept of insurance came first in the mind of merchants who used to transship their goods from one country to another and during the voyage their business used to suffer huge losses because of various risks including some sea perils or because of the Act of God risks. A time came when those merchants thought to raise a fund to meet such losses. Hence the concept of insurance came into their minds which went on flourishing day by day. By the time insurance Co's came into the existence and started offering various insurance covers under different policies. With the passage of time, insurance companies introduced a lot of many new insurance schemes so that almost everything at present could be covered.

General Insurance in India

The general insurance industry in India has made great strides in terms of physical growth during the last two decades with the premium income in 2001 at more than 10,000 crores. The growth figure indicates maximum potential growth in urban non traditional business (UNTB) along with normal growth in the traditional business which is directly linked with the industrial growth.

The main reason for tremendous potential of UNTB covers are:-

i) by the end of last decade the urban population in India has touched nearly 32% of total population i.e. nearly 32 crores of people will be urban dwellers.

ii) in nuclear families, a major phenomena of urbanization, the risk retention capacity is lowered unlike that of joint families of past.

iii) there has been increase in social tensions and social conflicts due to growing income disparities, unemployment, terrorism and religious fanaticism. This has invariably increased the risk to which urban family is exposed to.

iv) the spread of education and other social factors inculcated western materialistic values and Indian society is far turning into a quasi-legal one.

These factors coupled with growing movement of consumerism will increase further the demand for indemnity insurances. To meet the demand of urban sector, a large number of useful schemes have been introduced in past. At present, this industry has introduced a series of insurance covers starting from a cover of small businessman and a householder to a big industrialist, who can have a full cover to its industry for all movable as well as immovable assets against fire and allied perils. Besides this so many other covers are available for big industrialist as well as for others. Some of which are:-

1. Transit risks to goods during transit under marine insurance policy
2. Machinery breakdown to small and heavy machinery.
3. Burglary and Theft Covers.
4. Storage cum erection covers.
5. Covers to various types of motor vehicles.
6. Workmen compensation cover.
7. Personal Accident and Group personal accident.
8. Medi-claim covers.
9. Cancer insurance.
10. Plate Glass insurance.
11. Jewellers block insurance.
12. Money in transit covers.
13. Pedal cycle insurance.
14. Bhavishya Arogya cover.
15. Public liability insurance (Act liability).
16. LPG Dealers poiicy (Multi Peril).
17. Electronic equipment policy.
18. Contractors all risk insurance.
19. Contractors plant and Machinery insurance.
20. Boiler explosion.
21. Loss of profit (fire & engg) insurance.

Besides above covers there are other covers available for House holders and Shopkeepers as House holders insurance and Shopkeepers insurance under which various covers are available.

On the same pattern, there are various insurance covers available to professionals like lawyers, doctors, agriculturists, horticulturists, etc. These may be:-

1. Professional indemnity.
2. Doctors indemnity insurance.
3. Medical establishment professional negligence policy.
4. Cattle insurance.
5. Hut insurance.
6. Agriculture pump set insurance.
7. Domestic pump set insurance.
8. wind Mill insurance.
9. Horticulture/plantation insurance.

Further, there are covers available to School going children such as students safety insurance.

From the above we observe that at present insurance sector has tried to provide the cover in every field and to all constituents of society. It is also clear, how important is the insurance sector for smooth functioning of industries, banks and other financial institutions. In line with the economic reforms and to give boost to insurance sector, the Government of India appointed a committee on insurance sector reforms under the chairmanship of Mr. Malhotra. On the basis of the recommendations of this committee the opening up of insurance sector to private Indian and foreign companies was started which resulted in the following:-

i) so many new private Indian companies have been allowed to enter into joint ventures with foreign multinational firms to carry out insurance business in India. Consequently, for the insurance sector and for the India's economy at large the approval by the parliament marks a water shed.

ii) like other sectors such as consumer durables or the automobiles, competition is expected to benefit the consumer at large. Not only in terms of wider or big range of covers available but also in terms of much improved service as well as a lower premia. What sets insurance sector apart, however is that unlike other sectors the spin-offs will benefit a part of economy which is in dire need of funds i.e, the infrastructure sector. The huge funds raised by the insurance sector are the long term funds which typically are best suited to investment. In such infrastructure projects which have longer gestation periods.

It is also a fact that now the health insurance has been accorded much importance and it is estimated that only about 2 % of public in India stands covered under medical insurance and health schemes. In this way, insurance sector is able to tap only a marginal % of population and a large area remained unattended so far, in this sector. With the opening up of the insurance Market, some shift from public sector to private sector business firms will take place. However the extent of such "*demand* diversion" effect will depend on the relative cost different across these firms as well as "consumer risk aversion" but it is also possible that a major demand creation effect may occur with no substantial demand diversion with totally new business getting generated owing to aggressive publicity campaigns and hard work, dedication and will of the workers. It is a well known fact that Indian insurance companies despite their limitations are trying to face the new challenges. There is no dearth of dedicated and sincere workers in the industry who will like to take this development as an opportunity rather than a threat: The competition in this sector will help the insurance sector to show further encouraging results as well as help the consumer to get best service as the ultimate aim of the competition is to provide the consumer the best service at most reasonable cost. The positive effects of the competition are visible in the market in various other sectors of economy like banking, consumer durables, air and courier services. The insurance industry has already started to bring in various reforms in its functioning. They are taking up all steps to improve and increase operational efficiency by way of total computerisation in front offices. They are now stressing much on the trainings of staff to enhance their skills and capabilities to match with the higher standards and to bring the attitudinal change.

Suggestions for improvement

1. The present insurance companies will have to work hard for their survival and further progress. They will have to bring the rapid changes as and when desired.
2. It is not only for the insurance to remain careful in their working but the insured has also to remain vigilant and give attention to the insurance products, their terms and conditions/warranties etc. which are the basis for the insurance losses.
3. Opening up of insurance is likely to create hype and euphoria in the initial stages and clients may feel confused in such a market where a lot of players will come out with various schemes backed by a strong advertising. As these can be very crucial in the insurance coverages and admissibility of claims later on. The lower rates should not be the criteria of taking insurance policy rather proper risk management and cost benefit analysis should be the deciding factor.
4. The existing insurance companies will have to keep in mind that when their salesman moves ahead in achieving the customer satisfaction with whatever sincerity, he will have to overcome the following constraints.
   i) complexities of technicalities: It is not possible to tell everything of the insurance to every customer. Moreover the customer is a busy man, he does not find time to go into all the provisions of insurance contract. Hence it will be the skill of salesman which will play a vital role in planning to meet his customers scattered at different places and to impart his knowledge of goods and service in the limited time.
   ii) tariff and market agreements: This will play a vital role in giving the insured minimum premium rate for maximum risks. Here various provisions of discounts available in the tariff will have to be used properly.
   iii) audit and vigilance: A salesman always feels that whatever he tells in the best interest of procuring the business is watched by audit and vigilance. But they should not forget that these departments work

for accuracy and for correct interpretation of rules. Salesman should be always able to remain cautious.

iv) peculiarity of insurance contract: Unlike transactions of sales, the contract is quite peculiar in nature. In a contract of sale, the customer stands more to be defrauded where as in the contract of insurance, the insurer always becomes the victim of fraud of the customer. This is because, the customer being the owner of the property, possesses material facts which he quite often does not disclose for material gains of either getting the premium reduced or getting higher amount of claim. Here the salesman has to be careful and should watch the motive of his customer and check him in the initial stages and control as and when his occasion arises. The customer is never made aware of insurance rule that concealment of material facts can result into the contract to become null and void. Hence, the salesman must clear the same to his customer well in advance.

Insurers will also have to ensure that their sales man do not make any false promises and commitments which lateron will result into a bad impression in the mind of customer against the insurance company. As it is known fact that once impression is lost it is difficult to regain the public sympathy. It is said even though police display placard "Police are your friends, Please help us to help you" still the public in general have opinion that they are being harassed. Similar type of feeling has also crept in the minds of people that insurers do not settle claims on time or, pay adequate quantum, even they being fast and liberal. This agony of the customers is age long and the fears cannot be wiped off with a short cut approach to satisfy the customer. To this, insurers need constant and broad minded approach, they must know the agony of the customer and what are their constraints and how they should equip themselves to reach the requirements of the customer. Insurers should know the FACT by which they can achieve customers satisfaction.

The **FACT** is explained as under:-

F Faith

A Accuracy

C Confidence

T Tact

Faith: The nsurer should have the firm faith and belief in customers satisfaction. In this regard the people in field and also at the desk should work together with heart and soul for achieving the single word, "satisfaction".

Accuracy: Whatever may be the type of customer, his mood and temperament, the customer expects us to be accurate, in giving informations for deciding to insure, be short and to the point as the customer is a busy man and he has no time to hear lengthy matters. Be accurate in charging the premium and offering coverages is another thing that is expected by a customer.

Sales man must remain careful that other competitors are watching him. There must be accuracy of assessment of loss. Hence one must remain in touch with the customer, right from the time of accident; and customer be guided about the claim procedure, and assistance be given in assessment of loss.

Confidence: Customer should have confidence in insurers and its workers. Confidence is not a carbon copy. You will have experience with different types of customers but in general due to your approach, promptness and attention, the customer becomes your best friend, he automatically will appreciate your organization to others but at the same time it should be ensured that other customers also get similar treatment to have their confidence also.

Tact: Sometime while dealing with the clients, one will find rules coming in the way. Sometimes to win your clients, you may ignore some rules. Rules are framed for the good of all. Be tactful in dealing with clients. It is fair to be frank with the customer. In building one's success one should not forget one's official position and duty to the organization lest one would be distracted in the gloom of errors. It is wise to loose a client rather than breaking the rules. A tactful salesman neither breaks the rules nor will loose the customer. It will be the tact, Knowledge, experience and regular touch with the superiors for guidance and the same will bridge the gap. With the coming of private insurers in market, apprehensions have crept in, that government companies would suffer heavy fall in premium income. However, this could be proved wrong if the public sector insurance companies care for customer and provide him utmost satisfaction by acting upon the acdive of Mahatma Ghandi, which is "The customer is the most important visitor on our premises. He is not dependent on us. We are dependent on him. He is not an interruption in our work. He is the purpose of it. He is not an outsider in our business. He is a part of it. We are not doing him a favor by serving him. He is doing us a favor by giving us an opportunity to do so."

Conclusion

From the above description it can be delineated that with the onset of structural adjustment programme in India, the insurance sector got revolutionized. The liberalization policies followed by the Government of India and with the creation of IRDA, the scenario in insurance sector is completely changed. The new players, both foreign as well as domestic have started to establish their shops, the result being that the customer expected to get a choice of quality insurance products and also better customer services. However this poses new challenges for the existing insurance companies (both life and general). If they wish to be in the market, they will have to re-define their objectives, re-design their strategies and re-formulate their policies, programmes and procedures. They will have to act in a pro-active way, face the challenges, tap the opportunities & learn the new rules of the game to survive and thrive in the new business milieu.

-oo-

Section VI: Business and Commerce Education

25

EMERGING DIMENSIONS OF BUSINESS ENVIRONMENT AND IMPLICATIONS FOR COMMERCE EDUCATION

S. Fayyaz Ahmad

Being highly application oriented, the challenge of designing and implementing effective system of commerce and business education is a stupendous task, requiring constant upgradation and restructuring, so as to remain relevant to the changing needs of the industry. With the on-set of new millennium, the task has become more daunting as the forces shaping the business world have reached a critical level where their implications will be realised with amazing speed. These forces are transforming the whole spectrum of society so far as various economic, social, technological, ethical, political, and cultural factors are concerned, as a result of which the business environment is changing at an unprecedented pace, giving birth to a number of trends at national and international levels. The aggregate of these trends demand new roles to be performed by the institutions imparting commerce and business education. The forces of globalisation, privitisation and information technology have started revolutionizing the business environment. These fundamental changes have significant implications for restructuring the commerce and business education as a whole. One of the major forces of change is globalisation, which includes the process of integrating the world into a huge market. For a long time, businessmen believed that home markets were safe and adequate. They never felt the need to explore the overseas market in a big way. The scenario is different now. Globalise or perish is the order of the day. The signing of the WTO agreements by almost all the countries of the world has prepared the ground for an open world market, where only the fittest will survive. Multinational corporations are gradually reaching our doorsteps. The world class products and services are becoming available worldwide. Gone are the days of the protected industries, products, prices and markets. Businessmen face open and global competition. It has tremendous implications on our business education system, which has to cater to the requirements of global business. Our students shall have to be exposed to the international standards and practices so that either they get jobs in multi-national companies or help national companies to attain MNC status. This calls for changing the existing admission process, course curriculum, instructional methods. Course curriculum will have to include topics on globalisation, WTO, Intellectual Property Rights, Trans National Corporations, Foreign Direct Investment, International Trade, Export Marketing, ISO Quality Standards, International Accounting Standards, Cross Cultural Perspectives on HRD, HRM and OB, International Labour Standards etc.. Any complacency in this regard will result in serious negative results for our industry, economy and youth.

The second significant force of change facing the modem business is the privitisation drive. Governments all over the globe have started realising that it is only private sector which has the ability and the responsibility to start, run and sustain the activities of business. In other words, government has no business to be in business. Privitisation is the process whereby activities or enterprises that were once performed or operated by the government and its employees are being now performed, managed or owned by private business and individuals, often with much better results in terms of cost and quality of service. Privitisation achieves these results by replacing government monopolies with the competitive pressures of the market place. To encourage efficiency, quality and innovation in the delivery of goods and services. Privitisation implies liberalisation of regulatory restriction reforms in the labour laws, impetus to stock market function, fierce competition within private sector, disinvestment of government equity from the public sector enterprises etc.

The role of private sector is expanding to include hitherto restricted areas like civil aviation, postal services, telecom, power and insurance. The shift of focus from public sector to private sector has important implications for re-orienting business education. The students of business need to be fully exposed to the rationale of the free business enterprise and the shortcomings of the old command and controlled economy. The standard of business education has to be raised substantially to meet the competitive requirements of the private sector. New courses in the areas of insurance, banking, portfolio management, merchant banking, security analysis, entrepreneurship development, disinvestment policy etc. will have to be designed.

Alongwith globalisation and privitisation, the third important force of change is the technology. The revolutionary breakthroughs in the fields of information technology, bio-technology, automation, miniaturization, convergence artificial intelligence etc. have drastically transformed the business scenario. Information technology in particular, such as electronic mail, electronic data interchanges, video-conferencing, cellular phones, internet, personal computers, automatic teller machines etc. is not only helping business enterprises perform work faster and more efficiently but is also leading to downsizing, flat structure, decentralization of powers, a paperless revolution and mimics of human brains in decision making. The rate of change is so fast in the field of information technology that it is perplexing for the industry to face it properly. Such an information explosion has enormous impact on the business and business education.

Seemingly information technology related business courses like e-Commerce, Management Information System, and Computer Applications in Business will occupy the core of commerce education in future. Infact, a situation is fast emerging where all core business courses will have to be integrated with information technology system and perspectives. Thus a gradual shift from traditional commerce to e-commerce will take place or at least an integration between the two will become inevitable. The implications of this shift in focus in terms of faculty requirements, infra structural support, funding needs, curriculum development are far reaching. The universities shall have to grant more flexibility, autonomy and support to Commerce and Management Department in meeting the challenges of change. Attracting and retaining the professionally competent faculty members in the area of e-commerce and IT will be a big challenge. The Universities and colleges will have to adopt futuristic approach in attracting the IT faculty. The existing faculty shall have to be well versed with information technology and relate it with courses they teach.

Innovative ways of generating funds for building the IT infrastructure will have to be developed.

In addition to these challenges, the business education will have to respond more effectively to the issues of business ethics, corporate governance, social responsibility, quality management, consumerism, environmental pollution, workforce diversity, and service sector expansion. These issues will have to be incorporated in the curriculum in a reasonable manner.

Close collaboration with the industry will be imperative for business education to make it application-oriented and market-relevant. The industry will have to be actively involved in curriculum development, student training, job placement, guest faculty, sponsoring consultancy, executive development and research projects etc. Being autonomous, the role of private sector business education institutions particularly, foreign based institutions, will increase substantially. These institutions may attract best of students and faculty and marginalise the role of state universities. Similarly, the open and distance learning systems armed with the latest means of information technology and flexible procedures will grow fast, to cater to the continuing educational needs of the employees in private sector. Given these anticipated changes, it appears that the existing business education system in general and Commerce education is particular will have to be transformed to meet the challenges of change. There is a growing gap between the skill needs of the industry and what the education system can provide. Therefore today's educational institutions from reputed colleges to prestigious universities, will have to retool their business schools.

26

COMMERCE EDUCATION IN INDIA, USA AND UK: A COMPARATIVE STUDY

G. R. Akhoon

Abstract

Commerce Education develops such skills, attitudes and knowledge in students as are essential for the successful direction of business, trade, industry and service. The present paper attempts to highlight the development, status and position of commerce education in India and its comparative study with USA and Britain at the secondary level. The paper also concentrates on various problems of business education in general. At the end, efforts have been made to give some valuable suggestions to make commerce education effective and objective oriented in India.

Introduction

Commerce education had its origin in private commercial shops. It had never been an important activity of public education. In commerce education also a beginning was made with the teaching of book-keeping. In our own country the Munims used to train prospective munims under their apprenticeship. They took the prospective munims as their assistants and trained them on the job. Later on/with the development of business, the system of individual apprenticeship could not meet the needs of the enlarging business, and private commercial shops started the teaching of book-keeping and accountancy. In the great business expansion many more book-keepers and office workers were needed than the limited number trained by the apprenticeship system or by private shops. The private enterprise felt the need and started to satisfy the demand for trained workers. This resulted in the flourishing of private commercial schools because they provided essential vocational training for commercial jobs.

The teaching of commerce education started in Government schools and Government-aided schools very late. These schools starting the teaching of commerce subjects when people began to demand that vocational preparation for commerce and industry be provided at Government expenses. People insisted that this type of occupational training should not be available only to those who could afford to study in private commercial schools. As a result of this formal schooling, commerce started in Government schools and Government aided schools.

Growth of Commerce Education

Pre-independence era

The history of Commerce education dates back to 1886 with Madras, as' the pioneer State. "The Hunter Commission Report focussed attention on diversified courses as well as practical emphasis. The Government of Madras, under the British regime laid the foundation of commerce education by setting up commercial institutes in Madras. Ten years later the government established two other institutions in commerce education-one in Calicut and the other in Kelala. Upto 1900 A.D. these were the only institutions which were imparting commerce' teaching in the country. The most common subjects which were 'taught in these institutes were: (i) Business Methods, (ii) Letter Writing, (iii) Typewriting and (iv) Shorthand.

In the beginning of the 20th century in 1903, the teaching of commerce was introduced in Calcutta as well as in Delhi, but these institutions were designed as government commercial institutes. Another commercial institute was started in Bombay in 1912. Commerce education at the graduate level was started, in 1931 in Sydenham College of Commerce and Economics in Bombay and Presidency College, Calcutta. Besides, the commercial institutes and commerce colleges, attention was also paid towards professional education in commerce. A bold step was taken in 1920's in the field of commerce and industry by setting up the first Fiscal Commission (1921-22). In the light of the recommendations of the commission, some major improvements were witnessed in the field of iron and steel industry, sugar & tea industry, cotton and jute industry. Hence more and more professional institutions were set up in the field of commerce in twenties and afterwards. Although the Indian Companies Act was passed in 1913; but the real beginning of commercial and industrial growth was witnessed in early twenties as a consequence of the recommendation of the Indian Fiscal commission with emphasis on 'Developmental protection'. Although the Commission recommended for 'discriminating protection', it' really did not fulfil the desires and aspirations of the country. It had limited needs, in which It helped the development of certain industries like iron and steel, cotton textiles, Sugar, tea jute, etc. Real process of industrialization in India started from this period. All professional institutions in India also came up only after this period. The Indian Institute of Bankers was established in 1926 as a consequence of the report of the Young Hilton Commission. The institute of Chartered Accounts of Indian was established in 1934.

In 1944, Institute of Cost Accountants of India was established. This was felt more in order to justify the renewal of grant of protection to different industries, as the grant was dependent on the progress shown. In order to assess this need, the expert knowledge was greatly felt.

Post Independence Development

In the light of the Sargeant Report, commonly known as the Post War Education Development in India, two types of schools were recommended: (i) Academic, and (ii) Technical, though there were a few schools in the country with commerce even before the publication of Mudaliar Commission Report, the real growth and development was experienced in the field of secondary education only after the Mudaliar Commission Report in 1952-53. It recommended for diversified courses in Multi-purpose Higher Secondary Schools. The Ministry of Education, Government of India sponsored many conferences through All India Council for Secondary Education, D.E.P.S.E. for the orientation of the commerce teachers in the country at the secondary level, Several other seminar-cum-training courses were also organised at Taradevi, Simla, Bombay and other places.

Even after the publication of the report of the Secondary Education commission, commerce education could not develop much, as, comrr.erce was introduced in only few schools, the teaching of the skill aspect of the commerce programme was almost neglected. This was due to the following major causes:-

i) Lack of trained teachers.

ii) Lack of equipment and funds

iii) Lack of initiative on the part of teachers.

iv) Lack of co-ordination and administration

v) Lack of adequate instructional materials.

The problem of untrained teachers was most serious. It would be surprising to note that prior to the setting up of the four Regional Colleges of Education at Ajmer, Bhopal, Bhubaneswar and Mysore, there was not a single training college or department of university, which could provide pedagogy m Commerce for the benefit of the commerce teachers. So, the attention of the Government was diverted to this aspect. For the first time in India, Commerce as a pedagogy was started in 1963 in Regional College of Education, Mysore and in 1964 in other three Regional Colleges of Education at Ajmer, Bhopal and Bhubaneswar. These colleges are not only providing regular Commerce training but are also organising Summer School-cum-Correspondence Courses for un-trained commerce teachers of long standing. In addition to the in-service courses, workshops are also organised by these colleges for orienting the commerce teachers of the secondary level.

Besides training, much work has been done in improving the teaching aids and instruction material in various subjects of the commerce programme. Moreover there has been lack of coordination on the part of commerce· educationists with educational administrators for which both the parties are responsible. As a result, commerce graduates to not have any inherent advantage over other graduates and has not been considered in any way superior to other graduates either in the process of obtaining professional qualifications or as a .practitioner in profession. A commerce graduate, at one time, was accepted as a qualified Accountant or secretary, though not a professional accountant or secretary. Time has come now when a commerce graduate is not being accepted even as a qualified book-keeper or as a qualified drafting man in the Secretarial Department.

At the postgraduate level, present system of Commerce education does not fully equip students, either for taking up jobs or for acquiring knowledge of technical or specialized nature. The existing pattern of Commerce Courses does not prepare Commerce postgraduate for competing at all India/State Competitive Examinations like IAS, IFS, IES, ISS and other allied services. For professional jobs, they are not considered professionally qualified. A professional job in accounting needs a Chartered Accountant, a secretarial job needs a Chartered Secretary, a costing job needs a Cost and Works Accountant, and a Financial Analysis planning job needs a Chartered Financial Analyst. Imparting knowledge of Commercial law does not prepare the commerce students to practice at Bar, even if the case pertains to Commercial Law. An M.Com., in general, is considered unfit for managerial positions, allegedly on the ground that he is not exposed to various disciplines, which are essential to management, notwithstanding the fact, that he has studied the subject of management. While Economics, both theoretical and applied is considered to be the core of commerce courses, an

M.Com is not considered fit to teach in Economics Department. In practices, M.Com's are not only segregated, but positively discriminated against for such positions.

After completing post-graduation in Commerce, a student ultimately turns out to be neither a generalist nor a specialist for holding positions compatible with the level of his education. The Irony of the situation is that commerce education is regarded as a specialized branch of .knowledge, which surely, it ought to be, but unfortunately it is not in the employment market.

Status of Commerce Education in the Secondary Schools in India, USA and Britain.

Although commerce education started first at the secondary level in India, the real growth and development in commerce took place at the college level, up to the middle of the 20th century. The pattern of Indian education was such that for a long time commerce was regarded not as a separate discipline even at the college level. It was appendage' to the' department of Economics and thus had no separate identity of its own. The status of commerce education was reduced to an insignificant item of the twin departments Economics and Commerce, in which Economics had an upper hand. So, real progress could not take place in the field of commerce for a pretty long time. It was only after the publication of the reports of the Mudaliar Commission, that' the commerce education was expanded and its status raised. The multi-purpose Higher Secondary Schools were .started with a view to introducing practical" subjects, in various fields, commerce being one of them.

In the beginning when commerce was started, Letter-Writing, Business Methods, Shorthand and Typewriting were the subjects. Book-keeping was not a subject of .the commerce programme at that time. Later on, Book keeping was introduced in the Commerce curricula, which gained importance and popularity in the commerce programme. The Higher Secondary pattern was introduced with a view to developing employable skills among students, who could get jobs after having completed their career in the school. But, this objective was defeated because the commerce education lacked practical orientation. Teaching remained to be theoretical. So, this scheme could not create an impact on the society. There was a great criticism and so a special committee on commerce was appointed by the Government under 'the chairmanship of Dr. V.K.R.V. Rao. He recommended that commerce be introduced at the post-secondary stage, so that students could understand the basic concepts and work on the practical problems. But, this was too harsh an opinion and so it was not accepted and the country continued to have commerce stream at the Secondary and Higher Secondary stages through out the country.

As a consequence of the recommendations of the V.K.R.V. Rao Committee, National Diploma in Commercial Practice (NDCP) was started in the country to prepare qualified and skilled persons needed for the growing economy in the country. This N.D.C.P. Course was for two years after the secondary education and the products coming out of this course were considered to be superior to other commerce. With the rapid growth in the field of trade, commerce, and industry in the last few decades the need for proper education and the availability of the right type of commerce teachers was much felt.' So, for meeting the needs of teachers of practical subjects, a special type of institution was needed. Hence, the government of India entrusted this task to the N.C.E.R.T., an autonomous body, fully financed by the Ministry of education government of India. In the beginning, in collaboration. with the U.S.A., the U.S.A.I.D. expert consultants were also used in India, who helped in launching this project. Any how, the NCERT, and the Regional Colleges of Education could create a good impact on the educational horizon in the country, particularly in the field of commerce. It was only due to this institution, that the pedagogy of Commerce could be started in India. Before 1963, no training college or no University provided training facilities in the field of commerce. Now, right type of commerce teachers are being prepared through regular training, in-service courses, summer-cum-correspondence courses etc. ' Now, the status of commerce education has been better than what it was before; but, even now the practical aspect of the commerce programme, is far from being satisfactory. Much spade work has to be done in this field. The teaching of Shorthand and Typewriting and Office practice' has to be accelerated on a large scale as the future demand will be on a huge scale in these fields.

The recent thinking at the highest level in the Ministry of Education and Planning Commission is for the vocationalisation of commerce education at the secondary stage. If this is implemented, then certainly the practical subjects need to be over emphasised. Work-experience is another trend in the modern educational thinking in India. This has to be introduced at the secondary level so that students learn while they work and also earn something while they work on some useful craft some apprentice-ship training.

Comparative Study of Status of Commerce Education

Commerce education in India and U.S.A. has similarities as well as contrasts. In U.S.A., there has been tremendous change in the field of business education. Previously, this discipline was a new item in the field of education, and like many other subjects including science, it was in its infancy. The commerce discipline was not accepted by other prevalent disciplines even in U.S.A. Hence, for many years, Commerce education had an uncertain status. The same is true in the case of India also. In India, though the commerce teaching was started in 1886, it was not before 1903, that it was introduced at the college stage and 1952 onwards at the secondary stage though there were some conference schools even before 1952. For many years commerce education. India remained as an appendage to the department of economics in several universities, as mentioned earlier. Commerce as .a discipline was recognized by other disciplines very late.

Commerce education at the secondary level is under the rain-shadow area of science and some other subjects. Most of students take up science courses to prosecute their education at the college level and treat commerce education contemptuously due to the poor skills developed in the commerce discipline. The status of commerce education in the country is such that students passing out of schools as well as colleges do not find employment opportunities very certain. Commerce education in India is more' theoretical and less practical, more non-skill and less skill in nature. Hence, it does not do justice with the aspirations of the youth and the community. Hence, it could not make a strong headway in its field. In U.S.A. the growth and popularity of commerce education is due to sociological factors. Commerce education has been structured on the base of social needs. The country has developed tremendously in the field of trade, commerce, and industry particularly after World War II. In U,S.A. commerce education was geared to the needs of the country and aspirations of the students offering the courses. Employment was most secure after their school and college education, as they acquired the required skills during the course of their study. But, in case of India, reverse is the case. Even if some employment opportunities are there which should go to the commerce students, commerce students are not preferred; rather any students from any other discipline is appointed. The plea is that commerce students are less intelligent and less active than other students. This would not have resulted at all, had our commerce education been geared to the needs of business, trade and industry with practical bias. The curriculum in the field of commerce needs drastic changes. It should include those skills which may be employable.

Commerce education both in India and U.S.A. suffered from lack of social recognition in the beginning. But, in U.S.A. it got momentum; as it was possible to gear commerce education to the needs of the business community. But, in India, it needs to be yet recognized. The differences between the two may look to be in terminology, processes and content. But, the goals commerce education are the same. In India, the education in commerce is called commerce education; but, the same is called business education in U.S.A. Business education in U.S.A., is divided into various categories; vocational, pro-vocational and general in character.

Business education is a part of preparing the individual citizen for adjustment in the society. The individual is expected to develop such competence that he is able to become a productive member of the society. The goal in India can become securable only when commerce education at the secondary level becomes vocational in nature.

Towards Reforms in Commerce Education

Although Commerce education has shown tremendous growth in recent years, and use of latest education technology has not been very much adopted, mainly due to paucity of resources and lack or expertise. It is desirable that immediate attention should be paid (or use of various teaching methods which have been devised in western countries for teaching-business courses like those of case studies, simulation exercises. Various audio visual aids, Written exercises and assignments, syndicate discussions, seminars, tutorials and preceptorials. Well established university should take up the responsibilities of leadership projects for training college teachers on regular basis. Organising summer schools once a while does not serve much purpose. Young teachers should give exposure to latest educational technology. Sufficient financial assistance for acquiring latest teaching material and for undertaking faculty development programmes should be made available to universities by the public exchequer. There should be a closer cooperation and collaboration between universities, colleges, professional institutions and polytechnics. Part-time courses may also be designed to suit the need of various courses of students and trained. For designing courses at various levels there should be close collaboration between the universities and business houses. In order to avoid Overcrowding of classes, teacher-pupil ratio should be fixed for sanctioning teaching posts in colleges and Universities in the ratio of 1:20 for B.Com. (pass) course,. 1:12 for B,Com. (Honours) course, 1:8 for M.Com. course can very well be- recommended. For M.Com. course the ratio between senior positions (i.e. Professor and Readers) and junior positions (i.e., Lecturers and Tutors) should not exceed 2:1. Collaboration between industry and universities may be encouraged through academics-business interface programmes under which selected university teachers may be send to business houses for short period (preferably during vacations) and selected business executives are invited as visiting faculty to give courses and guide research. This will encourage sharing of expertise and experience available in academic institutions and business houses for mutual benefit. The main lines on which Commerce education should be reformed may be outlined as under:-

Plus 2 Course

These courses should be so designed as to give an elementary knowledge in the commerce sub-areas of Indian Economics, important institutions controlling, guiding and supporting country's economy, Book-keeping, law governing business entitles and operations and the like and should be so tailored as to suit the employers requirements in regard to subordinate positions of Book-keepers, clerks etc. These courses need not have any training input and should be so drafted and run as to equip the students for either of the two alternatives viz. (i) seeking subordinate jobs and (ii) going for better courses for the purpose of a better career.

Undergraduate courses

Objective of these courses should be to equip the students for lower middle level jobs in some specified profession e.g. tax assistant in a business or a tax consultancy firm, an accountant in a manufacturing undertaking, a local representative of a marketing division, a manager of a small bank branch and the like'. The designing of these courses should aim at providing to the students a better than elementary exposure in various sub areas of commerce along with a reasonably good working knowledge of the profession of his choice duly supplemented by a short period (say one month) on the job training in the choice profession. The organizational work relating to arranging and imparting of the required training should be entrusted to and be handled by the professional councils suggested hereafter.

Entry to these undergraduate commerce courses should however not be restricted to those who clear -plus two with commerce stream and should be kept open to the seekers of higher commerce careers but passed plus 2 with non-commerce streams.

Post-graduate Courses

The University post-graduate courses should be meant for those preparing for senior executive/consultancy jobs in an identified profession and should, therefore, be specified profession such as a PG course in Accountancy, A PG course in Banking, a PG course in Transport, a PG course in Insurance, a PG course in Taxation, a PG courses in Management, a PG courses in co-operatives and the like. These PG courses should cover various aspects of the specific profession in extensive details as per requirements of senior position in the profession and should include an on the job training for three months period. The training should be arranged by the proposed professional council in full cooperation with the Universities and should be so designed and executed as to expose the trainee to the niceties of the business problems, challenges and opportunities facing the senior executives in the profession.

27

VOCATIONALIZATION OF COMMERCE EDUCATION IN J&K- A FARCE IMPLEMENTATION

Zeenat Ara

Abstract

The phenomenal increase in education at all levels in the state has resulted in an increased number of graduates and post-graduates with limited or no jobs, aggravating the problem of the unemployment. The present education setup, therefore, calls for necessary changes so that the mismatch between the requirements of economy and educational system is mitigated. Towards this end, significant changes were made by educational planners at +2 and at undergraduate level. UGC also introduced scheme of vocationalization of education since 1996 at under graduate level. In commerce two vocational courses 1.

Tax Procedure and practices 2. Office Management and Secretarial Practice were introduced along with existing courses of study in colleges where commerce education is provided. The objective of the present paper is to analyze the critical issues involved in the implementation of the scheme in the state especially in the valley. The scheme has not achieved its basic objective due to the absence of on-the-job training, Non involvement of industrial establishments / concerned institutions, hasty decision in the selection of the courses etc. Attention of concerned authorities is drawn either to incorporate major changes suggested in this paper or to say good bye to this scheme without wasting time and resources. Multi –pronged approach is also recommended to strengthen the overall commerce education to meet the challenges of changing business and economic scenario.

Introduction

To begin with the words of Albert Einstein, "If mankind is to survive, then we need a completely new way of thinking". And to evolve a new way of thinking, there is no safe and easy way to follow than the way of Education" (Hasan, 1987). As a result of development programs in educational sector, large number of educational institutions have been setup at various levels in the state. The adoption of National Policy of Education 1986 and revised Program of Action 1992 laid constant thrust on univeresalization of education. There has been a phenomenal increase in the higher education also. Though, it looked encouraging, yet disturbing feature is that there is large number of educated un-employed youth wandering hither and thither for want of jobs. The inherited single-track system of education has resulted in alarming increase of graduates and postgraduates with limited or no jobs in their respective fields. So it is evident what is taught to the students does not help them in finding worth while jobs. It has, on the one hand generated dissatisfaction among the youth and their parents, the sign of which are already visible and on the other it posed serious problems to the education planners/academicians/administrative authorities. Teachers cannot absolve themselves from their responsibility just by saying that their job is to impart education only, and are not concerned with the employment part. The educational planners/educational authorities/administrators have to realize that education is a part of large socio-economic system and they have to perform their duty accordingly. Education must be made meaningful and relevant to the students because no country can afford to go on turning out educated un-employed manpower. (Shukla, 1988). The present educational system therefore, calls for necessary changes so that the mismatch between requirements of economy and educational system is mitigated.

Vocanalization in Commerce Education

As elsewhere in the country, commerce is an important part of our educational setup. Its importance has further increased in the light of vital economical change the world is passing through. This change is appearing like a storm which has swift away the restrictions of the business. The emerging global trade scenario, liberalization of industrial and fiscal policies, privatization, service industry expansion, computer and electronic revolution, internet etc., are placing special emphasis on business sector and in near future business environment is likely to change at much faster rate, which will affect commerce education. Moreover, the nature of work is changing from manual to mechanical, slow to fast, which in turn call for change in job skills. Presently we have number of jobs lying vacant for lack of properly qualified personnel. Therefore, to enable the youth, to enjoy the benefits of new environment, new technology, will definitely require new designs of human resource development. It has been observed that human being is a positive assets and a precious national resource, which needs to be cherished, nurtured and developed with tenderness, care coupled with dynamism (Shukla, 1988). Our traditional industrial sector needs to be modernized to face competition outside the state. Agro industrial sector has also realized the need of services and not only research scholars. All these factors taken together have changed the role of commerce education in recent years.

According to the growing needs of the economy and employment opportunities available in future, there is need of bringing about changes in the pattern and composition of the existing course contents of the Commerce education (Rao, 1985).

Again the needs of life go on changing, so is education. We cannot go on with a static curriculum. The content has to be selected according to the changing needs of the society in general and the subject in particular (Rao, 1995).

Realizing the need of re-designing the curriculum in commerce education and to make it job oriented the academic bodies of our state the board of school education, the universities, and other concerned authorities have effected significant changes. Besides, the UGC sponsored scheme of vocationalisation was implemented at under graduate level by introducing two vocational courses viz. (1) Tax Procedure & Practice; and 2. Office Management and Secretarial Practice

As part of the existing courses in few colleges where commerce education is provided, the object was to expose students to the world of work by including application oriented courses in the curriculum. It was expected to enhance individual employability, reduce mismatch between demand and supply of skilled manpower and to provide an alternative to those pursuing higher education without any particular interest and purpose Shukla, 1988). Commerce degree was bifurcated as B.Com General and B.Com Vocational with the object that the later may have an edge in the employment market. It is important to mention here that the concept of vocationalisation was not something new. The Program of Action 1992, drawn by Ministry of Human Resources Development in relation to National Policy on Education 1986 has already emphasized the need to explore the first degree level students to the world of work, by including application oriented courses in the curriculum. (Vocationalisation of 1st Degree Education, 1993), and U.G.C. has been assigned the task of launching of this program throughout the country. Accordingly, the U.G.C. identified 35 courses in 4 disciplines of science, Engineering and Technology, Arts and Humanities and Management (Annexure 1). These courses have a detailed syllabi framed by U.G.C. expert group. To quote "such a re-structuring of the existing courses with the introduction of one vocational subject integrated with the academic structure has been envisaged to provide knowledge and skills required for creative and productive functioning in the 21st Century, generating more employment potential and avenues for self entreprenieurship" (Rao,

Sethumadhava, 1995). So the goal of introduction of vocational courses is to develop knowledge, skills and attitude of students for gainful employment with major emphasis being given to possibility of self-employment.

Theoretically the scheme sounded very well and it appeared that its adoption in the commerce stream shall be encouraging to provide knowledge and skills required for creative and productive functioning but practically nothing concrete seems to have be done because of the under mentioned reasons:

1. On-the-job training is an essential requirement of vocational courses. This training was required to be given in the industrial establishments/ concerned institutions during vacations for a period of two months. The objective was to expose the students to the requirements of the world of work and to develop in them the skills necessary for specific jobs and various trades. In Tax Procedure and Practice, student is required to prepare various returns/forms/documents etc., relating to income tax and sales tax/Excise duty to acquire necessary skills, so that these documents can be prepared independently. (Vocationalisation of 1st Degree Education, Vol. 1st, 1993). For this purpose it was obligatory on the part of concerned colleges to sign Memorandum of Understanding with certain concerned establishments. But nothing has been done in this direction. Consequently two batches of vocational commerce graduates with Tax Procedure and Practice in Govt. Women College Nawakadal have come out without any practical training (see college records). Results are not encouraging even with those who have executed Memorandum of understanding because of the in-different attitude of the concerned institutions and in the absence of a required business environment in the valley.
2. Proper linkage between the colleges and the world of work alone can produce competent graduates in chosen vocations, but the concerned institutions are reluctant to impart on-the-job training on the plea that it will disturb their work schedule unnecessarily or mean little loss of production time and extra burden on supervisory staff.
3. The vocational courses introduced by UGC and opted by various colleges have somewhat become redundant and

superfluous so far as changes affected in view of the opening of the economy is concerned. For example, some provisions of Wealth Tax and Gift Tax are taught under Tax Procedure and Practice at under graduate level but they have since been abolished. The provisions are still incorporated in the course contents without any change (Syllabus 2001-2002).

Central Excise and Customs Procedure and Practice is also taught at under graduate level to vocational students. Since our state is devoid of central excise department and customs department, the students are unable to receive any practical training, not to think of their employment. Thus the selection of this course have proved a futile exercises.

4. The concerned colleges are required to choose one vocational course at their will, (out of eight courses) but are not authorized to effect any change or replacement with another course in line with the local requirements. Moreover, to go on turning manpower only in one vocational course, ignoring other courses, which are equally important, will only lead to saturation in the job market in the chosen course and consequently the student could be caught in a vicious circle.

5. As per the revised vocational course structure implemented from the session 2001, those vocational students who have opted for Office Management and Secretarial Practice (Syllabi 2001-2002) are required to surrender one compulsory subject Income Tax Law and Practice, thereby ignoring the utility of taxation for a Commerce graduate. Similarly, students who have opted for Tax Procedure and Practice are required to surrender a paper on Economic Environment in Business (Syllabus 2001-2002), the knowledge of which is essential for a Commerce graduate in the fast changing economic environment of today.

6. The basic objective of vocationlisation was to adjust vocational graduates in concerned institutions/industrial concerns and also make them ready for self employment, but students seem to be reluctant to go for these courses because (i) no preference is being given to vocational commerce graduates in the job market over their counterparts with Science and Arts streams respectively. (ii) they prefer to go for wage

employment in contrast to self employment because self employment culture is almost absent in the valley of Kashmir.

7. The four important components of the scheme are (i) preparation of reading material for teachers and students (ii) monitoring and evaluation of scheme in colleges (iii) training for teachers and (iv) creating awareness among public through media etc. Unfortunately no requirement has been fulfilled except providing some funds. Thus no serious effort has been made by the U.G.C/particular University/particular college to popularize the concept of vocationalisation.

Future Role and Recommendations

World has entered into an era of technology – an age where industries are moving from market place to cyber space and products are moving from shelf to disc space, a virtual revolution that is re-defining the very concept of commerce education and business. After analyzing the existing pattern of commerce education at under graduate level in the state along with the failure of vocational commerce education to serve the specific objective, increasing trend towards commerce education, changing business environment and requirements of economy, a multi-pronged approach is needed. Broadly speaking, two options are available to cope up with the situation :-

i) to incorporate major changes in the existing vocational set-up, or

ii) to say good-bye to the vocational scheme and adopt multi-pronged approach -- academic and administrative to strengthen the commerce education in the state.

If the first option is chosen, the concerned college principals should rise to the occasion and put forth their efforts to make vocational stream operational, strengthen it by taking various corrective measures and not to keep it a mere sacred cow in the colleges. In this direction, need is urgent to:-

i) involve industrial establishments/concerned institutions in this academic activity by signing Memorandum of Understanding (MOU) and arrangements need to be made to provide on-the-job training as per the requirements of the scheme. Need is also felt to open production-cum-training centers within the college, run on commercial lines for which students should also contribute financially.

ii) courses which have proved less useful or have no utility in our state, particularly in the valley, should be replaced by those which prove beneficial to the student community in the long run enabling them to find worth while jobs or divert them towards self-employment which is the basic objective of the scheme. This is the right time for such replacement as the scheme is yet in its infancy stage and has not involved large investment. Further the colleges be authorized to replace the courses (from among the approved list by UGC) after a certain period of time in order to avoid saturation in the job market in that particular course.

iii) In order to keep students well-equipped with the latest and up to date knowledge of the subject, the syllabi/course contents should be thoroughly revised, redundant and out dated parts scrapped and new changes incorporated. In this connection there should be direct and close co-ordination between the UGC and colleges as UGC is the sole authority to frame syllabi of the vocational courses.

iv) it is obligatory on the part of the college principals to continuously monitor and evaluate the courses introduced. Guest faculties be invited regularly, audio visual aids be introduced to make the studies of these courses more interesting and motivational. Special teaching materials be made available in the colleges and necessary training arrangements for teachers be made possible which is an important requirement of the scheme.

v) if the concerned authorities opt for second option, the following suggestions need to be taken care of.

Academic Front

The scheme of vocationalisation in commerce though in its infancy stage presently seems a futile exercise and hence be withdrawn. Need is urgent to have only one common stream at under graduate level. Division of B.Com general and B.Com vocational should be done away with. Again the utility of the vocationalisation vary from subject to subject and place to place, for example, Tax Procedure and Practice may prove fruitful in states which have highly developed business environment and industrially developed, but not in the valley where small scale industries are mostly run on subsidies. Tax is not a problem for them at present. It may prove fruitful in subjects like Tourism and Travel Management, Functional Hindi, Functional Sanskrit, Communicative English, Industrial Chemistry, Bio-Technology, Sericulture or Mushroom Cultivation or in Mass Communication, but not in Commerce. Commerce itself is a special field of knowledge related with trade, industry, business and ancillary services. What is required is;-

a) to enrich the courses of study after regular intervals;

b) keep them up to date and in tune with latest developments in various subjects;

c) keep them at par with other universities of the country;

d) the courses must be relevant the applicability aspect of subject must be borne in mind; and

e) classroom teaching should be reinforced by practicals

In this direction, the Department of Commerce at University level has already taken initiative by way of framing modules and grouping of various subjects and from the current session 2001 implemented a revised course structure at under graduate level where far reaching changes have been made e.g., Computer application has been made compulsory subject for all the three classes. Course contents of various papers have been enriched with latest changes certain papers which had become less practicable have been scrapped. This effort is expected to go a long way in raising the quality of commerce education, thereby making it relevant to the needs of the society.

Commerce graduates are befitting input for industrial and business institutions. Present businesses demand services of specialists in various fields like Accounting, Taxation, Computer Application, Marketing etc. Need is to involve business institutions and have close co-ordination between academicians and business managers. They should be given representation in academic bodies of the universities. This will help to know: (i) the type of man power they require and thereby to make curriculum more effective and result oriented (ii) to enable the students to get on the job training in various areas taught in the classroom.

There has been no improvemental expansion regarding the introduction of allied (related and professional courses) other than graduation in commerce in the colleges. Need is to follow Islamia College of Science and Commerce and Degree College Bemina and introduce BBA, BCA and other job oriented diploma courses, keeping in view the aspirations of student community and latest technological changes in trade, industry and commerce.

Administrative Front

In this regard it is suggested that :

a) Overhauling of Commerce Education needs investment, and government should provide adequate funds and facilities to the concerned colleges so that the advantages of modern information technology are availed.

b) Under 10+2+3 pattern of education, commerce education is provided at +2 stage in few selected Higher Secondary Schools. To cope up with the increasing demand for skilled man power to transact commercial and government jobs, government should introduce commerce stream in all Higher Secondary Schools of the state and make it at par with Science and Arts streams. These schools in turn will be the feeding centres at degree level.

c) The Commerce departments in these selected Higher Secondary Schools are understaffed. The Directorate of school education should realize the utility of the subject and should put forth their efforts to provide adequate staff to these departments.

d) Presently, the student has to go through qualifying/competitive test and subject specialization carries no weight in the job market. Need is to give preferential consideration to Commerce graduates over Arts and Science graduates in banks, Industrial establishments and financial institutions in respect of jobs.

e) Lastly, teacher is a central figure in any educational system. Therefore, the teachers should put forth their sincere efforts to produce young men and women, who can successfully meet the challenges of fast growing technology, thereby, the challenges of competitive job market in and outside the state. It is also needed to improve our professional capabilities in order to keep up the standards of the education.

References

"Vocationalization for 1st Degree Education', UGC Guidelines, Volume I, Curriculum for Arts, Humanities and Social Science, Commerce & Economics and Management subjects. Published by UGC, New Delhi, (1993) Section I, V, VI.

Hassan, Ijlal, (1987) 'Education for Today and Tomorrow', Chattan Publications, Srinagar: 132.

Office Records, Department of Commerce, Govt. College for Women, Nawakadal, Srinagar.

Rao, Seema, (1995) 'Teaching of Commerce', Anmol Publication, New Delhi: 17

Rao, Sethumandhava, P. H. (1995) "Vocational Education at First Degree Level" 'Professional Competency in Higher Education, Published by CPDHE, New Delhi: 17.

Shukla, P. D. (1988) 'The New Education Policy in India', Sterling Publication Pvt. Ltd., New Delhi: 72.

Syllabi, B.Com, Vocational Part I, II and III published by the University of Kashmir, 2001-2002.

ANNEXURE I

PROPOSED VOCATIONAL SUBJECTS

Discipline/Area	Subjects
1) Art, Humanities & Social Sciences	1) Functional Hindi 2) Functional Sanskrit 3) Communicative English 4) Archaeology and Museology
2) Commerce, Economics & Management	5) Principles and practice of Insurance 6) Acturial Science 7) Tax Procedure and Practice 8) Office Management and Secretarial Practice 9) Foreign Trade, Practice and Procedure 10) Tourism and Travel Management 11) Advertising, Sales Promotion and Sales Management 12) Computer Applications
3) Science	1) Industrial Chemistry (seven streams) 2) Food Science and quality control 3) Clinical Nutrition Dietetics 4) Industrial Microbiology 5) Bio -Technology 6) Biological Technique and Specimen preparation 7) Speed Technology 8) Sericulture 9) Industrial Fish and Fishery 10) Instrumentation

	11) Optical Instrumentation
	12) Geoexploration and Drilling Technology
	13) Mass Communication and video Production
	14) Still Photography Audio Products
4) Electronic Equipment Maintenance	1) Computer Maintenance.
	2) Electrical Equipment Maintenance.
	3) Environmental & Water Management.
	4) Rural Technology.
	5) Automobiles Maintenance.
	6) Refrigeration & Air Conditioning.
	7) Construction Technology Management.
	8) Manufacturing Process

Source: UGC Guidelines for Vocationalisation for 1st Degree Education published by UGC 1993, Section V, page 18.

28

VOCATIONALISATION OF COMMERCE EDUCATION: A CASE STUDY

G. M. Baqal

Abstract

Vocational subjects were introduced with the objective of providing knowledge and skill required for creative and productive functioning in the 21st century, generating more employment potential and avenues for self entrepreneurship. Vocational education though not inherently defective, is fraught with some problems. In this paper, an attempt has been made to identify these problems and offer some suggestions to make the vocational course meaningful.

Introduction

The educationists strongly feel that the traditional education system should undergo a change in accordance with the changing environment so that we are able to produce professional and skilled manpower. Professional and skilled manpower has a place to occupy in modem age of automation. Therefore, the demand of the students to have opportunities can be generated by offering vocational education. It is in view of this realization that the U.G.C has drawn a very pragmatic proposal to introduce vocational scheme of teaching and learning at the college level. These courses were recommended by an expert group appointed by the commission after deliberating upon the issues exhaustly. The group observed that vocationalisation would help generate a skilled class of technocrate-entreprenuers and professionals who in the 21st century are expected to take up the responsibility of speeding up the business and industrial activity in consonance with the changing scenario in the world. The significance of vocational education is well illustrated by the example of Japan and Germany which could achieve their progress mainly because of their superior vocational training system (National Commission on Excellence in Education U.S.A, 1983.).

Vocationalisation of Education in J&K.

Since early 1990s, the Jarnrnu & Kashmir State implemented the UGC policy of vocationalisation so as to produce graduates with job oriented courses which involve professional and on the job training alongside the general education. Vocationalisation of commerce education was also started in some of the institutions in the state during the same period. Some of the vocational courses in commerce introduced in various institutions are Office management, secretarial practice, Tax Procedures & Practices, EDP .Before vocationalisation of commerce in J&K State, the employer hardly made any difference between the commerce and non-commerce graduates. The vocationalisation aimed at removing this indifference because of its following objectives:

1. to familiarise students with the world of work. :
2. visits to enterprises for familiarisation with equipments, materials, services and work processes through observation and discussion with supervisory personnel.
3. application of theoretical content of the vocational subject through practicals, field trips.
4. preparation of project report.

The college faculty incharge of the vocational subject is supposed to continuously liaison with the personnel of the enterprise and plan different aspects of on the job training.

Performance of the Programme

On the job-training being imparted to commerce students under vocational programme is expected to differentiate them from the students belonging to general courses. However, the vocationalisation could not work to the expectations of the society. This fact is revealed by the field survey undertaken by the author. The field survey revealed that vocational education though not defective, suffers from certain problems as are pinpointed by the anti-vocational group. A change in college curriculum demands for change in teaching methods, change in evaluation methods etc. (Matto, 93) and to some extent teaching methods. But the introduction of Vocational subjects in commerce was not followed by the change in examination and evaluation mechanism that continues to be traditional in nature. The employers don't observe difference between vocational and non-vocational students. The survey revealed the following causes for failure of the Vocational education in commerce.

Causes of failure:

For a programme to be successful, there are certain basic preparations which should be made before launching the programme. However, the programme of vocationalisation of commerce seems to have been launched in haste. Before launching the programme of vocationlisation in the state, the necessary ground work was not done in respect of-

i) preparation of reading material for teachers and students.

ii) training for teachers.

iii) creating awareness about the programme.

iv) creating Monitoring & Evaluation Mechanism.

The guidelines for the preparation of reading materials have not been prepared for the teachers concerned with vocational education. In order to differentiate the vocational students from the general course students, traditional teaching methods was not changed. Arrangement for imparting training to teachers have not been made. Awareness programmes through print or electronic media have not been organised. The evaluation and examination mechanism for vocational examination are traditional in nature. There is no continuos process for evaluating the students performance. Examination continues to dominate the education process. Passing an examination is more important than acquiring any education (Nadeem 93). The cases of anti-vocational group can be seen from the analysis of Castro (1987). However, the present field survey conducted by the author revealed the low priority for vocational education. It is because of various reasons shown as under:-

S. No.	Nature of Reason	% of students
I	Importance not known	5
2.	No specialization, no market	75
3.	Only college level, not at school level	20

Source: Field survey conducted by the author in Kashmir valley in 2001.
Note: Single reason sought from the respondents for ineffectiveness of vocationalisation.

Eighty students belonging to general & vocational courses were interviewed. The maximum number of students i.e. 75% were observed having doubts about the importance of vocational education on the ground of "No Specialization, No market". Till now vocational education in colleges is being imparted in class rooms and students are enriched only with theoretical knowledge of the subjects. They are not put to the world of work. On the job training is given in final year of vocational courses. The change in the current employment market has made these teaching techniques inadequate, incomplete and obsolete. Further vocational course does not keep pace with the changes in the policies. For example in the case of vocational course on tax procedures, some provisions of Wealth Tax Act which stand abolished are being taught under these courses. As a result, the output from colleges find itself misfit in the employment market. Much of the pre-employment vocational training is isolated from market force (World Bank 1991). 5% of students were found unaware about the nature and importance of vocational education. The face to face discussions revealed that the traditional subjects have got deep roots in the minds of students/parents.

The ground for criticizing vocationalisation of commerce education is that it has been introduced at college level, not at, school level. A commerce student to be worthwhile should have vocational subjects right from Higher Secondary Level. School based vocational education has become indispensable (Balbir 92) The other reason for failure of vocationalisation of commerce education is that general commerce received a set back in Jammu & Kashmir when 11th and 12th classes were started at Higher Secondary Level under 10+2+3 pattern. The reorganisation was not so comprehensive tó give boost to commerce education. The planners did not take necessary steps to introduce commerce at +2 level in all Higher Secondary Institutions. 7 out of 10 higher secondary institutions where commerce is taught were found with one commerce teacher only. As a result single teacher plays like "Jack of all, master of none". This discourages the students to opt for commerce subjects. Moreover, no arrangement was made by the government /private schools, to introduce commerce at higher secondary level in the areas where this subject is taught in colleges. For instance, Girls Higher Secondary School, Baramulla and Udhumpur are examples in this behalf. As a result, the colleges don't get optimum number of students which leads to wastage of infrastructure and frustration of basic purpose. This approach of our planners is well expressed by a Kashmiri proverb YEN NE KUNE WONUNE LAGOON (Weaving without warp & weft).

Conclusion

In commerce education, there is ample scope for vocationalisation in the field of Management, Taxation, Travel & Tourism, Advertising, Finance etc. vocationalisation of subjects has become inevitable due to shift towards privatization where right person is placed at right place. But to think of vocationalisation of commerce, when general commerce is in shambles, means unwise planning so, the policy needs to be re-framed. Commerce education should be introduced in all the higher secondary institutions with sufficient infrastructure. Vocational students should be put to the world of work throughout the course. The courses should match with the changes that occur from time to time in the market. Proper training needs to be imparted to the teachers concerned with the teaching of vocational courses .On the job training should be the part of curriculum. It should not be a single visit to some enterprises but placement for sufficient time for on-the-job training is must for making a vocational programme successful. In the present system of examination, memorization occupies an important place because the questions set require recall of information on the part of students. Therefore, the need of the hour is to introduce problem solving approaches than working through theoretical pedagogy to know what the students have been able together. Viva-voce test should be conducted after the termination of examination so that the student's depth of knowledge can be ascertained. This would discourage the practice of being bookish. Continuous process of evaluation system should be introduced. Continuous process of evaluation scheme will ensure constant monitoring of the progress of students, which will discourage the cramming on the part of students.

In short, education is closely related to changes in environment. Any changes in the environment must be followed by the changes in the course curriculum so that education can make one's life in harmony with existence.

NC/25-99
18.10.04